A Covenant with Death

A Covenant with Death,

The Constitution, Law, and Equality in the Civil War Era

Phillip S. Paludan

UNIVERSITY OF ILLINOIS PRESS
Urbana   Chicago   London

Publication of this work has been supported by a grant from the Oliver M.
Dickerson Fund. The Fund was established by Mr. Dickerson (Ph.D., Illinois,
1906) to enable the University of Illinois
Press to publish selected works in American history, designated by the executive
committee of the Department of History.

LIBRARY OF CONGRESS CATALOGING IN PUBLICATION DATA

Paludan, Phillip S.   1938–
A covenant with death.

Bibliography: p.
Includes index.
1. United States—Constitutional history.
2. Reconstruction. I. Title.
KF4541.P34   342'.73'029   74-34324
ISBN 0–252–00261–x

FOR MARSHA

Contents

Preface

The study of the legal-constitutional history of the second and third quarters of the nineteenth century has suffered from the brilliance that comes from narrowness of focus. We have able studies of small periods and topics by men of great insight and energy. Perry Miller has pointed to the demand upon legal thought to bring order and stability to the pre–Civil War world. Arthur Bestor, Harold Hyman, and James G. Randall have written that the Civil War must be seen as a constitutional crisis, and Randall described the problems that this crisis posed for Lincoln's administration. Alfred Kelly, W. R. Brock, Eric McKitrick, and Stanley Kutler have suggested how Reconstruction was limited in its consequences by the tenacity with which postwar legislators and judges clung to familiar constitutional havens. But no one has yet attempted to include the insights of all these authors, to write a history of Reconstruction that escapes the restrictions imposed by the arbitrary division of United States history into separate periods for the era of Andrew Jackson and the Civil War and Reconstruction.

The present work is an attempt to place the history of Reconstruction in a perspective broader than that of the post-Appomattox or even the post-Sumter years. There is no profound originality in my conclusion that constitutional ideas and preconceptions limited and perhaps destroyed the possibilities for permanent equal justice which the Civil War and Reconstruction spawned. I hope to show that the roots of Reconstruction's failure rest in a period when men thought little about civil war and nothing about reconstruction. If we want to understand the immensity of the Reconstruction tragedy, we must see it as part of the legal-constitutional history of America in the age of Andrew Jackson. As American judges, lawyers, and political leaders developed responses to the problems, real and imagined, of the 1830s, they built patterns of thought which structured the ways in which they would perceive the prewar crisis, the war, and Reconstruction. Simply stated, my contention is this: the concern for the stability of society in the Jacksonian years caused men to see the disunion crisis as a challenge to the existing order. This, in turn, made it impossible for them to develop a new legal and constitutional order which would guarantee equality for the Negro.

The inquiry poses a problem in method; two options suggest themselves. The first is to read all the available speeches, pamphlets, and books on constitutional and legal topics and to synthesize from them a composite legal mind of the Civil War era. This method can often be illuminating and most suggestive. In the hands of Perry Miller, it can result in extraordinary achievement. Used by George Fredrickson or David Davis or Winthrop Jordan, it can offer profound scholarship and invaluable insights. But this method has its pitfalls. It frequently reveals as much about the mind of the historian as about the mind of the era. The process of selection and synthesis offers too many opportunities for culling from a body of thought only those comments that conform to the historian's generalization.

In addition I think this method is insufficiently historical. While it may tell what happened, it does not tell it the way it happened. Certainly the thought of an era exists, but it does not come into being as "the thought of an era." It is created in the minds of individual men who think of themselves, not as having "the mind of their era," but as unique human beings reaching conclusions based on personal experience and dictated by previous conclusions.

These difficulties are most easily avoided by the more modest method used here: to take what appear to be representative thinkers of an era and analyze their thought in relation to their time. The result, of course, is a narrower focus. Conclusions about the nature of thought during the period must be drawn more tentatively. But the method's merit is that it respects the reality of an enormously complex past. It recognizes that the thought of an age is a composite, not a homogenization, of the thoughts of individuals.

Having said that, let me express my belief that the individuals chosen represent more than just themselves. There are mutual consistencies in their thought, and my reading of congressional debates and the works of other jurists of the period convinces me that their responses, while individual, were not unique. My goal is still to discern the outlines of the legal thought of the Civil War era—but I have taken individual samplings from the many layers of that thought, rather than making a wholesale excavation.

Here then are Francis Lieber, a nationalist without deep concern for the Constitution, but with profound concern for a stable Union; Joel Parker, a rigid constitutionalist and believer in states' rights, yet withall a bitter opponent of secession; Sidney George Fisher, a racist admired by Gobineau, yet a man who could create a constitutional theory with vast promise for the Negro; John Norton Pomeroy, a Whig nationalist and proponent of congressional Reconstruction who willingly abandoned the freedmen; and Thomas McIntyre Cooley, Jacksonian Republican and advocate of equal liberty for all men, yet an opponent of federal efforts to secure that equality.

A study of the thought of these men can help to answer important questions about the struggle for equality and the disunion crisis which gave that struggle hope. What turned conservative legal thinkers, men who deplored the excesses of abolitionism, into enemies of slavery and the South? How did the pervasive racism of nineteenth-century Americans shape the uses of that national power which the Civil War unleashed? What were the consequences of saving the *federal* Union? How revolutionary was this "Second American Revolution"?

The underlying issue studied in these pages is the ability of law to adapt to demands for change. How much can and should a society's legal ideas and institutions shape, and even control, equally imperative requirements and opportunities for reform? There can and should be no total victories for either side in such an encounter. The important issue is, which side should be acceded to in which circumstances? We must paraphrase a question asked by Lincoln as he sought a balance in the Civil War: "Must a legal tradition of necessity be too strong for the liberties of its people, or too weak to preserve itself?" America during the mid-nineteenth century provides a profoundly important and happily complex opportunity to confront that question.

Acknowledgments

This book exists because throughout my life people have in varied ways offered encouragement, assistance, criticism, and inspiration. As an undergraduate I attended Occidental College, where I met Professor Ray Lindgren, now of Long Beach State College. He listened, cajoled, and said, by the example of his warmth and humanity, "Be a college teacher." As I began work on my master's degree, Merlin Stonehouse took an interest in me, made me a friend as well as a student, and showed me the dimensions of critical historical writing. My Ph.D. advisor, Harold Hyman, combined the talents of these two and in addition offered the example of energetic and insightful scholarship to emulate. Colleagues at the University of Kansas by their questions, counterproposals, and sincere interest helped me become healthily distrustful of the figures in this book. John Clark, David Katzman, and especially Clifford Griffin deserve mention. Griffin read the entire work with devoted attention, disbelieved everything and thereby added immeasurably to whatever merit it may have. Unfortunately, even this keen criticism has at times been unavailing when matched against my stubbornness. The errors of this work are thus my own.

Two libraries offered their resources and staff to reinforce my efforts, the University of Illinois Library and the Henry Huntington Library in San Marino. Mary Isabel Fry of the latter, along with her most helpful staff, deserve thanks.

The University of Kansas General Research Fund provided assistance which was of great help. *The Journal of the History of Ideas* and the *American Journal of Legal History* granted me permission to reprint the chapters on Pomeroy and Cooley which appeared in their pages in various stages of completeness. Richard L. Wentworth of the University of Illinois Press has been a demanding and, thus, most helpful editor.

Finally, my mother, my children, Karin and Kirsten, and most especially my wife, Marsha, have conspired at various times to provide the nonacademic sustenance which is indispensable to my intellectual efforts.

"I would rather commit an injustice than countenance disorder."
—Goethe, July 25, 1793
Campaign in France

Law and Equal Rights:
The Civil War Encounter

July 4, 1854, was a hot day even for a Massachusetts summer. But despite the heat, a crowd of about ten thousand gathered in Framingham to commemorate the day. Recent events in Boston insured a large crowd and gave the gathering a special moral fervor. Only a few days earlier Anthony Burns, a fugitive slave, had been captured and confined in the courthouse. A mob of abolitionists, preachers, transcendentalists, and other angry citizens had attacked the building; in response, a detachment of U.S. Marines, two companies of fully armed artillery, and over a hundred U.S. marshals and deputies surrounded it. Judges, jurors, litigants, and lawyers, as well as ordinary citizens, had been forced to pass through a cordon five men deep and to prove their right to enter. The scene recalled an experience four years before when the same courthouse was wrapped in chains to make sure that another fugitive slave, Thomas Sims, did not escape. Burns and Sims shared the same fate. The armed might of the federal government executed the legal authorities' judgment that both men were indeed slaves. They were returned to bondage.[1]

Massachusetts had long been agitated by the fugitive slave issue. In 1837 the state had passed a personal liberty law which interfered with the federal apprehension of runaways. This law was held unconstitutional by the state's chief justice, but six years later a petition bearing over 65,000 names led to the enactment of another. The passage of the 1850 Fugitive Slave Act had led to protests and one slave rescue which attracted national attention, but it was not until 1855 that the state's greatest wrath was exposed. Then anger over the

---

1. *The Liberator*, July 7, 1854; Henry Steel Commager, *Theodore Parker* (Boston, 1936), 220–240; Leonard Levy, *The Law of the Commonwealth and Chief Justice Shaw* (Cambridge, 1957), 92–106.

Kansas-Nebraska question and the treatment accorded Burns produced the most extreme personal liberty law of the age. Conservatives attacked this law as they had the others, seeing in all of them violations of the Constitution, threats to the Union, and possible harbingers of war. But many people were in no mood for constitutional arguments which made Bay Staters into slave-catchers. Longfellow had given voice to the mood in 1851: "Shame that the Great Republic, the 'refuge of the oppressed,' should stoop so low as to become the Hunter of Slaves."[2]

Few conservatives were there at Framingham. The vast majority had come to hear a denunciation of slavery and the laws that supported it. They stood before a platform decorated with symbols of their anger. A large banner proclaimed, "Redeem Massachusetts." Two black-bordered white flags bore the words "Kansas" and "Nebraska." Most noticeable of all was the flag of the United States, draped in black, hanging upside down.[3]

The major figures of northeastern abolition had gathered for the occasion. Wendell Phillips was there, ready to delight the crowd with his biting irony. Sojourner Truth, the former slave, was there, prepared to prick their consciences and appease their guilt with incisive comments about how northern white men—yes, even those of Massachusetts—were responsible for the endurance of slavery. Henry Thoreau was to read a poem written for the occasion. Beside these three sat other antislavery veterans, some recently scarred in the fight to free Burns. But the day belonged to William Lloyd Garrison.

"We have degenerated in . . . our reverence for the higher law of God," he told them. A government theoretically of the people was "in the hands of party demagogues . . . who are the vassals of the Slave power." Only the forms of a republic remained where once there had been the determination to establish a government dedicated to the equality of all men. Now "the most high handed acts of usurpation are submitted to with slavish servility." Popular liberty

---

2. Levy, *Law of Commonwealth*, 92–106; *A Memoir of Benjamin Robbins Curtis*, ed. Benjamin R. Curtis (Boston, 1879), I, 173–178; II, 205–212; Stanley W. Campbell, *The Slave Catchers: Enforcement of the Fugitive Slave Law, 1850–60* (Chapel Hill, 1968), 119–120, 124–131, 148–150, 171.

3. *The Liberator*, July 7, 1854.

lay denigrated, and the government directed its attention and its fortunes in service of securing slave property and expanding slavery's domain into the West. Men seeking to serve this government would discover that the price to be paid was "a ready acquiescence in whatever the Slave Power may dictate."

A government so enchained should be repudiated, Garrison insisted, and the symbols of its servitude destroyed. He picked up a copy of the Fugitive Slave Act, set fire to it, and said in the language of the Bible, "And let the people say Amen." The vast crowd responded, "Amen!" He picked up a copy of the decision which had sent Burns back to bondage, and copy of a charge to the jury which had tried Burns's erstwhile rescuers. He burned these, too, and asked the crowd to cry "Amen"; it did so eagerly.

Then he reached for a copy of the Constitution, held it in his hand and declared that it was the "parent of all the other atrocities." "A convenant with death," he called it, "An agreement with hell." He set it afire and cried out as it burned, "So perish all compromises with tyranny! 'And let the people say Amen.' " A huge shout of "Amen" echoed. But this time hisses and angry outcries were also audible.[4]

The changed reaction of the crowd probably reflected more general dismay at such abuse of a treasured national symbol than disagreement with Garrison's constitutional views. Some of the editor's abolitionist colleagues had argued that the Constitution was in fact an antislavery document, but their efforts could have convinced only believers. Despite the fact that the word "slavery" did not appear in the Philadelphia document, the price of southern ratification had clearly been protection for the peculiar institution. Arguments that the absence of the word signified opposition to slavery, that the three-fifths clause in fact denied two-fifths of the South's voting power, that the fugitive slave clause applied only to indentured servants, and that the guarantee of republican forms of government condemned slavery were ingenious, but only that. After eloquence had done its best, the fact remained that the Constitution protected slavery where it existed, whatever arguments might be made about the question of expansion. This was a reality recognized

4. *Ibid.*

by practically all of the nation's responsible leaders and endorsed by Lincoln even during the secession winter.[5]

The necessities of war tore slavery from the Constitution; apparently the covenant that Garrison had so dramatically condemned was broken. With the passage of the Thirteenth Amendment, four million slaves became free men. The Reconstruction Congress, motivated by a combination of humanitarianism and political expediency, showed its intention to secure freedom by the exercise of federal power if necessary. Civil rights laws, capped by the Fourteenth and Fifteenth Amendments, seemed to promise equal liberty under law for all men.

The promise was quickly broken. Southern hostility to the new status of former slaves provoked challenges to the legality of postwar legislation. The Supreme Court was called upon to determine the lawful dimensions of the freedmen's liberty—to determine the extent to which there might be federal protection for it. Then men discovered that the covenant with death had not been broken. Its extent was wider and deeper than they had supposed.

In case after case the Court insisted that the Constitution did not permit extensive federal efforts to protect the freedmen. Giving sanction to the national mood, the judges increasingly limited the extent of federal responsibility. In 1873 the Slaughterhouse Cases produced the decision that the protection of vital civil rights remained in state hands. In 1876 and 1883 in *United States* v. *Cruikshank* and the Civil Rights Cases the Court announced that private individuals who attacked those Negroes who forgot their place might not be prosecuted by the national government. Then in 1896 *Plessy* v. *Ferguson* demonstrated the complete abandonment of Civil War guarantees. States might legally create two classes of citizenship if they could convince judges that the separate facilities thus created were "equal."[6] Looking back in 1917 at the failure of Re-

5. *The Antislavery Argument*, ed. William H. Pease and Jane H. Pease (Indianapolis, 1965), 343–394; Aileen S. Kraditor, *Means and Ends in American Abolitionism* (New York, 1969), 185–217; *Collected Works of Abraham Lincoln*, ed. Roy P. Basler (New Brunswick, 1953), IV, 162, 199.

6. 16 *Wallace* 36 (1873); 92 *United States Reports* 542 (1876); 101 *United States Reports* 3 (1883); 163 *United States Reports* 537 (1896); Loren Miller, *The Petitioners* (Cleveland, 1966), 102–182; Albert P. Blaustein and Clarence C. Ferguson, *Desegregation and the Law* (New York, 1962), 76–113; John R. Lynch,

construction, former Mississippi political leader John R. Lynch insisted on the powerful influence of Supreme Court decisions in snatching liberty from the hands of his race. "By those unfortunate and fatal decisions," Lynch declared, "the vicious and mischievous doctrine of States' rights, called by some State sovereignty, by others self-government, which was believed to have perished upon the battlefields of the country, was given new life, strength and audacity. . . ." Black hopes for freedom were thus legally taken away.

Not until over half a century had passed would the Court respond to changes in the national mood and discover a Constitution that protected the Negro instead of obstructing his protection. A vast depression and the resulting New Deal accustomed Americans to a powerful, active federal government. The activities of that government on the home front during World War II reinforced the image. The struggle against Nazi racism diluted America's commitment to her own. The movement of large numbers of Negroes to the cities brought the pressure of voting masses to the struggle for equality, and the nation was willing to allow what had been denied for so long. Finally in 1954 the Supreme Court announced that it was retaking the territory it had surrendered in the last half of the nineteenth century. The *Brown* v. *Board of Education* decision was the opening declaration that federal laws would protect equal liberty. It was followed by the passage of sweeping federal legislation, by the establishment of permanent federal civil rights officials in the South, and by the presence of federal troops when necessary. The Constitution blessed it all. Although there remained the enormous problem of de facto inequality, constitutional inhibitions no longer paralyzed the struggle for equality. The covenant with death was broken.[7]

Reconstruction historiography mirrors this judicial journey. As the nation complacently accepted the abandonment of the Negro, historians wrote descriptions of the post-Appomattox era that blackened the motives of northern congressmen and denounced the cor-

---

"Some Historical Errors of James Ford Rhodes," *Journal of Negro History*, II (Oct., 1917), 366.

7. 347 *United States Reports* 483 (1954); Alfred H. Kelly, "The School Desegregation Cases," *Quarrels That Have Shaped the Constitution*, ed. John A. Garraty (New York, 1966), 262–265.

ruption of radical southern governments. The period was described as a "tragic era" and an "age of hate." The momentum of such writing carried through the 1920s and 1930s, but weakened by the mid-1940s even as the Court moved toward the *Brown* decision. By the 1950s and 1960s historians were echoing the sentiment of the Warren Court. The tragedy of Reconstruction came to be not that it happened, but that it failed. Reconstruction legislators changed from vindictive villains to a "vanguard for racial justice." Like the bench, historians were implicitly apologizing for generations of lost equality, seeking perhaps to redeem the tragic history of the Negro after Appomattox by giving that history more glorious beginnings.[8]

In recent years, orderly progress within the legal framework has come under attack. Black militants and their supporters have insisted that the moderate method of institutionalized reform is too slow and might be a sham. Growing sentiment suggests that progress within existing institutions is impossible, since these institutions themselves are incurably racist. Some have claimed that equality will have to be wrenched from the white establishment, irrespective of the imperatives suggested by existing structures.

Modern scholarship seems to reflect a reaction to this belief. Implicit in two of the most recent studies of Reconstruction is an attempt to defend the orderly process of law by insisting that the legislation of the post-Appomattox period is now relevant and vital, despite a century-long burial. Hans Trefousse in *The Radical Republicans: Lincoln's Vanguard for Racial Justice* and Kenneth Stampp in *The Era of Reconstruction* both argue that the long-range result of Reconstruction was beneficial to the Negro, and that therefore the era itself deserves admiration. In Stampp's words,

> The Fourteenth and Fifteenth Amendments, which could have been adopted only under the conditions of radical reconstruction, make the blunders of that era, tragic though they were, dwindle into in-

8. Claude Bowers, *The Tragic Era, The Revolution after Lincoln* (Boston, 1929); George F. Milton, *The Age of Hate: Andrew Johnson and the Radicals* (New York, 1930); Hans L. Trefousse, *The Radical Republicans: Lincoln's Vanguard for Racial Justice* (New York, 1969). Rembert Patrick, *The Reconstruction of the Nation* (New York, 1967), 305–308, lists the major articles on Reconstruction historiography and briefly discusses major trends.

significance. For if it was worth four years of civil war to save the Union, it was worth a few years of radical reconstruction to give the American Negro the ultimate promise of equal civil and political rights.[9]

Reconstruction promissory notes, long term though they were, may be redeemed now. The law provides what it so long denied.

This sentiment may be correct; indeed, the dominant modern constitutional view suggests that it is. But it may be too late. Having at long last rejected a constitution which protected inequality, we may now discover that constitutional guarantees are considered irrelevant. Despite the claims that blacks are a people slighted by written history, perhaps many have learned history too well. For the fact is that law and the Constitution failed the Negro in the Civil War era and for almost a century thereafter; whatever our sentiments concerning the methodology of modern Reconstruction, we cannot undo the past simply by making heroes out of yesterday's villains. Historians should not be satisfied simply to glorify the efforts of dead radicals. It is less important to venerate far-sighted Reconstruction frontiersmen than to understand why their dreams were stillborn. However exalted their vision of equal justice may have been, that vision was insufficient to change permanently the condition of the Negro in America.

Reconstruction did not happen as it did because the participants were vengeful radicals or visionary dreamers. Whatever their motives, these men had to deal with events in terms of the possibilities and imperatives which history provided. They were to be guided by their preconceptions about race, politics, and law. These would shape whatever legislation they adopted.

The influence of racial attitudes and political necessities on the failure of Reconstruction is a subject of much current study, but the ability of legal and constitutional beliefs to cripple the era's civil rights advances has not been widely investigated. This is unfortunate, for the modern civil rights struggle challenges the law to adapt and play a role in expanding equality or to become irrelevant.

9. Kenneth M. Stampp, *The Era of Reconstruction* (New York, 1967), 214–215; Trefousse, *Radical Republicans*, 408–409, 435, 470.

Therefore it may be especially useful to examine how law failed the Negro in the past so that it can more successfully serve the nation today. Moderates need to understand the roots of black distrust of merely legal guarantees, and militants need to recognize that men are not always free to create a new world out of whole cloth. Men's inability to question fundamental legal and constitutional principles may make basic change impossible. Their frightened belief that certain legal structures are imperative for the survival of ordered liberty may lead them to exalt order and to deny liberty.[10]

In writing this book I have had to consider the possibility that constitutional arguments are simply excuses or rationalizations for not acting to protect the Negro. I have rejected such an idea because it rings too much of the twentieth century, rather than the nineteenth. The rationalization of one era may well be the reality of another. Most Americans laugh when a well-known comedian explains his misdeeds with "Da debble made me do it." But this explanation was no laughing matter to the vast majority of colonial Americans, and probably to most in the nineteenth century. When it is asserted that someone is making excuses or rationalizing, what may be meant is that he is not giving the reasons *we* would give for *our* behavior. This is hardly the best foundation for beginning historical study.

I am not, of course, pleading for abandonment of a critical attitude toward what historical figures say and do. When people of the past ignore facts which they can reasonably be expected to know, the historian has an obligation to consider this "ignorance" and to try to explain it. When hypocrisy and sophistry are shown in the

10. See Richard Curry, "The Abolitionists and Reconstruction: A Critical Appraisal," *Journal of Southern History*, XXXIV (Nov., 1968), 527–545, for a discussion of race-centered analyses of the failure of Reconstruction. The four major studies of the era which mention the impact of the Constitution on shaping policy are W. R. Brock, *An American Crisis: Congress and Reconstruction, 1865–67* (New York, 1963); Eric McKitrick, *Andrew Johnson and Reconstruction* (Chicago, 1960); Harold M. Hyman, "Reconstruction and Political-Constitutional Institutions: The Popular Expression," *New Frontiers of American Reconstruction*, ed. Harold Hyman (Urbana, 1966), 1–39; and Alfred Kelly, "Comment on Hyman's Paper," *ibid.*, 40–58. Only Hyman's article mentions constitutional thought outside Congress. I have tried to open this area of study in "John Norton Pomeroy: State Rights Nationalist," *American Journal of Legal History*, XII (Oct., 1968), 275–293.

past, we should point them out and seek sources. But to assume *a priori* that men are rationalizing or making excuses for their real feelings is to warp our perception of the past with the impossible demand that the mind of the past be that of the present.

It is also too easy to make the mistake of the so-called legal realists and assume a dichotomy between "real" reasons and what are called rationalizations. Such an assumption takes too simple a view of human motivation; it gives too little attention to men's ability and desire to convince themselves even as they are convincing others. Rationalizations are not necessarily lies, nor are all public explanations with which we happen to disagree necessarily deceits or even excuses. Explanations and justifications affect speakers as well as listeners. They are the articulated forms of inarticulated feelings, or they may support reasons and conclusions already developed. In so doing they become part of the motivation for action.[11]

In an age as concerned with legal-constitutional matters as the nineteenth-century United States, in the midst of a crisis in which legal and constitutional questions attracted vast amounts of oratory and writing, men who were lawyers, judges, and legal thinkers, as well as congressmen who swore to uphold the Constitution and who operated in a system created by that Constitution, were very likely to be seriously concerned with constitutional questions. It strains credulity to believe that they would not express their concern for the constitutionality of their actions as sincerely as they would their racism, political ambitions, or other feelings. It is most likely that their motivations were combinations of all these feelings and attitudes. I have tried in this work to take constitutional motives as seriously as others have taken racial and political ones.[12]

Constitutional and legal preconceptions were not the only impediments to achievement of equal liberty. Probably most funda-

11. Wilfred Rumble, Jr., *American Legal Realism: Skepticism, Reform, and the Judicial Process* (Ithaca, 1968), contains both a description of the realist argument and a criticism of it. See especially pp. 88–95.

12. For emphasis on racial ideas in Reconstruction, see material in note 10. The most direct argument asserting the political motivations underlying Reconstruction is in David Donald, *The Politics of Reconstruction* (Baton Rouge, 1965). The previously cited works by Brock and McKitrick also focus on this theme, as does most of the literature of Reconstruction.

mental was the widely accepted and scientifically affirmed belief that Negroes were an inferior race.[13] But racism showed itself far beyond individual attitudes and encounters between blacks and whites. Surely racism was there when local vigilantes beat or murdered "uppity niggers." But it was also there when blacks could not testify in courts, when they could not attend schools with whites, when they could not exercise the right to vote because of their color, when they could not freely migrate to seek employment. In short, racism appeared in the institutions of government and law which gave inequality the stamp of legality.[14]

Racism also showed itself in more subtle ways. It was preserved by institutions whose growth and development had no obvious relationship to preserving inequality. The problem of the Negro freedman was primarily a problem of power. He neither expected nor asked to be loved—he sought and needed protection from the frequently demonstrated fact that he was not loved. He suffered from the inability to exercise power or to have it exercised in his behalf. This might mean that he could not utilize local and/or state law enforcement agencies to protect himself against violence, or it might mean that he could not elect officials who would provide security. Most significantly, given the fact that he lived surrounded and outnumbered by former masters, it might mean that should these avenues fail, he had no recourse to an outside agency with the power to protect him.

In 1865 the federal government did not have the constitutional power to interfere when state and local agencies failed to provide equal justice; it had been denied the power to interfere with such

13. There were few nineteenth-century Americans who did not hold what Dante Puzzo describes as the two basic assumptions of racism: "that a correlation exists between physical characteristics and moral qualities; that mankind is divisible into superior and inferior stocks." Puzzo argues that racism begins to show itself after the sixteenth century. George M. Fredrickson sees it rising to full stature by the mid–1830s. Dante Puzzo, "Racism and the Western Tradition," *Journal of the History of Ideas*, XXV (Oct.–Dec., 1964), 579–586; George M. Fredrickson, *The Black Image in the White Mind: The Debate on Afro-American Character and Destiny, 1817–1914* (New York, 1971), 47.

14. The Ku Klux Klan during Reconstruction claimed that it was protecting the South against threats to the law and order of the community posed by "dangerous" freedmen. See David M. Chalmers, *Hooded Americanism: The History of the Ku Klux Klan* (New York, 1965), 13–15.

racist conditions for reasons that transcended the condition of the black man. Of course, the institution of federalism has its powerful uses as an instrument of intolerance—time and again the idea that states have rights which the federal government may not transgress has cloaked bigotry. In the twentieth century states' rights have impeded or stopped anti-lynching laws, equal schooling, fair trials, and access to the ballot box. No one doubted the racial views of presidential candidates Strom Thurmond, Orville Faubus, or T. Coleman Andrews, who carried the banner of the States' Rights party in 1948, 1956, and 1960. Nineteenth-century politicians were equally adept at saying "states' rights" when they meant "keep the black man in his place."[15]

But our very familiarity with the modern phenomenon can mislead us when we try to understand the nineteenth century and the failure of Reconstruction. It is far too simple to conclude that men of that era (or even our own) simply brandished federalism and the Constitution to cover their anti-Negro bias. Some did, but the vast majority had reason to cherish the Constitution and the federal system it secured. Basic to any understanding of the struggle for equality in the nineteenth century is a recognition that states' rights and liberty were not generally viewed as antithetical a hundred years ago. States' rights was not usually an incantation to scare away federal protection for blacks.

The states' rights idea then stood for local control of the character of daily experience. It meant that a local or regional majority might determine the way in which it wanted to live and basically live that way without outside interference. The federal government could not and would not interfere, unless (as happened very rarely) a constitutional issue was raised. Then the resolution took place in a distant courtroom after the event, and it predominantly involved only the parties to the suit.

Obviously this constitutionally endorsed dominance of state over federal government secured the blessings of slavery for slaveholders and their supporters. But it also protected a way of life for which colonists had fought British imperialism for almost twenty years.

15. Mark De Wolfe Howe, "Federalism and Civil Rights," *Massachusetts Historical Society Proceedings*, LXXVII (1965), 15–27; Charles Coleman, *The Election of 1868* (New York, 1933), 19–23.

It conformed to the necessities of a vast land, to the nation's complexity and multitude of local differences. It made sure that the citizens of Maine would be free from the evil influence of alcohol, that Georgia could deal as she chose with Indians, that New York might pass health regulations that fit local conditions, that Maryland might value public improvements over the destruction of an individual's property. In short, it provided Americans with the cherished experience of controlling their own destiny. An 1850 observer described both the dominance and the benefits of states' rights and localism:

> The President has one postmaster in every little village; but the inhabitants of that village choose their own selectmen, their own assessors of taxes, their own school-committee, their own overseers of the poor, their own surveyors of highways, and the incumbents of half a dozen other little offices corresponding to those which, in bureaucratic governments, are filled by the appointment of the sovereign. In all these posts, which are really important public trusts, the villagers are trained to the management of affairs, and acquire a comprehensiveness of view, a practical administrative talent, and a knowledge of business which are, or ought to be, among the chief objects of every system of education. And this training is very general; for owing to our republican liking for rotation in office, the incumbents of these humble posts are changed every year or two, till every decent man in the place has had his turn.[16]

Thus the institution of federalism, potent though it was in depriving the Negro of protection, served more beneficent and popular purposes as well. For obvious reasons this fact was ominous for the success of the struggle for equality. To secure his equality, the freedman would require a major constitutional upheaval. The federal government would have to override almost a century of history and break down the lineaments of a federal system which permitted states, but forbade Washington, to protect and defend the civil and political rights of citizens. While this upheaval might help the Negro, it endangered a treasured institution of most white Ameri-

---

16. Francis Bowen, "The Rebellion against the Magyars," *North American Review*, LXX (1850), 502; Alexis de Tocqueville, *Democracy in America* (New York, 1863), I, 537; Leonard D. White, *The Jacksonians: A Study in Administrative History, 1829–61* (New York, 1954), 509–512.

cans. The black man might be deprived of equal protection of the laws not because he was hated, but because constitutionally established federalism was loved.[17]

This commitment to federalism and constitutionalism did not exclude any substantial body of American nationalist thought. The form of American nationalism enlivened constitutional concern even as it succored states' rights. Whatever may in fact have been the origin of American nationalism, its existence and nature were verified by two written documents, the Declaration of Independence and the Constitution. The first announced the fact of nationhood and proclaimed its ideals; the second described the structure of the government that would administer the nation and delineated the sinews of allegiance. By acceding to these documents, people whose predominant experience had been and would be essentially local made themselves a nation. They also came to understand the nation by specific reciprocal legal obligations. Sidney Hyman's words may clarify the point. "In contrast to the usual course of a nation's development, American nationhood did not evolve out of the experience of a particular ethnic group rooted in a particular stretch of soil. It was a self-consciously created historical experiment based on an ethic of citizenship." Similarly, Yehoshua Arieli has written, "National identity was not a natural fact but an ideological structure." They echo the 1859 idea of Francis Lieber, "Our feelings of loyalty center in these . . . the constitution, or rather the Union. . . ." The nationalism, then, was inescapably bound together with the constitution, and even the strongest nationalists insisted on their passion for the Philadelphia document.[18]

17. In the 1833 case of *Barron* v. *Baltimore*, 7 *Peters* 243 the Supreme Court declared that the Bill of Rights limited the federal government, but not the state governments. Marshall said for the Court, "In almost every convention by which the Constitution was adopted, amendments to guard against the abuse of power were recommended. These amendments demanded security against the apprehended encroachments of the general government—not against those of the local governments." This decision has never been overruled, although the Fourteenth Amendment has increasingly been interpreted to limit the powers of the states to infringe on the rights of citizens.

18. Sidney Hyman, "Rips in the Fabric of the Law," *Saturday Review*, July 11, 1970, 21; Yehoshua Arieli, *Individualism and Nationalism in American Ideology* (Cambridge, 1964), 30; Francis Lieber, *Civil Liberty and Self Government* (Philadelphia, 1959), p 361n. Perry Miller notes with approval Alfred North Whitehead's

Similarly, states' rights devotion was not incompatible with firm nationalism. American nationalism was unique (and therefore most admirable in a nation that prided itself on uniqueness) because here nationhood was maintained by gentle ties of sentiment, not strong reins of centralized command. Here was a nation where men were left alone to pursue their own vision of happiness. The United States garnered devotion because it tolerated and respected local differences. David Potter has argued persuasively that "national loyalty flourishes not by challenging and overpowering all other loyalties, but by subsuming them in a mutually supportive relation to one another." Morton Grodzins agrees: "Direct national loyalty [is] a misnomer. It does not exist. Loyalties are to specific groups, specific goals, specific programs of action. Populations are loyal to nation as a by-product of satisfactions achieved within non-national groups, because the nation is believed to symbolize and sustain those groups."[19]

Even as nineteenth-century Americans trumpeted the uniqueness and superiority of their nation by demanding its expansion, the governmental feature they emphasized was the great merit of federalism. It allowed local units, the states, to administer the vast reaches of territory—a feat impossible for a faraway national government. The nation would not become tyrannical in its expansion, the advocates of manifest destiny and mission argued, because the federal principle, which was part of the expanding national domain, would not allow it. Nationalist Edward Everett spoke for many:

> By the wise and happy partition of powers between the national and state governments, in virtue of which the national government is relieved from all the odium of administration, and the state gov-

---

observation that the United States and the Roman Empire shared a similar fact of birth. In both cases there was the "creation of a nation and an administration by conscious effort . . . statesmen assumed control of historic destinies and refusing to let nature take its course, erected by main force a society . . . to read the history of the first sessions of the Congress under President Washington in 1789 and 1790 is to be driven either to laughter or to tears or to both. Even more than in the first years of the Augustus principate, I suspect, it presents the spectacle of men trying to live from a blueprint." *Nature's Nation* (Cambridge, 1967), 4.

19. David Potter, *The South and the Sectional Conflict* (Baton Rouge, 1968), 48; Morton Grodzins, *The Loyal and the Disloyal* (Chicago, 1956), 29.

ernments are spared the conflicts of foreign politics, all bounds seem removed from the possible extension of our country, but the geographical limits of the continent.

Respect for federalism, the most potent institutional obstacle to the Negroes' hope for protected liberty, was strong throughout American society. It portended difficulty, if not tragedy, in the struggle for equality in the disunion crisis.[20]

Another powerful legal obstacle was the dominant attitude about the proper uses of law to affect the way Americans lived.With few exceptions, traditional American ideas about the role of government did not encourage federal activity. National abundance, a yet undeveloped national economy, and memories of prerevolutionary oppression combined to discourage extensive government action. Creators of and constant participants in local administration, Americans distrusted a governing power which they rarely encountered and almost never needed. Even Thoreau, who was extremely hostile toward government, admitted that he encountered an agent of the government at most once a year. What was the shape of government in the United States? Thomas Carlyle answered, "Anarchy, plus a street constable." "America," he added, is "the most favored of all lands that have no government."[21]

Carlyle's comments accurately described one dominant characteristic of American society, but they overlooked the fact that there were Americans who sought and found government support for their enterprises. From Alexander Hamilton to Henry Clay and beyond, a substantial body of opinion advocated federal government assistance in behalf of the American economy. That government responded with protective tariffs in 1816, 1818, 1824, and 1828, the establishment of two national banks, and the financing of internal improvements such as the national road which linked the states of Maryland, Pennsylvania, Ohio, Indiana, and Illinois together. Wash-

20. Quoted in Albert K. Weinberg, *Manifest Destiny: A Study of Nationalist Expansionism in American History* (Baltimore, 1935), 106; Fredrick Merk, *Manifest Destiny and Mission in American History* (New York, 1963), 26–27.

21. Thomas Carlyle, "Horoscope," *Collected Works*, Sterling ed. (Boston, n.d.), XII, 356–357; Henry David Thoreau, *Walden and Civil Disobedience* (New York, 1966), 232.

ington also assisted states in their own internal improvement efforts and provided surveyors for coastal and interior exploration.

After Andrew Jackson became president, a growing states' rights sentiment diminished federal involvement, but states continued to support the growth of the economy through corporation laws, tax exemptions, granting private use of the power of eminent domain, and occasionally investing public money in corporate securities. Such local activity was, however, insufficient to satisfy many Americans who supported the Whig and Republican parties in order to gain renewed national assistance in their drive for wealth.[22]

Though apparently more promising to the Negro than the states' rights attitudes of Jeffersonians, in fact these ideas offered nothing particularly useful to him. They rested on premises about the nature of America and Americans which were irrelevant to his circumstances. The very success and prosperity of the United States, combined with a potent work ethic, produced a legal environment inimical to those excluded from success by circumstances, incompetence, and the force of law. Slavery and prejudice insured that the Negro often qualified in all three categories. The image behind the legal structure was that of a man capable of achievement who wanted only an environment which made sure that his talents would be allowed to flourish: that the resources of the land might be his for the taking, that the market would secure his transactions, that his enterprises would be allowed to burgeon, that his products would find their way to market. The law that most Americans wanted supported enterprise but seldom regulated it. Not until 1887 would the first federal regulative agency exist.[23]

This law assisted competence; it did next to nothing to compensate for the lack of it. It was the sort of ideology about the uses of law which shamed poverty and only reluctantly and rarely provided state expenditures to help the needy. The federal government was even less active—it completely denied its funds even to such worthy prewar proposals as that of Dorothea Dix, which would

22. James Willard Hurst, *Law and the Conditions of Freedom in the Nineteenth Century United States* (Madison, 1956); Alfred H. Kelly and Winfred Harbison, *The American Constitution: Its Origins and Development* (New York, 1970), 330–332.

23. *Ibid.* The Interstate Commerce Commission was created by Congress in 1887.

have used money from the sale of public lands to aid the insane. Miss Dix had reasoned that, if such money was available to aid private enterprise, it should be available to help the sick. She was mistaken. During and after the war the federal government showed the same reluctance to extend charity. The wartime Freedman's Bureau depended on the sale of abandoned southern lands for its funding; the postwar bureau was given money only to purchase buildings for schools. It depended on private charities for its survival, and even its leader, General O. O. Howard, thought that its very existence was temporary.[24]

When Americans used their governments, they used them to open channels for action, to release energy, but seldom to interfere with individual lives. For example, Chief Justice Lemuel Shaw of Massachusetts handed down decisions which encouraged railroads to grow and prosper and discouraged potentially restraining forces. Did a mill pond owner complain that a railroad right of way destroyed his pond? The right of the road must take precedence, Shaw replied, for railroads expanded the prosperity of the commonwealth. Did a worker claim damages against a railroad because a switch went unattended and he incurred injury? Shaw answered with a fellow servant doctrine of negligence which made damage suits almost impossible. His celebrated pro-labor decision in *Commonwealth* v. *Hunt* reflected his view that all participants in an economy deserved an equal opportunity to engage in free and open competition.[25]

Law was used to open the environment for enterprise. Pure laissez faire did not exist, of course; all government agencies did not step aside and let anything and everything transpire which might. But the action that did take place was predominantly action in favor of freedom. It removed barriers to the full exercise of individual talent. The thoughtful arguments of James Willard Hurst, Louis Hartz,

24. Willie Lee Rose, *Rehearsal for Reconstruction* (Indianapolis, 1964), 352–353, 374–376; Alice Felt Tyler, *Freedom's Ferment* (Minneapolis, 1964), 286–287, 291–292, 306–307; John Cox and Lawanda Cox, "General O. O. Howard and the 'Misrepresented Bureau,'" *Journal of Southern History*, XIX (Nov., 1953), 441; George H. Bentley, *A History of the Freedman's Bureau* (Philadelphia, 1955), 172; William S. McFeely, *Yankee Stepfather: General O. O. Howard and the Freedmen* (New Haven, 1968), 1–9.

25. Levy, *Law of the Commonwealth*, 140–170.

and the Handlins against a purely laissez faire perspective on American history are useful correctives to an oversimplified viewpoint,
but they do not change the basic fact that few Americans ever
encountered an agent of government above the local level, and fewer
still wanted to. Most people wanted a free field and no favor, an
open run at acquisition. The law might be used to grease the wheels,
but it would seldom draw the map to direct enterprise. Americans
were using law and government to encourage each individual to
acquire all that he could, to own his environment and to master it
by himself. People were mastering the continent by bits and pieces
and using law to insure the continued individual enterprise necessary
for continued conquest. Law did not get in the way—it cleared the
way.[26]

This was selfishness, of course, but selfishness robbed of its usual
brutality by the fact of abundance. The simple abundance of land
and opportunity kept open for almost all white men the chance to
pursue, acquire, and bank "happiness." Americans were realizing in
large measure Jefferson's ideal—a nation of individual landowners,
masters of their environment, experiencing the feeling of freedom
that only those who were such masters could know. They were
doing so under Jefferson's ideal government, one which hardly
ever governed. The American form of laissez faire worked, and
gave the endorsement of personal experience to prevailing constitutional views.

The government which would be tested by the Civil War could
and did stay out of the lives of practically everyone because it was
not needed to make those lives abundant and generally happy. As
the contest over the second Bank of the United States demonstrated,
most people distrusted connections between power and wealth because it suggested a control which they seldom sought and felt they
did not need. It was as if Americans were saying, "We can. Let us."

26. Hurst, *Law and the Conditions of Freedom*; Louis Hartz, *Economic Policy
and Democratic Thought: Pennsylvania 1776–1860* (Cambridge, 1948); Oscar and
Mary Handlin, *Commonwealth: A Study of the Role of Government in the
American Economy, Massachusetts 1774–1861* (New York, 1947). Robert A. Lively,
reviewing the literature of the extent of government aid to enterprise in the
nineteenth century, observes, "The substantial energies of government were employed more often for help than for hindrance of enterprise." *Business History
Review*, XXIX (March, 1955), 85–96.

Happily for them, most white Americans could. But it was hardly the sort of environment to help black Americans who most emphatically could not.

This optimistic legal attitude was manifested in the political sphere by the expansion of democracy. Faith in the ability of all men showed itself in the growing dominance of legislatures over executives, and especially over judicial branches of government. Movements developed to elect judges and to allow further chances for white men to own and control a piece of the continent.

Most legal thinkers opposed this trend. As Perry Miller has brilliantly shown, they were afraid that such freedom might be license, might destroy the existing necessary legal sinews of society. They feared for both liberty and property and worried about dangers to order. Victories by Jackson's Democratic party threw Supreme Court Justice Joseph Story into somber musing. "I am sorry to be obliged to take a gloomy view of the future prospects of the Republic," he wrote. "I read nothing in what is now going on which may not be read in the history of every other Republic which has existed and has perished." A glimmer of hope appeared for the Negro in this reaction to assumed democratic excesses. Insofar as his freedom would require militant opposition to what Lincoln called the "anarchy" of secession, a strong sentiment for order was being generated here. Perhaps frightened by Jackson, the legal establishment would espouse a fight against secessionists that would inevitably destroy slavery.[27]

But even this hopeful element in prewar legal thought did not promise creation of the energetic and concerned government required to provide the Negro with meaningful freedom. Both democrats and apprehensive lawyers shared a similar idol—liberty from government. Anti-Jacksonians were afraid that government in the hands of untutored democrats would endanger individual rights. Jacksonians feared government in hands other than their own. Neither were consistent apostles of the kind of powerful government which equality would demand.

27. Perry Miller, *The Life of the Mind in America* (New York, 1965), 99ff.; Daniel J. Boorstin, *The Americans: The National Experience* (New York, 1965), 35-39; Joseph Story to Francis Lieber, February 9, 1836, Lieber Papers, Henry Huntington Library, San Marino, Calif.

The idea of freedom from government dominated the American mind so strongly that, on the verge of a great outreach of federal power, even Lincoln described the war in Jacksonian terms.

> This is essentially a People's contest. On the side of the Union, it is a struggle for maintaining in the world that form and substance of government whose leading object is to elevate the condition of men —to lift artificial weights from all shoulders—to clear the paths of laudable pursuit for all—to afford all an unfettered start, and a fair chance in the race of life. Yielding to partial and temporary departures, from necessity, this is the leading object of the government for whose existence we contend.[28]

Such was the legal environment in which the struggle for equal liberty was begun. In 1860 the signs were not hopeful, but when secession was followed by civil war, prospects brightened. To preserve the Union, war was being waged against the South, and that would ultimately mean against slavery. No longer would the Negro's freedom have to depend on the white man's compassion for his bondage. When the South seceded to preserve slavery, it bound with links of steel the survival of the Union with the death of slavery. The numbers of Northerners interested in the condition of the Negro increased dramatically, supplemented daily by the legions of those willing to crush the rebellion by any means necessary.

Driven by the need to insure the loyalty of pro-Union slave states, and concerned over the question of constitutional limitations, Lincoln disavowed his intention to make the Civil War an antislavery crusade. But soldiers in the field, their friends and relatives at home, and millions of other Northerners quickly came to know better. It was impossible to separate the fight against the Confederacy from blows against the slavery which supported Confederate efforts. Soon the President accepted this reality. Beginning with the Emancipation Proclamation and culminating with the Thirteenth Amendment, he joined survival of the nation with freedom of the Negro. The over 170,000 Negro Union soldiers made this connection inescapable.

Constitutional questions provoked by the war also seemed auspicious for equality. For almost twenty years the South had demanded

28. Basler, ed., *Collected Works of Lincoln*, IV, 438.

that national power be exerted on behalf of slavery. But in defending secession, Southerners raised the states' rights–state sovereignty banner and attempted constitutionally to march out of the Union under it. In reaction many Northerners, though they supported states' rights "properly construed," damned the state sovereignty fetish and spoke of a federal government with expanded power over the states. In fact, federal power did expand during the war, and it appeared that the restrictive influence of federalism would be correspondingly diminished. Further grounds for hope existed in the very fact that a disunion crisis had occurred at all. Some observers suggested that this crisis was encouraged by profound constitutional defects which would have to be remedied, perhaps by expanding federal power over state domains.[29]

But while the disunion crisis might foster hopes for equality, it might also defeat them. The imperative precondition for an end to slavery was a war which would permit the nation to forget its negrophobia and its constitutional compunctions. When both sides accepted the war that resulted from secession, the slaves gained their freedom. Yet the very goal of the war itself, the Union, endangered the possibility that their freedom would be protected. The Civil War was a struggle for the familiar federal Union, a fight for a constitutional system under which Americans had achieved unparalleled prosperity and liberty. Although prospects existed for vast constitutional change, they might be undone by a respect for constitutional traditions so powerful that men would die for them. Although there could be no freedom without the war, it might be that to win the war would be to lose the peace insofar as gains for blacks were concerned. That would depend on the extent to which the problems of disunion, war, and reunion produced changes in the nation's constitutional and legal thought.

The war revealed a broad spectrum of constitutional thought

29. Arthur Bestor, "The American Civil War as a Constitutional Crisis," *American Historical Review*, LXIX (Jan., 1964), 327–352; Bestor, "State Sovereignty and Slavery: A Reinterpretation of Proslavery Constitutional Doctrine, 1846–60," *Journal of the Illinois State Historical Society*, LIV (Summer, 1961), 148–174; E. L. Godkin, "The Constitution and Its Defects," *North American Review*, XCIX (July, 1864), 117–145; Sidney George Fisher, *The Trial of the Constitution* (Philadelphia, 1863); Leonard P. Curry, *Blueprint for Modern America: Nonmilitary Legislation of the First Civil War Congress* (Nashville, 1968).

among its supporters. On one end stood the radical belief that in time of war the Constitution was best ignored— that the law would sanctify whatever was demanded for survival of the Union. On the other stood the conservative insistence that respect for constitutional limitations was vital if the nation was to emerge from the conflict with liberty as well as union intact. Men's thinking fell all along this continuum; even the most vocal radical could be found revealing his constitutional scruples, and conservatives usually found something that they wanted enough to allow a deviation from constitutional precedent. Consistency of viewpoint is less important than the fact that constitutional debate was constant and voluminous throughout the disunion crisis. If we want to understand that era, we must study that thought. The constitutional argument was not "interesting but essentially irrelevant"; it shaped the legislative and judicial response to the era and thus changed (or, more importantly, failed to change) lives.[30]

If the Negro was to achieve equal liberty, the Civil War would have to produce vast constitutional change. The federal government would have to transgress almost a century of history and break down the constitutional division of power which allowed states but not Washington to determine the civil rights of citizens. No such change was possible in peacetime, but perhaps a fight for national survival might provoke it. The crucial question was: how much respect for the Constitution is commensurate with the demands of war?

That query brought despair to many men. Chief Justice Taney could not visualize the Constitution surviving a civil war; thousands of Peace Democrats or Copperheads felt the same way. They argued repeatedly that the war killed liberty as efficiently as it killed rebels. Indiana's Daniel Voorhees voiced the fears of many: "What is there to America worth preserving if the principles of liberty, the doctrine of the Constitution, shall perish?" It was said that the life of the nation was in danger. He agreed—but the life of a nation was its liberty, as well as its territory. Without the preservation of liberty, "the mere form of our Government will be a cold and lifeless corpse. We are asked to make war on this vital principle and to submit to

30. The comment about the essential irrelevancy of the constitutional discussion comes from Stampp, *The Era of Reconstruction,* 25.

its destruction, in order to preserve the Union. You might as well ask me to plunge a dagger into my heart in order to preserve my life."[31]

But despite such gloomy counsels, the war went on. The constitutional debate between earnest supporters of the war continued as well; it was no less bitter because the participants were quarreling over means rather than ends. And it was of immense importance to the Negro as well as to the nation. If the view prevailed that the existing constitutional system was the prize of war, then, even though the Union might be saved, the freedom of blacks would be only half won. If the view prevailed that the Constitution was at best a symbol and at worst an impediment to national survival, there might be reason for the black man to hope for secure equality. The two most prolific writers for these contending viewpoints were the German-born political theorist Francis Lieber and the more conservative Harvard professor of constitutional law Joel Parker.

Lieber's prewar writings had given him an international reputation and won him the respect of Americans of all sections. Joseph Story stated a widespread opinion when he wrote to Lieber, "You know ten times as much as [Tocqueville] does of the actual workings of our system and of its true theory." A modern scholar concurs as to Lieber's importance. Merle Curti insists that Lieber "may be regarded as the most significant figure during the [Civil War] period, in articulating and promoting among intellectuals and public men a theory of nationalism in general and American nationalism in particular." During the conflict the theorist was chairman of the publications committee for the Loyal Publication Society, a militant pro-Unionist organization. He wrote ten of the society's ninety pamphlets and managed to implant his own radicalism in the others. He corresponded for over thirty years with radical senator Charles Sumner, advising Sumner and other congressmen on matters of war and reconstruction. If there was a single individual who spoke most consistently for the radical nationalists of the North during that era, Lieber was the man.[32]

31. *Congressional Globe*, 37th Cong., 3rd sess., p. 1062; Carl Brent Swisher, *Roger Brook Taney* (New York, 1935), 456; Frank Klement, *The Copperheads in the Middle West* (Chicago, 1960).

32. Story to Lieber, May 9, 1840, Lieber Papers; Merle Curti, "Francis Lieber

Parker was less known to the public but needed no introduction to a generation of American lawyers. In addition to a twenty-year tenure at Harvard (1848–68), he had served an outstanding decade as chief justice of the New Hampshire Supreme Court. In 1844 Sumner called Parker "one of the ablest judges of the country." His best-known student, Oliver Wendell Holmes, Jr., referred to him as "one of the greatest of American judges . . . who showed in the chair the same qualities that made him famous on the bench."

In addition to teaching, Parker was the author of the most consistent statement of respectable conservative opinion to appear during the war. He wrote seven lengthy articles for the wartime *North American Review* covering every major constitutional question of the disunion crisis. He commented with intelligence and insight on the right of secession, the legality of the suspension of the privilege of the writ of habeas corpus, the legitimacy of emancipation, the proper extent of the power to conduct war, and the relationship of civil to international war. Some of his wartime arguments would later echo in the Supreme Court. After Appomattox he continued to offer the nation his opinions on the major constitutional questions of Reconstruction. Of the widespread criticism of expanded national government, Parker's best combined breadth of commentary with depth of analysis.[33]

Since the major concern of the present work is that of national protection for Negro rights, it is important to consider the relationship between national power and the Negro during the war. The man whose writings most clearly reflect that relationship is the relatively obscure Sidney George Fisher. Fisher wrote on most major questions of the prewar period and commented on a wide range of issues after the war. His most important work, however, is *The Trial of the Constitution*, an original and thoughtful analysis of the weaknesses of the Constitution and the way to remedy them. His remedy involved the first argument against the separation of

and Nationalism," *Huntington Library Quarterly*, IV (1941), 263–292; Frank Freidel, *Francis Lieber, Nineteenth Century Liberal* (Baton Rouge, 1947), 345–353, 378–382.

33. George S. Hale, "Joel Parker," *American Law Review*, X (Jan., 1876), pp. 235–269; Mark De Wolfe Howe, *Justice Oliver Wendell Holmes: The Shaping Years* (Cambridge, 1957), 184–186; John Philip Reid, *Chief Justice: The Judicial World of Charles Doe* (Cambridge, 1967), 47.

powers to appear in this country, an assertion of British constitutional principles which he hoped would save the American Constitution. Most intriguing about Fisher's thought, however, was the result when his profound racism encountered his insistence on the vast extent of federal power.[34]

As the 1880s and 1890s heard the death knell for promises of equal justice, two lawyers were making their reputations. By the closing decades of the century, Thomas McIntyre Cooley and John Norton Pomeroy were revered and respected by the legal profession. Cooley's *Constitutional Limitations* had become the bible of corporation lawyers seeking to protect clients from the regulatory efforts of state and federal governments. Pomeroy's *Remedies and Remedial Rights* was the guidebook for recent nationwide movements to codify the law, and his *Equity Jurisprudence* shaped equity law in the United States. Both men had witnessed the disunion crisis and had analyzed the extent of constitutional revolution produced by Reconstruction. As their reputations expanded in the last third of the century, so would the influence of their opinions on the question of protection of Negro rights. Their views became those which prevailed for almost a century.[35]

Of course, none of these men waited until the war began to develop his legal and constitutional views. The origins of the constitutional thought of the disunion years lie in the Jacksonian era. Americans who experienced and responded to conflict were educated and grew to maturity when the spirit of Old Hickory dominated society, and as late as 1868 men were still calling themselves "Jacksonian Democrats." With this fact in mind I have sought to provide, where possible, the background of their responses to war and reconstruction by describing their reactions to Jackson's America.[36]

---

34. Clinton Rossiter, *Constitutional Dictatorship* (Princeton, 1948), 224n; *The Trial of the Constitution* (Philadelphia, 1862); William H. Riker, "Sidney George Fisher and the Separation of Powers during the Civil War," *Journal of the History of Ideas*, XV (June, 1954), 370–412.

35. Sidney Fine, *Laissez Faire and the General Welfare State* (Ann Arbor, 1956), 128–129; John Norton Pomeroy, Jr., "John Norton Pomeroy," *Great American Lawyers*, ed. William D. Lewis (Philadelphia, 1909), III, 89–136.

36. Francis Lieber to Martin Russell Thayer, Oct. 7, 1868, Lieber Papers. Kenneth Stampp is wrong in calling Andrew Johnson "The Last Jacksonian"

As a starting point, however, it is important to demonstrate the extent to which the war itself was a constitutional and legal crisis, and to reveal how tenaciously men clung to the Constitution in responding to disunion. This widespread constitutional concern was not confined to private studies, libraries, or lecture halls. Legislators continually sought in the Constitution justification for their efforts to save the Union. Although this study focuses on five representative legal thinkers, the most significant measure of their insights is the way in which efforts to solve practical constitutional problems reflected similar concerns and imperatives. Indeed, it was the political-constitutional institutions' failure to respond successfully to the disunion crisis which provoked jurists to express their views and to seek to exercise influence in that expression. A brief investigation of the constitutional concern of congressmen and judges may clarify the nature of problems faced by the subjects of this work and may indicate their role.

(*The Era of Reconstruction*, ch. 3), as I trust the present work will demonstrate. The legal-constitutional ideas of Jackson's era would retain potency years after Lincoln's successor died.

War for the
Constitution and the Union

In October, 1865, a writer in the *Nation* magazine reflected on the Civil War just passed and noted a singular fact: "Nothing has been more remarkable during the war than the rapidity with which 'legal fictions' sprang up as the strife progressed. Generally the sword tears all the lawyer's fine-spun webs to pieces, and lays the naked facts of the case before the world, but our war has furnished an exception to the rule."[1]

The writer, probably English-born E. L. Godkin, should not have been surprised at the respect for law demonstrated by Americans in the disunion crisis. The issues which had provoked the conflict were largely constitutional: Did Congress have power over slavery in the territories? Were the rights of slaveowners national rights? What was the structure of the Union? And, as historian Arthur Bestor observes, "The very form that the conflict took was determined by the pre-existing form of the Constitutional system."[2]

When war broke out, sensitive observers were quick to understand that more than a question of armed might was at issue—the foundation of law itself had been challenged. Andrew Preston Peabody, editor of the *North American Review*, declared that the fight was for the Constitution itself, a document which "claims our allegiance because it is law and order—the only government possible for us, the only bond of peace and beneficent relations by which our nation can be held together, and can maintain its place among the nations of the earth. The theory of the Secessionists resolves itself into universal distintegration and anarchy." Five days after Sumter, Stephen A. Douglas had declared that the conflict just begun was

1. "Legal Fictions," *Nation*, I (Oct. 12, 1865), 455–456.
2. Bestor, "The American Civil War as a Constitutional Crisis," 329, 332.

"not a question of Union or disunion. It is a question of order; of the stability of government; of the peace of communities." He was echoing Lincoln. "Plainly, the central idea of secession," the newly inaugurated President had said, "is the essence of anarchy."[3]

Decades of oratory had forged an ill-defined bond between union and the nation's fundamental law. When inaugurated as vice-president, Thomas Jefferson told the Senate, "I consider the Union of these States as the first of blessings, and as the first of duties the preservation of that Constitution which secures it." Years later, South Carolina's Robert Hayne told an Independence Day crowd that "the Union I revere and which is dear to my heart is founded on the Constitution of my country. It is a constitutional union, which we are sworn to preserve, protect, and defend." Antagonist Daniel Webster agreed with that. The Constitution was "the band which binds together twelve millions of brothers." The *Whig Review* joined the chorus: "Our Union is but the symbol of Constitutional freedom." The *Democratic Review* harmonized: "The Constitution of the United States is the Union and the only Union known to the American people." And in 1858 Jefferson Davis came to Boston and told an enthusiastic crowd, "We became a nation by the Constitution, whatever is national springs from the Constitution; and national and constitutional are convertible terms."[4] By the time disunion came, Northerners were ready to believe that their fundamental law was threatened and had to be fought for.

Of course, Southerners could find a different meaning in these words. If the Union was founded on the Constitution, then a violation of that Constitution by Northerners was a justification for disunion. But both sections shared a respect for the Philadelphia document and what it represented which was strong enough to shape the course of the war. When the South seceded, it demonstrated its reverence by framing a constitution similar in marked degree to the one written in 1787. Given the opportunity to create a

3. "Loyalty," *North American Review*, XCIV (Jan., 1862), 156; *Rebellion Record*, ed. Frank Moore (New York, 1862), I, 40–41; Basler, ed., *Collected Works of Lincoln*, IV, 268; Kenneth M. Stampp, *And the War Came: The North and the Secession Crisis, 1860–61* (Baton Rouge, 1950), 33–34, 54, 75, 200.

4. Quoted in Paul C. Nagel, *One Nation Indivisible: The Union in American Thought* (New York, 1964), 53–58.

new government structure, the rebels chose to copy the old one.[5]

In the North respect for the Constitution was constantly and loudly expressed as men took seriously the belief that the war was for the Constitution and the Union. The attitudes of Copperheads are the most obvious example. Basically extreme advocates of Jeffersonian government, they objected passionately to measures used by Lincoln to prosecute the war. Combining negrophobia with pro-southern sentiment, small government ideology with civil libertarian rhetoric, Copperheads posed a serious obstacle to the success of Lincoln's wartime orders. By 1862 Union leaders had reason to believe that the small government philosophy, expressed with special eloquence in the Middle West, would bring major influence to the Democratic party there and elsewhere.[6]

This constitutional concern was not the sole property of antiwar protestors. In developing their strategy of loyal opposition, the War Democrats grasped the Constitution as their standard. In the midst of the war powerful Democratic leader Samuel Tilden told his political allies that the Lincoln administration had yielded to "fatal radical influence." It was the duty of the Democrats to support the war but to "serve as a counterpoise in . . . constitutional opposition." New York's Governor Horatio Seymour asserted that by ignoring the Constitution the Republicans endangered support for the fight to save the Union. He sought to gather into the Democratic Party "the great masses of conservatives who still battle for the time-honored principles of government." It would be their job to "stand between this government and its own destruction." As of 1862 the motto of the northern Democratic party was, "The Constitution as it is; the Union as it was."[7]

The Republican party was equally sensitive to the pervasive con-

5. Charles Robert Lee, *The Confederate Constitutions* (Chapel Hill, 1963); Roy F. Nichols, *American Leviathan* (New York, 1966), 164–181.

6. Frank Klement, *Copperheads in the Middle West*; Ralph H. Gabriel, "Constitutional Democracy: A Nineteenth Century Faith," *The Constitution Reconsidered*, ed. Conyers Read (New York, 1938), 247–258.

7. Society for the Diffusion of Political Knowledge, *The Constitution* (New York, 1863–64), 11–13, 105. This work is a collection of anti-administration speeches, letters, and writings emphasizing Lincoln's alleged transgressions against the Constitution.

stitutionalism of the people. Despite the innovative use of national
power by the Lincoln government, the 1864 platform still managed
to insist on the party's staunch constitutional commitment five times
in an eleven-part platform. These words echoed the President's
attention to such questions. When Lincoln declared at Gettysburg
that the war tested the U.S. government's ability to survive, he was,
in large measure, striking a constitutional note. The nation could
not endure unless it resolved the conflict between liberty and power
which had always troubled it. As early as July, 1861, the President
had emphasized his compelling concern with the problem of fundamental law: "Must a government of necessity be too strong for the
liberties of its people, or too weak to maintain its own existence?"
These were signals of a pervasive constitutionalism in a nation whose
rule of law had been challenged. In addition, the crisis and the response to it tended to generate respect for specific aspects of the
constitutional system, primarily for states' rights.[8]

This respect rested on a secure foundation. As Edward S. Corwin
observes, "Secession had been the serious threat that it was in
1860 not because the states' rights theory was strong in the South,
but because it was strong throughout the whole country." Although state sovereignty arguments had justified secession, the
states' rights sentiment was not seriously damaged. Indeed, the vitality shown by most northern states in response to secession provided
strong reasons to respect these local governments.[9]

Lincoln's post-Sumter program was given energetic implementation by the states. Even before Sumter fell, Wisconsin and New
York had enacted military measures providing hundreds of thousands of dollars to support prospective regiments. Rhode Island and
New Jersey were similarly active, as were Massachusetts and Pennsylvania. In the early days of war Governors Morton of Indiana,
Andrew of Massachusetts, and Yates of Illinois were the true secre-
taries of war of the endangered United States. They raised troops,
gathered supplies, and offered money to pay for both. It was, Fred

8. Basler, ed. *Collected Works of Lincoln*, IV, 426; *Documents of American History*, ed. Henry Steele Commager (New York, 1948), I, 435.

9. *Federalism as a Democratic Process, Essays by Roscoe Pound, Charles H. McIlwain, Roy Franklin Nichols* (New Brunswick, 1942), 86–87. Corwin's comment on Nichols's paper.

Shannon notes, "a striking contrast between a feeble and tottering federal government and a group of lusty state governments which were both stable and financially sound."[10]

Indiana's Oliver P. Morton constantly gave evidence of his state's concern for her soldiers. He kept in touch with them through his personal secretary. Indiana casualties were cared for by the Indiana Sanitary Commission, which provided not only medical care, but also food, clothing, bedding, soap, whiskey, wine, tobacco, writing paper, Bibles, and other books. Morton's efforts embroiled him in conflicts with federal officials, and the Indiana commission was never on good terms with the U.S. Sanitary Commission. The state agency opposed union with the national because it feared losing its special ability to take care of Hoosiers. Federal commissioners responded to this insularity by charging that Indiana's efforts manifested "that obnoxious heresy of State sovereignty, against which the whole war [is] directed."[11]

Ohio also provided medical care for its soldiers after having raised and equipped them. Governor David Tod took a personal interest in the welfare of Ohio troops and continually telegraphed Washington, demanding attention to the wants of these men. In 1864 John Brough replaced Todd, but harassment of federal officials on behalf of Buckeye warriors did not slacken. Brough also acted to increase the amount of aid given to soldiers' families, and he carefully supervised state agencies engaged in this work. Their welfare efforts expanded; the U.S. Sanitary Commission reacted with its usual objections.[12]

The Illinois picture was similar. An active governor, Richard Yates, raised troops with great vigor in war's early days. His legislature provided the necessary funds to supply these troops; behind the lines the women of Illinois made clothing, bandages, and other personal items. They promoted benefit concerts and performances to raise money for the men in arms. By 1863 Illinois ladies had orga-

10. Fred A. Shannon, "State Rights and the Union Army," *Mississippi Valley Historical Review*, XII (June, 1925), 51–71.

11. Emma Lou Thornbrough, *Indiana in the Civil War Era* (Indianapolis, 1965), 104–110, 175–176, 188–190.

12. Eugene Roseboom, *The Civil War Era, 1850–73* (Columbus, 1944), 396, 426–427, 443.

nized themselves into ladies union leagues to substitute for male clerks and other workers who had enlisted. The state had no sanitary commission of its own but still provided the support for one. When word arrived of the capture of Fort Donelson and the resulting casualties, the state constitutional convention took an unprecedented step and assumed the responsibility for raising $500,000 to give relief to the wounded. The next year $10,000 more was set aside by the state legislature.[13]

These activities and others like them throughout the North certainly demonstrated and encouraged the belief that states were worthy objects of admiration by their citizens, deserving devotion as well as allegiance. Small wonder, then, that the federal government did not confuse a war against state sovereignty extremism with a war endangering states' rights. As James G. Randall observes, "The national government, especially in the early part of the war, showed a scrupulous regard for state functions, this attitude being carried even to the point of hindering the Government. On the other side, States were jealous of retaining important activities, and their actions frequently encroached upon Federal jurisdiction."[14]

The war in fact proved the vitality of all elements of government within the American leviathan. It proved in the end, of course, that the federal government could preserve itself. But it proved continually the energy of state and local governments as well. As Roy F. Nichols notes,

> Among many a particularly significant question was resolved—the question whether the federal system could continue to function under the strain of its two specified strata; whether legislators on two levels, state and federal, could cooperate; whether state legislatures, state governors, and state courts could operate in sufficient correlation with Congress, the President, and federal courts to make possible the bringing of such a full scale war to a conclusion.[15]

13. Arthur Charles Cole, *The Era of the Civil War, 1848–70* (Springfield, 1919), 273–284.

14. James G. Randall, *Constitutional Problems under Lincoln* (Urbana, 1951), 406.

15. Nichols, *American Leviathan*, 257; Daniel J. Elazar, "Comment," *Economic Change in the Civil War Era*, ed. David T. Gilchrist and W. Davis Lewis (Greenville, 1965), 94–108. For an elaboration of the important role played by states throughout the nineteenth century, see Lance Davis and John Legler, "The Gov-

Federal government did expand during the war, but this expansion did not necessarily come at the expense of the states. Randall issued a warning on this point in his benchmark work on constitutional questions during the Civil War. "The national government," he observed, "did not extend its power by the assumption of State functions so much as by taking to itself the conduct of its own affairs. Nationalizing measures were for national objects."[16]

Government activity increased at the state and local level, too. As a result of the war, state per capita expenditures increased throughout the North. New England recorded the greatest increase, jumping from $1.28 in 1860 to $9.36 in 1865. Other regions showed a similar rise in per capita spending. The middle Atlantic states spent $1.94 on each citizen in 1860; by 1865 that figure was $3.47. In the Old Northwest the war brought a change from $1.19 in 1860 to $2.21 in 1861, $2.13 in 1862, $2.19 in 1863, $1.74 in 1864, and $1.61 in 1865. Even in the region comprising Iowa, Missouri, Minnesota, Kansas, Nebraska, and the Dakotas, where the per capita spending was $.04 less in 1865 than in 1860, the war era witnessed the beginning of a general increase in state spending and activity. Daniel Elazar is correct in his assertion that during the disunion decade the "expansion of government was not primarily a centralization of power within the traditional system at the expense of the state and local governments, but a growth of government activity (and, with it, real power) at all levels—federal, state, and local."[17]

State governments earned the respect of their citizens by energetic efforts to protect state regiments and support the war. They demanded the respect of the federal government by jealously upholding their rights in state courts. When Congress passed the 1863 Habeas Corpus Act, it had inserted a provision which provided protection from prosecution for federal officers performing military duties. In state after state, judges either struck down the measure or evaded it and asserted the traditional lineaments of the federal sys-

---

ernment in the American Economy, 1815–1902: A Quantitative Study," *Journal of Economic History*, XXVI (Dec., 1966), 514–527.

16. Randall, *Constitutional Problems*, 432. For another view see Nichols, *American Leviathan*, 273–274.

17. Davis and Legler, "The Government in the American Economy, 1815–1902," 514–551; Daniel Elazar, "Comment," 94–95.

tem. Despite a war for Union and against the ultimate assertion of
state sovereignty, state judges insisted on affirming their own prerogatives. The Union they envisioned was a union of states. Before
the Democratic party had adopted the slogan "The Constitution as
it is, the Union as it was," state judges had insisted on the slogan as a
fact.[18]

Perhaps the most revealing explanation of states' rights feeling
came from Illinois Governor Yates in January, 1865. Yates was a
militant radical in the Reconstruction era and anticipated such sentiment before Appomattox. During the war he was most vigorous in
urging greater effort by the federal government against the rebellion. He led the way in demanding the radical step of using black
troops as combatants. Yet such beliefs did not preclude a marked
commitment to preserving state influence and integrity.

There was, he told the state assembly in January, 1865, no "political heresy so dangerous to our existence as the doctrine of the right
of secession." But it was dangerous because it was similar to ideas
rightly cherished by Americans everywhere. Southerners had taken
the poisonous doctrine of secession and "sugar coated [it] with
the plausible sobriquet of State Sovereignty." Beguiled by the
southern view of what constituted such sovereignty, unprincipled
Northerners had attempted to inhibit the ability of the government
to preserve itself.

That did not mean that state sovereignty was in itself wrong.
After all, Yates explained, the motto of Illinois was "State Sovereignty and National Union." When understood properly, this was
"the best and most beautiful motto which adorns the armorial bearing of any state in the Union." He continued:

> I am for unlimited state sovereignty in the true sense, in the sense
> that the State is to control all its municipal and local legislation and I
> would be the first to resist all attempts upon the part of the Federal
> Government to interpose tyrannical usurpation of power in con-

18. The state cases are *Griffin* v. *Wilcox*, 21 *Indiana* 370 (1863); *In re Kemp*, 16
Wisconsin 382 (1863); *Warren* v. *Paul*, 22 *Indiana* 276 (1864); *Short* v. *Wilson*, 1
Bush 350 (1866), (Kentucky). Randall (*Constitutional Problems*, 428–429) describes
as "frequent" cases where federal officers were held answerable by state courts despite the 1863 bill.

trolling the legislation of States. The States are sovereign in every sense in which it is desirable they should have sovereignty. . . .[19]

Crucial in any analysis of the proper dimensions of such sovereignty was a determination of just where it would be desirable. Yates described his view in terms broad enough to give a sense of power to state sovereignty proponents of the most militant cast. Such sovereignty was properly exercised in those areas where "the people know and understand their immediate wants, social, agricultural, commercial, mechanical, educational, municipal." If Congress interfered with these without the consent of the people of the state, then there would be "a flagrant abuse of power which every patriot son of Illinois would resist with all his energies and all his life." Even to this militant radical, the dimensions of state sovereignty were vast.

He even suggested that the war might expand and not decrease the vitality of states, thus making them even less subject to interference from Washington. The recent experience, "the rapidity in growth and population of the States[,] makes them feel their consequence and strength more and their dependence less sensibly on the Federal Government," he concluded. Vigorous states, sensitive of their rights and sovereignty, with a broad view of their legitimate domain—this was a most significant legacy of the Civil War. It suggested little change in the federal system which the Constitution enshrined.[20]

Federal legislators also showed marked concern for constitutional restraints. Lincoln expanded the role of the President far beyond limitations suggested by tradition. Faced with unprecedented circumstances, he explained, "I suppose I have the right to take any measure which may subdue the enemy." But Congress did not always share this supposition. Legislators showed considerable opposition to the unrestrained exercise of executive prerogative. The antebellum experience of legislative dominance and respect for legal structure among lawyers of House and Senate produced demands

19. *Reports Made to the General Assembly of Illinois*, 34th sess. (Springfield, 1865), I, 28; Edward Gambill, "Who Were the Senate Radicals?" *Civil War History*, XI (Sept., 1965), 237–244.
20. *Reports to General Assembly*, 29.

that written law replace, or at least define, executive orders.

The desire of even radicals to impose their will on the President may have been rooted partly in a desire to replace presidential fiat with the rule of law. As Ben Wade explained, "The president cannot lay down and fix the principles upon which war shall be conducted. . . . It is for Congress to lay down the rules and regulations by which the Executive shall be governed in conducting a war." Charles Sumner echoed these sentiments and made more specific a congressional desire that traditional legal ideas control the necessities of war. When Lincoln appointed military governors for occupied southern states, Sumner observed that such action was "without sanction in the Constitution and laws . . . its effect is to subordinate the civil to the military authority, contrary to the spirit of our institutions and in derogation of the powers of Congress."[21]

Wade and Sumner were not apostles of constitutional restraint, yet there was in their statements an argument that was often heard and believed during wartime congressional debates. Noticeable in most discussions was an effort to provide order and restrictions, legal boundaries, to potentially unregulated action. Congressional action regarding civil liberty is an instructive example of this sentiment.[22]

Initially Congress tried to avoid major legislation on the issue. Americans were notoriously sensitive where their civil liberties were concerned, and few congressmen relished the idea of having to explain to constituents any apparent tampering with their civil liberties. Nevertheless, early in the war Illinois Senator Lyman Trumbull, chairman of the Senate Judiciary Committee, presented a bill to regulate the exercise of martial law in areas under army control.

21. *Congressional Globe*, 37th Cong., 2nd sess., p. 2596. Earlier, Congressman Fernando Beaman, in arguing against executive military control, called such control "incompatible with the spirit of our institutions" (*ibid.*, 1555). James G. Randall, *Lincoln, the Liberal Statesman* (New York, 1947), 127; T. Harry Williams, "Lincoln and the Radicals: An Essay in Civil War History and Historiography," *Grant, Lee, Lincoln, and the Radicals*, ed. Grady McWhiney (Evanston, 1964), 109–110. Williams contends that legislators "wanted to set up a kind of Congressional dictatorship," and uses the Wade quotation. Seen in the context of the material below, Wade's words suggest a greater concern for law than Williams implies.

22. For Wade's opposition to constitutional restraints, see *Congressional Globe*, 37th Cong., 2nd sess., pp. 1735–1737.

The bill authorized suspension of the privilege of the writ of habeas corpus by army officials and defined procedures for trial and punishment of active rebel sympathizers. The senator argued for the bill in terms which hardly indicate radical design.

Trumbull was not interested in vengeance as much as in regulation, in providing a legal roadmap for the unexplored jungles of American martial law. Responding to widespread public antagonism over habeas corpus suspension, he announced his concern that the rights of all citizens—North and South—be protected, and his dismay at arbitrary arrests. "I think that the idea that the rights of the citizen are to be trampled upon and that he is to be arrested by military authority, without any regulation of law whatever, is monstrous in a free government," Trumbull declared. When Senator Cowan, later to support Andrew Johnson during Reconstruction, argued that a rebel had no rights and could be dealt with under the laws of war, Trumbull was furious. "The idea that the laws of war prevail is the most monstrous proposition I ever heard enunciated anywhere." The President and his aides were exercising prerogatives ill-suited to a government of laws. Their action cried out for regulation by Congress. "The object of this bill," Trumbull insisted, "is to place the actions of the government in crushing this rebellion under the Constitution and the law, and I think it is the most important object that can engage the attention of Congress."[23]

Trumbull's fears of military rule, even in the midst of war, were widely shared. Oregon Senator Edward Baker agreed with Trumbull. "Look at the fact," he said. "The civil power is utterly overwhelmed, the courts are closed, the judges banished [in the South]." Baker thought that the President certainly had the right to have his commanders issue orders to stabilize conditions, but the crucial and controlling question was, "Are they to [execute the laws] with regulation, or without it?" It was the duty of the legislature "to preserve . . . the liberty, lives and property of the people of the [seceded states] by just and fair police regulations." Ira Harris of New York was also worried about potential chaos in Dixie, where in many places "a perfect state of anarchy prevails . . . civil authority

23. *Ibid.*, 37th Cong., 1st sess., pp. 337–342. For further evidence of constitutional concern from Trumbull and other congressmen, see Donald Morgan, *Congress and the Constitution* (Cambridge, 1966), 125–133.

disappeared, civil government no longer exists." Congress would
have to bring order and stability, Harris believed. Although more
conservative than many of his colleagues, New Jersey Republican
John Ten Eyck saw a Virginia where "all law was beaten down
and disregarded . . . the machinery of the courts . . . run out, no one
there . . . to enforce law. Some restriction and restraint" was needed,
he said, "rather than suffer the military to regulate the whole thing
according to their own will and dictation."[24]

Similar motives were evident in the passage of the severe Confiscation Act of 1862. Again, military actions were outracing congressional control as battle necessity demanded action now and
regulation later. To supply this regulation, Trumbull, though radical in his proposal to confiscate forever the property of rebels,
displayed concern that the needs of war had outrun constitutional
provision. Reacting to the need to bring order into this protean
realm, Trumbull presented a bill which used traditional structures
to restrain contemporary necessity. By terms of the confiscation
statute, the federal courts, the attorney general, and federal district
attorneys enforced the forfeiture of rebel property in non-military
areas.

> So far from admitting the superiority of the military over the civil
> power [Trumbull explained] in time of war, or that there is neces-
> sity that it should be so, I hold that under our Constitution, the
> military is as much subject to the control of the civil power in war
> as in peace. . . . I want no other authority for putting down even
> this gigantic rebellion than such as may be derived from the Con-
> stitution properly interpreted. It is equal even to this great emer-
> gency; and the more we study its provisions, the more it is tried in
> troublous times, the greater will be our admiration of the instrument
> and our veneration for the wisdom of its authors.

Throughout the discussion of confiscation, Trumbull showed a
marked concern for law, not an abnormal concern for retribution.
"This concern for constitutional procedures and for the integrity
of civil courts," a recent Trumbull biographer says, "was typical of
his stand throughout the war."[25]

---

24. *Congressional Globe*, 37th Cong., 1st sess., pp. 336, 372, 342.
25. *Ibid.*, 37th Cong. 2nd sess., p. 18; 12 *Statutes at Large* 589; Mario Di-

In giving control over confiscation to the attorney general, congressmen insured that a conservative construction would be placed on the procedure. In his constrictive interpretation of the act, Attorney General Edward Bates practically squeezed it to death. He told his attorneys general and marshals to ignore a severe interpretation of the measure suggested by Secretary of State Seward and asserted that concrete proof was required to prosecute. Action in the rebellion by a property-owner was not sufficient to permit confiscation; prosecutors would have to provide evidence that the property itself had been used to further the rebellion. Accordingly, the Confiscation Act was never vigorously enforced.[26]

Another apparently radical measure, the 1863 Habeas Corpus Act, revealed again the conservative inclinations of legislators in responding to the needs of war. This measure was the final result of Trumbull's abortive earlier efforts to regulate arbitrary arrests. Congress had avoided action on the senator's earlier bill, but by 1863 arbitrary arrests had increased, and Democratic victories in late 1862 were partly due to reactions to an administrative policy of arrests that had become, in Harold Hyman's words, "incredibly harsh." Once more conditions in the field demanded legislative control, and again congressmen of both parties demonstrated a serious concern for constitutional liberties. This concern would continue even to the final days of the war, when a man as radical as Henry Winter Davis would speak out repeatedly against the military trial of civilians in the North.[27]

Trumbull's earlier speeches against military arrest forecast the sentiments of 1863. The Illinois senator shared his colleagues' fear that the disorders of wartime might portend danger for traditional American liberties. He repeated an 1861 demand that the secretary in charge of arbitrary arrests provide Congress with specific information whenever an arbitrary arrest was made. In this way courts might have access to information which would allow some control

---

Nunzio, "Lyman Trumbull, United States Senator," Ph.D. dissertation, Clark University, 1964, p. 118.

26. Marvin Cain, *Lincoln's Attorney General, Edward Bates of Missouri* (Columbia, 1965), 157.

27. Benjamin Thomas and Harold M. Hyman, *Stanton: The Life and Times of Lincoln's Secretary of War* (New York, 1962), 281; *Congressional Globe*, 37th Cong., 3rd sess., pp. 534–535, 538; 38th Cong., 2nd sess., pp. 1323–1329, 1421–1422.

over imprisonments by military tribunals. Otherwise, Trumbull
and his supporters feared that these tribunals might suppress civil
courts.[28]

Trumbull's demand was reflected in the 1863 Habeas Corpus Act.
It required that the secretary of state provide courts with the names
of persons arrested outside civil procedures. If a grand jury had met
after the prisoner was in custody and had failed to indict him, he was
to be set free. After the war a Supreme Court which applied this
law (with rather effusive rhetoric, to be sure) would be criticized
for excessive sympathy for rebel supporters. Here, in the heat
of conflict, Congress was providing the legal means to express such
sympathy; it was saying that, where civil courts existed, they should
control the actions of military tribunals. While the bill did validate
Lincoln's previous policy, it also provided legal procedures to replace personal fiat. Doing so, it reflected the serious commitment of
legislators to established legal traditions.[29]

The wartime discussion that most clearly revealed congressional
concern for constitutional tradition was held over the question of
Reconstruction. As Union armies occupied the South, Lincoln
placed military governors over the conquered areas. Worried by
such martial rule, Congress debated civilian alternatives. The debate
remained alive from the first session of the war congress to the
Wade-Davis Bill of 1864. This latter measure has traditionally been
viewed as the epitome of the conflict between Lincoln and radical
"vindictives." In fact, the measure was a comparatively conservative answer to a problem which might have had a more radical
solution.[30]

The initial congressional Reconstruction proposals were based
on the idea that the seceded states had lost their status as states and

28. Horace White, *The Life of Lyman Trumbull* (Boston, 1913), 191–199; Orville Hickman Browning, *Diary*, ed. T. C. Pease and J. G. Randall (Springfield,
1925), I, 630–633; Allan Nevins, *The War for the Union* (New York, 1960),
II, 310.

29. 12 *Statutes at Large* 755; "Hoosier Justice: The Journal of David Mc-
Donald," ed. Donald Dewey, *Indiana Magazine of History*, LXII (Sept., 1966),
175–232; Robert G. McCloskey, *The American Supreme Court* (Chicago, 1960),
108; Stanley Kutler, *Judicial Power and Reconstruction Politics* (Chicago, 1968),
92.

30. Herman Julius Belz, *Reconstructing the Union: Theory and Policy during
the Civil War* (Ithaca, 1969), 285–291.

hence had reverted to territorial status and could be governed by Congress. Even these measures had the weight of American legal tradition on their side, compared to Lincoln's policy of martial rule over American states. In its practical application, however, Lincoln's plan set conservative governors like Andrew Johnson of Tennessee and Edward Stanley of North Carolina over the conquered states, while initial congressional proposals did suggest that major changes would take place in southern society.[31]

But these early congressional proposals based on territorialization could not pass in Congress. Often they were not even voted on. Ohio Republican Samuel Shellabarger, later to provide the theory of Reconstruction which Congress accepted, explained the failure of wartime radical measures. "Those words of the Constitution— 'The Union'—take into their high import not the idea of unimpaired territorial domination alone, but involve as well the indestructability of the States themselves." Any proposal "which gives to void state action validity for the purpose of destroying itself, misconceives, as its kindred error the right of secession, misconceives, the very foundation principle upon which the entire structure of Government rests." When Congress finally found a measure it could agree to, it was the Wade-Davis Bill, which rested not on the radical idea of territorialization, but on the essentially moderate constitutional concept that Congress could guarantee to every state a republican form of government.[32]

Congress thus accepted the idea that states retained their status as

31. *Congressional Globe*, 37th Cong., 2nd sess., p. 934; Belz, *Reconstructing the Union*, 277-303. Even the archconservative Garrett Davis of Kentucky at one point supported territorialization. "If the people of any State cannot or will not reconstruct their State government and return to loyalty and duty, Congress should provide a government for such State as a Territory of the United States, securing to the people thereof their appropriate constitutional rights." *Congressional Globe*, 37th Cong., 2nd sess., p. 786. I am greatly indebted to the work by Belz for the entire discussion of wartime Reconstruction.

32. Belz does insist that the Wade-Davis Bill was as radical as any measure based on territorialization insofar as its assertion of congressional power over southern territory was concerned. But his argument does not demonstrate this suggested equality of severity. It rests on the indisputable fact that both plans limited states' rights. The critical issue, however, is how much these rights were limited. Belz himself emphasizes that radical supporters of territorialization had to back away from their proposal and accept the more moderate idea of reconstructing states. See *Reconstructing the Union*, pp. 205-206.

states even though they were guilty of rebellion. That concession
to legal tradition had great meaning, both for what it revealed about
congressional constitutional concern and for what it portended for
future reconstruction measures. Men of truly radical constitutional
views recognized the immense danger of accepting state status in
Dixie. William Whiting, solicitor of the War Department and a
radical thinker who urged that the Union government conduct
the Civil War like an international war, perceived immediately what
dangers lurked behind viewing seceded states as states. "Beware of
committing yourselves," he warned, "to the fatal doctrine of recognizing the existence in the Union, of States which have been declared by the President's Proclamation to be in rebellion, else, by
this new device of the enemy, this new version of the poisonous state
rights doctrine, the secessionists will be able to get back by fraud
what they failed to get by fighting." Congress rejected Whiting's
warning.[33]

Congressmen at odds with Lincoln were not simply "Vindictives"
or "Radicals." Engaged in something more complex than a conspiracy against Lincoln's good will, they were trying to find and
make law in the midst of mutating circumstances. They were trying
to cope with secession and with what they feared might be anarchy
before both overwhelmed the nation.

Consistency of constitutional viewpoint was not always the rule
in this process of law-making. Senator Fessenden warned in May,
1862, that "the present of all times in the world is the last when we
ought to enlarge the organization of the government." Later he
vigorously urged a stronger prosecution of the war by Lincoln
and defended arbitrary arrests. Yet he was called faint-hearted by
Trumbull on matters of confiscation while the latter, outraged by

33. William Whiting, *War Powers under the Constitution of the United States*
(Boston, 1871), 234. This work originally appeared as a series of pamphlets during
the war. Whiting also predicted that, "clothed with State Rights under our constitution, they will crush every Union man by the irresistible power of their legislation." Whiting was more influential with Lincoln and Stanton than with Congress.
He advised the President in favor of the constitutionality of emancipation, permanent confiscation of rebel property, and wide-ranging powers for provost marshals.
Thomas and Hyman, *Stanton*, 280–281; Allen Thorndyke Rice, ed., *Reminiscences
of Lincoln by Distinguished Men of His Time* (New York, 1886), 59; Edward S.
Corwin, *The President: Office and Powers, 1787–1957* (New York, 1957); Belz, *Reconstructing the Union*, 132–133.

arbitrary arrests, led the confiscation movement in Congress. For all their talk about the need for the rule of law in the conquered South, both Senators Harris and Baker had supported territorialization as the foundation for Reconstruction.[34]

In fact, the Civil War Congress wrote much innovative legislation—legislation which expanded the power of the federal government far beyond its prior dimensions. A national banking and currency system was created, and the first federal income tax law was passed. Congress subsidized the building of railroads, encouraged the establishment of public higher education, and provided homesteads at practically no cost. These were important new federal activities, and legislators responsible for them were both impressed and nervous about what they had done. When John Sherman looked at the legislation of the Thirty-seventh Congress, he remarked that the laws "cover such vast sums, delegate and regulate such vast powers, and are so far reaching in their effects, that generations will be affected well or ill by them." William Pitt Fessenden was equally impressed. "We have assumed terrible responsibilities, [and] placed powers in the hands of the government possessed by none other on earth short of a despotism."[35]

But such comments must be seen in the perspective of a federal government that had been singularly inactive before the war, and which remained one of the least energetic in the world long afterward. As late as 1902 the Russian observer Moisei Ostrogorski could note "how small is the place which government occupies in the existence of the New World, how limited are its powers. . . . The inhabitants of the American Republic are hardly 'governed,' a citizen may spend his whole life without coming in contact with representatives of the government."[36]

The federal government had been expanded far beyond its prewar

34. Charles A. Jellison, *Fessenden of Maine* (Syracuse, 1962), 146, 155; *Congressional Globe*, 37th Cong., 2nd sess., p. 2016. Allan Nevins (*War for the Union*, II, 355) calls Trumbull and Fessenden radicals.

35. John Sherman to William T. Sherman, March 20, 1863, in *The Sherman Letters: Correspondence between General and Senator Sherman from 1837 to 1891*, ed. Rachel Sherman Thorndike (New York, 1894), 194; Fessenden quoted in Leonard P. Curry, *Blueprint for Modern America*, 251.

36. M. Ostrogorski, *Democracy and the Organization of Political Parties*, ed. Seymour Martin Lipset (Garden City, 1964), II, 310.

dimensions. If federal expenditures are any indication, it would never again approach its prewar levels of inactivity. But this expansion had taken place within the existing constitutional system and only with the blessing of the national charter. Wartime measures were not just questions of survival; they were constitutional questions, and congressmen engaged in a constant search for legal legitimacy for their legislative goals. Solutions to the most compelling problems of the war—confiscation, civil liberties, reconstruction— were all ultimately shaped by the respect men held for the Constitution.[37]

Underlying it all was the sentiment which had led, in part, to opposition to Lincoln—a desire that the structure of law replace personal whim, however well intentioned. Congressmen insisted that the war for the Union was a war for law, and they often mentioned their fear (shared by Lincoln) that successful secession might precipitate anarchy. They were fighting for a government of laws, and most insisted that law prevail during the fight. They struggled and sacrificed for their long-treasured union of states, and they demanded that that Union, not one radically altered in war's crucible, be maintained.[38]

Emancipation was, of course, the most radical result of the war. But even abolitionists showed a growing respect for the nation's charter, or at least respect for other Americans' respect for the document. In antebellum days many abolitionists had been enraged by a constitution that covenanted with the hell of slavery, but they became more admiring when the war promised to destroy slavery. Frederick Douglass called the war a war "in order to save the Constitution." George B. Cheever argued that the end of slavery and protection for freedmen were perfectly consistent with the nation's charter. Fearing that the Emancipation Proclamation might only be a wartime expedient, abolitionists lobbied effectively for the enduring protection of the Constitution in an amendment. George

---

37. *Statistical History of the United States* (Stamford, 1965), 711.

38. For congressional fear of anarchy, see John Sherman to William Sherman, July 24, 1864, Thorndike, ed., *Sherman Letters*, 237; Phillip S. Paludan, "The American Civil War Considered as a Crisis in Law and Order," *American Historical Review*, LXXVII (Oct., 1972), 1017–1019.

Julian was typical of these law-respecting abolitionists. In early 1862, fearful that democratic institutions would suffer with continuing war, he told congressional associates that the rebellion was "a gigantic conspiracy against the Constitution and the laws." He demanded that the Southerners be punished by the loss of their slaves, yet he insisted that no destruction of the federal system would be required. "I think," Julian said, "there are such things as State Rights, notwithstanding the efforts of rebels to make them a cloak for treason." He went even further in his respect for federalism: not only would states' rights exist unharmed by proposed emancipation, but "there is such a principle as State Sovereignty, recognized, while limited, by the Federal Constitution itself."[39]

Throughout the war men criticized the weaknesses of the federal system and the failures of the Constitution. Concurrently, however, they insisted on respect for the law and the Constitution, and often for states' rights. "Poor Constitution," Francis Lieber observed with mock distress, "she, that ought to be treated respectfully and courteously like a chaste woman and lady of highest standing, has become violated and forced to go to bed with all sorts of company." But Lieber spent much of his time writing pamphlets to show the constitutionality and legality of wartime measures. His private belief that the war was outside the Constitution was not widely shared. Much more common were the sentiments that a Baptist minister expressed to veteran troops bivouacked near Fredericksburg, Virginia, on July 4, 1862:

> Never before had I so strong a faith in the great Republican idea, and in the Constitution given us by our Fathers. Exposed to a rebellion which would have torn in pieces any other nation taken unawares ... unprepared for war, we have found all the powers in the Constitution necessary for the most vigorous measures. ... A Con-

39. George Julian, *Speeches on Political Questions* (New York, 1872), 154; Philip S. Foner, *The Life and Times of Frederick Douglass* (New York, 1955), III, 378–383; George B. Cheever, "The Slaves Are Free by Virtue of the Rebellion and the Government Is Bound to Protect Them," *New York Independent*, Jan. 16, 1862. These speeches are conveniently available in *The Radical Republicans and Reconstruction, 1861–70*, ed. Harold M. Hyman (Indianapolis, 1967), 25–50, 84–89. James McPherson, *The Struggle for Equality: Abolitionists and the Negro in the Civil War and Reconstruction* (Princeton, 1964), 125–126.

stitution which will stand such a shock as this, a Union which will
bear without ruin such a fearful strain as this, is well worth living
for, nay, more, it is well worth dying for. . . .[40]

Throughout the war constitutional questions were constantly
debated. Men were fighting for the Union and law, and they were
vitally concerned about keeping war circumstances within traditional legal restraints. "The innumerable speeches in Congress and
out of Congress, within the last few years," Harvard professor Joel
Parker noted, "may serve to show with what diligence, if not with
what success, constitutional law has been recently studied." The
war stimulated what one historian has called "a massive constitutional inquiry." In so doing it encouraged respect for such a durable
and vital Constitution. Opinions differed on what the true meaning
of the law might be, but almost no one of influence suggested solutions to the problems of the war which abandoned traditional
principles. In January, 1862, James Russell Lowell spoke for most
Americans: "Our Constitution gives us a government second to
none in strength."[41]

Much of this applause for the Constitution was part of the usual
glorification of flag and country in time of crisis. In addition to
provoking critical discussion of the document, the war naturally
produced its share of nationalistic prose, poetry, and oratory. But
American conditions gave oratory about the Constitution a special
significance. Having a written constitution meant that uncritical
reverence still attached men to a framework of ideas. Constitutional
idealization may have been a form of nationalistic glorification, but,
unlike purely nationalist oratory, it was not all-justifying. When a
man declared that we fought for the nation, he implicitly justified
whatever the survival of that nation required. But when men expressed devotion to a written constitution, they imprisoned themselves with their rhetoric. They built an enclosure whose boundaries
were defined by the words of the document itself, court decisions

40. George F. Noyes, *Celebration of the National Anniversary by Doubleday's Brigade* (Philadelphia, 1862) as quoted in Hyman, ed., *Radical Republicans,*
66; Lieber to Martin Russell Thayer, Jan. 2, 1864, Lieber Papers.

41. Joel Parker, "Constitutional Law," *North American Review,* XCIV (April,
1862), 441; Harold M. Hyman, "Reconstruction and Political-Constitutional
Institutions," 14, 22-23; and see chapters below.

based on that wording, and whatever writings about the document had gained popular acceptance. The restrictiveness of such a condition had been shown by the legislation of war and would continue to reveal itself after Appomattox.

Since the Constitution had been proven adequate to the needs of war, it was only natural that men would seek its guidance in dealing with Reconstruction. Indeed, as the postwar period opened, many influential congressmen of both parties wished to retreat from the expanded boundaries of constitutional possibility required by war and return to a more limiting document.

An important reason for the respect for American legal tradition was the fact that more and more congressmen were lawyers. By the war era the primacy of the legal profession in Congress was obvious. In the Thirty-ninth Congress which assembled in December, 1865, 54 percent of the House and 85 percent of the Senate were lawyers. The Fortieth Congress had over 160 lawyers in it. This legislative dominance led congressmen to pass measures which increasingly left to courts the implementation of legislation. It also meant that constitutional limitations were matters of familiarity and concern. It may have been the easiest course to have done what men like Thaddeus Stevens wanted to do: to ignore the Constitution in Reconstruction insofar as it impeded a complete reorganization of the South. But that course was not taken. "[I]n a world governed by lawyers," historian W. R. Brock observes, "the idea of suspending the Constitution seemed to offer far more difficulties than remedies." They chose to work within the existing legal structure; consequently, revolution was not the result of Reconstruction.[42]

The war had demanded many innovations in constitutional procedures. Arbitrary arrests, confiscation, emancipation, and efforts at reconstruction all involved legislators in novel legal experiences. Seeking to give the blessings of the Constitution to these extraordinary acts, congressmen during the war often relied for justification on the doctrine of war powers. They insisted that they were at war and that the salvation of the Union was the primary need; hence measures necessary for that salvation were constitutional. Like Senator Lot Morrill, many believed that "the Constitution . . . pro-

42. Donald Morgan, *Congress and the Constitution*, 133–138; W. R. Brock, *American Crisis*, 6–8.

vides for revolutionizing itself." Yet most leading figures in Congress recognized that wartime constitutional justifications would not easily support postwar actions.[43]

Maine's Senator Fessenden retained his wartime influence after Appomattox. His position as chairman of the Senate Finance Committee and his recent tenure as secretary of the treasury, combined with widely admired personal qualities, gave him special authority in the Thirty-ninth Congress. Fessenden had some important comments on the nation's entry into a new legal environment as Reconstruction began:

> We have just gone through a state of war. While we were in it it became necessary all around to do certain things for which perhaps no strict warrant will be found; contrary at any rate to previous experience. . . . In time of peace, when we live under a written constitution, it is our duty to come back as fast as possible; to forget, if necessary, any precedent which might, if made in times like these, have occasioned very serious difficulty and trouble.

Faced with truly extreme changes in traditional federal structure, legislators were likely to balk. In May, 1866, a cholera epidemic threatened the eastern seaboard, and a bill was presented which ignored states lines in establishing quarantine corridors. Senator Henry Anthony of Rhode Island asserted that he would rather have cholera itself than such a bill. Iowa's James Grimes feared that the wartime tolerance of exceptional measures was overwhelming postwar sensibilities. The war had indeed encouraged Congress to draw to itself "authority which had been considered doubtful by all and denied by many statesmen of this country," Grimes said. But the time for such actions had passed. "Let us go back to the original condition of things," he pleaded, "and allow the States to take care of themselves as they have been in the habit of taking care of themselves." The influential *Nation* agreed. The belief that the Constitution ought to bow to or tolerate bowing to necessity "is a dangerous theory, which has been endured rather than sanctioned through the war and cannot any longer be tolerated."[44]

43. *Congressional Globe*, 39th Cong., 1st sess., p. 570.

44. *Ibid.*, 27–28, 236–237, 2446; *Nation*, II (April 26, 1866); Brock, *American Crisis*, 54; McKitrick, *Andrew Johnson and Reconstruction*, 269–273.

These were signals of conservative feelings in and outside of Congress. In the postwar conflict over how to get the rebel states into their "proper practical relation" to the rest of the Union, they signaled a longing for familiar legal havens which would show itself when men got down to the business of making laws rather than speeches. The Reconstruction theory which Congress accepted revealed this fact. Given the opportunity of choosing to treat the southern states as "conquered provinces" or as "suicides," congressmen chose neither. They rejected the Southerners' view that Appomattox had miraculously restored the status quo ante Sumter. They also rejected the minimum conditions plan of Andrew Johnson. They accepted the theory of Samuel Shellabarger, who insisted on the continued existence of states and state boundaries: "I shall not consider whether, by the rebellion, any State lost its territorial character or defined boundaries or subdivisions, for I know of no one who would obliterate these geographical qualities of the States." Shellabarger added that the state governments had, however, lost their rights as states of the Union.[45]

This addition might have allowed a vast number of changes in federal-state relations. It might have enabled the federal government to claim from that moment the power to interfere vigorously in the states to protect the rights of freedmen. But this did not happen, partly because Congress accepted the idea that it was dealing with states. This apparently simple acceptance of prewar state boundaries carried with it profound consequences. The return of states as states meant that men were going to respect traditional ways of thinking about the federal union. The moment the word "states" was uttered, habitual patterns of thought began. Only great restraint would keep that thought from reaching states' rights conclusions in one form or another. Few congressmen were able to escape their past, to escape the compelling tradition that states, as states, were worthy of respect. They retained a commitment to states' rights and to constitutional limitations which helped keep Reconstruction basically a conservative process.

45. McKitrick, *Andrew Johnson and Reconstruction*, 93–119; *Congressional Globe*, 39th Cong., 1st sess., p. 142; John W. Burgess, *Reconstruction and the Constitution* (New York, 1902), 60, says that Shellabarger's theory was "sound political science and correct constitutional law."

The debate over Negro suffrage in the District of Columbia reveals the respect that Congress showed in questions involving federalism. Legislators moved to grant that suffrage in Washington
more than two years before they could pass the Fifteenth Amendment. The House legislated equal suffrage there on January 18,
1866, preceding reconstruction measures of any kind in the South
by almost a month. Senate action was delayed for a year due to
other business and fear of a presidential veto.[46]

The white voters of the District had rejected Negro suffrage by
overwhelming margins in recent elections. But Congress was not
concerned about the wishes of these voters, nor would it listen to
their arguments about the right of self-government. Freed from
constitutional restraint on congressional action in the District,
legislators quickly overrode such arguments. As George Julian put
it, Congress was the sole and complete judge of all measures in
Washington, and to think that white voters, many of questionable
loyalty, could deny black ballots was "superlatively ridiculous . . .
sublimely impudent." When Henry Wilson introduced the bill in
the Senate, he lamented that Congress lacked a similar sovereignty
in dealing with questions that involved states. In the District, he
noted, men could act in accordance with their consciences. They
could recall that black men had died to defend the Union and repay
that sacrifice. But, when dealing with the states, "State constitutions
and State laws, covered with the wreck of human rights block up
the way, and we may not overleap the barriers."[47]

Similar concerns about traditional federal-state boundaries were
demonstrated when Congress debated the Civil Rights bill. The measure itself legislated rights which had been requested for black men
before the war by reformers seeking the amelioration of slavery.
It secured for freedmen the right to make and enforce contracts, to
sue and be parties in suits, to give evidence in court, to have and to
transfer private property. This bare minimum of rights received
support from conservatives as well as reformers. States' rights pietist

46. Constance McLaughlin Green, *Washington: Village and Capitol, 1800–
1878* (Princeton, 1962), 300.

47. *Ibid.*, 298–300; *Congressional Globe*, 39th Cong., 1st sess., pp. 173, 255–
259, 286; *Diary and Letters of Rutherford Birchard Hayes*, ed. Charles R. Williams (Columbus, 1924), III, 25.

James Henderson of Missouri said, "The declaration of citizenship does not confer any rights the exercise of which cannot be restrained by a State Legislature so as to protect the general peace and welfare of the States. I am sure of that." Conservative editor and congressman Henry J. Raymond told his readers, "We can find in [the bill] nothing conflicting with the constitution as it now stands." Senator John Sherman told his conservative brother, General William, "The Civil Rights bill and the constitutional amendment [the Fourteenth] can be defended as reasonable, moderate, and in harmony with Johnson's old position, and yours." Yet even such a moderate measure could not find support from the man who would write the important first section of the Fourteenth Amendment, former abolitionist John Bingham. Violations of the bill were to be tried in federal (not state) courts, and Bingham feared this expansion of national judicial power. "I have always believed that the protection in time of peace within the States of all the rights of person and citizen was one of the powers reserved to the States," he announced. "And so I still believe."[48]

These moderate sentiments became more radical as Andrew Johnson's political ineptitude combined with southern obstinance to evoke congressional rancor. This story has been told with great skill by Eric McKitrick, Lawanda and John Cox, and W. R. Brock. It requires no retelling here. Worth emphasizing is the fact that, even after the split between Congress and President had inflamed passions, legislators still wrote a Reconstruction record far less radical than many advanced reformers demanded. Surfacing constantly in the stormy confrontation in Washington were signs of continued constitutional respect, signs portentous of the doom of equal rights.[49]

The Fourteenth Amendment was intended to overcome the constitutional objections provoked by the Civil Rights bill. It was meant to provide the possibility of changing the federal system so

48. *Congressional Globe*, 39th Cong., 1st sess., pp. 1293, 572–574, 1152, 1117, 483; Thorndike, ed., *Sherman Letters*, July 8, 1866, p. 276; *New York Herald*, March 17, 1866; Brock, *American Crisis*, 112.

49. Thomas A. Bailey, *Presidential Greatness* (New York, 1966), 293–295; McKitrick, *Andrew Johnson and Reconstruction*; Brock, *An American Crisis*; Lawanda Cox and John H. Cox, *Politics, Principle, and Prejudice, 1865–66* (New York, 1963), 145–146, 190–192.

that equal rights might be protected by the national government.
It fell short of these goals. The most radical wordings of the amendment were rejected by Congress; wording which would have
granted the federal government the direct power to provide protection was turned down. Wording which would have granted
Negroes the right to vote was rejected. The measure which passed
was open to dangerously broad interpretation and was certainly
disappointing to true radicals. It was presented to the people as
leaving control over suffrage in state hands, as representing no
change in previous constitutional conditions so far as protection of
rights was concerned, as stripped of radical character. Abolitionist
George B. Cheever reflected his colleagues' feelings that the amendment was practically meaningless—federalism remained a barrier to
equal rights. The amendment, Cheever said, "is State reconstruction
on the basis of popular disintegration; the reconstruction of state
rights, by taking away the people's rights. . . . The black man's
personal rights are annihilated, in order that the white man's state
rights may be equalized."[50]

The Fifteenth Amendment similarly sold out freedom to federalism. Three major possibilities for a voting rights amendment were
discussed in Congress. The most radical would have given the federal government complete control over the right to vote in every
state. A slightly more moderate proposal would have prohibited the
states from denying the right to vote on grounds of race, color, or
previous condition and would have forbidden literacy, nativity, or
property requirements for voting. The measure which passed permitted such tests (indeed, anticipated them) and kept in state hands
the control of voting rights.[51]

The Reconstruction Acts of 1867–68 imposed a national presence

50. Howard J. Graham, "Our 'Declaratory' Fourteenth Amendment," *Stanford Law Review*, VII (Dec., 1954), 3–39; Charles Fairman, "Does the Fourteenth
Amendment Incorporate the Bill of Rights?" *Stanford Law Review*, II (Dec., 1949),
5–139; Joseph B. James, *The Framing of the Fourteenth Amendment* (Urbana,
1956), 156–157; McPherson, *Struggle for Equality*, 356; George B. Cheever, *The
Republic or the Oligarchy? Which? An Appeal* (New York, 1866), as quoted
in Hyman, *Radical Republicans*, 332–333, 341.

51. McPherson, *Struggle for Equality*, 424–427; William Gillette, *The Right to
Vote: Politics and the Passage of the Fifteenth Amendment* (Baltimore, 1965),
52–57.

within the states that was unique in American history. But only presidential stubbornness and southern intransigence had called forth this radical action. Left to themselves, most influential congressmen would have imposed minimum reconstruction requirements; even these measures of 1867–68 were more satisfactory to moderates than to radicals. The Reconstruction Acts did not disrupt the traditional federal structure for long. As soon as southern states complied with congressional insistence that southern black men have the same legal rights as whites, military reconstruction would end. John Sherman, author of the first Reconstruction Act, could insist with only a small exaggeration that he had "carefully [left] open to the South the whole machinery of reconstruction."[52]

Legislators varied in their commitment to the Constitution of their fathers. Some insisted that their most radical dreams were enshrined in the Philadelphia charter; all worked to give the blessing of the Constitution to their proposals. Therefore, even while legislating an expanded federal government concern, they showed a serious apprehension of too radical a deviation from the security of the American legal past. As Alfred Kelly observes, "No one can read the debates of 1866 to 1868 in the [*Congressional*] *Globe* without being forcibly impressed with the fact that the overwhelming number of so-called Radical Reconstruction leaders—Bingham, Boutwell, Trumbull, Conkling, Fessenden, Sherman, Wilson, Howard, Morrill and others—staged their arguments within an essentially conservative frame." "After the war," historian W. R. Brock has written, "the Constitution continued to exert its old magic." Why not? Proven adequate to the needs of preserving the Union, it was the obvious blueprint for Reconstruction.[53]

The most effective adversary of a complete and enduring egalitarian Reconstruction was not the practically moribund Democratic congressional minority. Nor was it Andrew Johnson or the conquered South which had fought so well and learned so little. Rather,

52. Thorndike, ed., *Sherman Letters*, March 7, Nov. 1, 1867, pp. 289, 299; John Sherman, *Recollections of Forty Years in the House, Senate, and Cabinet: An Autobiography* (Chicago, 1895), 371; Larry George Kincaid, "Legislative Origins of Military Reconstruction Acts, 1865–67," Ph.D. dissertation, Johns Hopkins University, 1968; *Nation*, II (Mar. 1, 1866), 263.

53. Alfred H. Kelly, "Comment on Harold Hyman's Paper," 52; Brock, *American Crisis*, 250–273.

the most effective adversary to lasting protection of equal justice was the natural devotion of men to the Constitution and the federal system it enshrined. Subtly, in the darkness of unexplored preconceptions, openly, in clear admiration for a constitutional system proven adequate in the stress of war, Reconstruction measures were fitted with conservative constitutional shackles.

Federalism, by no means the casualty of war, limited the extent of nationalizing Reconstruction efforts. The expansion of federal government activity which did occur failed to create any enduring institutional innovations in the power of Congress or the President. The existing institution which was most changed was the one most likely to preserve the law and the Constitution in their traditional forms—the judiciary. Legislators tried to work within existing governmental structures in passing Reconstruction bills and amendments. They realized that the American people were unlikely to tolerate anything else, and they usually shared their constituents' views. The deviation from normal federal-state relations seen in the Reconstruction Acts, the 1871 Force Acts, and the 1875 Civil Rights bill were all transitory. As soon as the South accepted the legality of equal rights for the freedmen, Reconstruction would cease, whether those rights were actually protected or not. The nation would wait another hundred years before attempting to make legal demands enforceable by an active federal government.[54]

Much of the delay was due to a racism as pervasive during Reconstruction as after. Americans clung firmly to a belief in the basic inferiority of the Negro race, a belief supported by the preponderance of nineteenth-century scientific evidence. George Julian hit the mark when he lamented to his congressional associates in 1866 that "the real trouble is that we hate the Negro. It is not his ignorance that offends us, but his color."[55]

54. "Neither the Civil War nor the Spanish-American War left much impression on civil institutions." Leonard D. White, *The Republican Era: A Study in Administrative History, 1869–1901* (New York, 1958), vii; Kutler, *Judicial Power and Reconstruction Politics.*

55. George W. Julian, *Speeches on Political Questions* (New York, 1872), 299; C. Vann Woodward, "Seeds of Failure in Radical Race Policy," *New Frontiers of American Reconstruction*, ed. Hyman, 123–147; William Ragan Stanton, *The Leopard's Spots: Scientific Attitudes toward Race in America, 1815–59* (Chicago, 1960); Richard O. Curry, "The Abolitionists and Reconstruction," 527–545.

This widespread hostility toward the black man naturally showed itself in Reconstruction politics. George Clemenceau's description of the 1867 election portrayed the tactics of the era: "Any Democrat who did not manage to hint in his speech that the Negro is a degenerate gorilla, would be considered lacking in enthusiasm." But notable is the way in which the Democracy showed an awareness of the fact that civil rights questions involved not only racism, but also questions of law and the recently won constitutional order.[56]

The Democratic party recognized the connection between respect for federalism and opposition to Negroes in its 1868 platform. Instead of outright opposition to the idea of Negro suffrage, the party simply declared that suffrage was a state matter, not subject to federal control. Presidential candidate Horatio Seymour had sounded a similar call three years before. He told a crowd in Seneca Falls, New York, that the question of Negro suffrage "is not merely a proposition whether we will or will not give to the African freedman the right to vote. It is an attempt on the part of the General Government to assert the power to determine the right of suffrage in the different States." In the following years Republicans became concerned enough over the northern respect for states' rights to echo the Democratic platform of 1868 in their own. The "question of suffrage in all loyal states," Grant's party promised, "properly belongs to the people of those states."[57]

Such widely expressed respect for states' rights suggests that constitutional concern played an important role in determining the outcome of Reconstruction's egalitarian promises. Was it more important than racism? That question is unanswerable. As time passed, pervading prejudice certainly contributed to the increasing reluctance of Northerners to provide protection for the freedmen. But one of the strongest arguments for not acting was provided by the profound respect of Americans for constitutional limitations and federalism. It gave men the chance to say "I cannot," rather than "I will not."

The first constitutional test of the protective nature of the Fourteenth Amendment, and thus of most of the legislation that pro-

56. Clemenceau quoted in Fawn M. Brodie, *Thaddeus Stevens, Scourge of the South* (New York, 1959), 316–317.
57. Charles H. Coleman, *The Election of 1868* (New York, 1933), 19–21.

tected the Negro, came in the 1873 Slaughterhouse Cases. A group of New Orleans butchers protested against a state-established slaughtering monopoly. They insisted that the monopoly took away their right to make a living. Most crucially, they insisted that this was one of many rights now protected by the federal government as a result of the amendment. The specific phrase at issue was: "No State shall make or enforce any law which shall abridge the privileges or immunities of citizens of the United States." The butchers asked the court to agree with them on an expanded view of federally protected privileges or immunities. No Negroes were directly involved in the case, but the degree of liberty they would enjoy in the future hinged on the number of rights that the Supreme Court would determine as now under national protection.

Justice Samuel Miller, one of the most nationalist members of the Court, emasculated the latent power of the amendment in a 5–4 majority opinion which strictly limited those rights. Although he declared that the purpose of the amendment was to protect the black man, he limited the dimension of federal protection under the privileges and immunity clause to minuscule size. The only rights which he mentioned as subject to national security were the rights to go to the seat of government, to run for federal office, to demand protection from foreign governments, and to use the rivers of the nation. These were hardly rights on which the basic freedoms of Negroes rested. Absent from this list was almost every important civil right, and every Bill of Rights guarantee.

Miller and the court had been able to snatch these freedoms from black hands by resting the majority opinion on that same devotion to federalism which had pervaded Reconstruction debate. The Civil War, Miller observed, had indeed encouraged a widespread feeling that stronger federal government was necessary. "But, however pervading this sentiment, and however it may have contributed to the adoption of the [Fourteenth Amendment], we do not see . . . any purpose to destroy the main features of the general [federal] system."[58]

This decision was the foundation on which future courts would

58. 16 *Wallace* 82; Charles Fairman, *Mr. Justice Miller and the Supreme Court, 1862–90* (Cambridge, 1939), 124, 137–138.

build impediments to federal protection of rights. Its potency in this regard was recognized almost immediately. In 1874, when Congress debated the measure that would become the 1875 Civil Rights Act, opponents waved the Slaughterhouse Cases in the faces of advocates, and even previously favorable persons began to show doubts. *Nation* magazine changed its earlier position and asserted that the civil rights measure was "so unconstitutional that probably not ten respectable lawyers in the country could be found who would be willing to father it." When the bill did pass, it seems not to have been taken seriously in the North because of its dubious legality. For example, the *Boston Commonwealth*'s Washington correspondent believed that the federal government would make little effort to enforce it, and that the Supreme Court would use the Slaughterhouse precedent to strike it down.[59]

The Slaughterhouse decision affected Negro rights both in state courts and in later Supreme Court action. At the state level judges used the precedent of 1873 to uphold laws which limited the practice of law to whites, segregated schools, and made it a crime for blacks and whites to intermarry. The precedent was also used to deny federal protection to black men who had been attacked by whites for exercising their rights.[60] But more important was the way in which the view of federalism presented in the Slaughterhouse Cases pervaded civil rights cases in the Supreme Court. When the court began to interpret the other clauses of the Fourteenth Amendment, it guided itself by the constitutional image of 1873. In the 1875 case *United States* v. *Cruikshank*, the court again argued that no changes in the federal system had been made. The U.S. government, Justice Waite said for the majority, cannot grant protection for "any right or privilege not expressly or by implication placed under its jurisdiction." The only such right that Waite granted was the right to

59. Newspapers quoted in James McPherson, "Abolitionists and the Civil Rights Act of 1875," *Journal of American History*, LII (Dec., 1965), 504, 509. See also his discussion of the decision's impact on congressional debate on the 1875 bill (p. 504).

60. *Marshall* v. *Donovan*, 73 *Kentucky Reports* 681, 687–688 (1874); *In the matter of Charles Taylor*, 48 *Maryland Reports* 28, 32 (1877); *Green* v. *The State*, 73 *Alabama Reports* 26 (1882); *State* v. *Jackson*, 80 *Missouri Reports* 175, 177 (1883); *Lehew* v. *Brummel*, 103 *Missouri Reports* 550 (1890).

petition. Although this case was decided on grounds different from the Slaughterhouse precedent, the view of the federal system which Miller had proposed in 1873 was still crucial in leading judges to their result.[61]

Similarly, the concept of federalism announced by Justice Miller formed a fundamental buttressing for the 1883 Civil Rights Cases. As in the Cruikshank case, the precise constitutional issue here was not privileges and immunities, but once more the Court built its decision denying Negroes protection on the view of restricted federal power announced a decade before. Page after page of the Civil Rights Cases opinion described a Congress limited in the ways it could provide security for citizens. The Fourteenth Amendment "does not authorize Congress to create a code of Municipal law for the regulation of private rights," Justice Bradley declared. Repeating himself a few paragraphs later, Bradley insisted that Congress may not "enact a code of laws for the enforcement and vindication of all rights of life, liberty and property." Had the Slaughterhouse decision accepted an expansion of federally protected rights, such a code could have been drawn and the Civil Rights Cases and similar decisions destructive to Negro rights would have been legally untenable.[62]

But of course the 1873 decision went the other way. In so doing, it violated the intentions of the framers of the Fourteenth Amendment. John Bingham explained in March, 1871, that the purpose of the amendment had been to reverse the decision of John Marshall in the 1833 case of *Barron* v. *Baltimore*. There Marshall had declared that the guarantees of the Bill of Rights applied only to action by the federal government; states might violate them without federal response. Historians have debated whether or not to accept Bingham's sweeping description of new federal power. Yet even if the amendment's framers did not intend in 1868 to incorporate Bill of Rights freedoms under federal protection, they indisputably sought to secure more rights than the Slaughterhouse decision allowed. Judging by the 1866 Civil Rights Act, which formed the basis for the Fourteenth Amendment, the intentions of the framers were

61. 92 *US* 542.
62. 109 *US* 3.

to give Negroes and whites equal opportunities to exercise at least fundamental civil rights. These rights should be withdrawn from state purview and made the subject of federal government attention. But Miller's decision recaptured for the states the protection of those rights. It restored the federal system to pre–Fourteenth Amendment status in the realm of personal liberties. Miller did not see "any purpose to destroy the main features of the general system."[63]

But the same men who had written the amendment provided him with reasons to believe as he did, and for other Americans to agree with him. Bingham's assertion of vast intention had been followed with an ominous constitutional caveat. There were rights of citizens of the United States which could be "contradistinguished from rights of citizens of a State." These might still be under the control of vital states with significant rights. "God forbid," Bingham declared, "that by [the amendment] we should strike down the rights of the States . . . I believe our dual system of government essential to our national existence." Similar assertions had punctuated the debates of 1866 when the amendment was framed. The avowed respect for the federal union of states was strong enough that Lyman Trumbull, author of the Civil Rights and Freedman's Bureau bills and supporter of the amendment, could declare in 1871, "The States were, and are now, the depositories of the rights of the individual against encroachment . . . the fourteenth amendment has not changed an iota of the Constitution as it was originally framed."[64]

In the years that followed, the Supreme Court, with little outcry from the public or legislators, decreased the dimension of federal protection and diminished the hopes of egalitarian dreamers. Yet in the arguments and the legislation of Reconstruction there were the seeds of that court action. In the respect and admiration of Americans for an enduring union of vital states and a Constitution

63. *Congressional Globe*, 42nd Cong., 1st sess., appendix, p. 84; Graham, "Our 'Declatory' Fourteenth Amendment," 3–39.

64. *Congressional Globe*, 42nd Cong., 1st sess., p. 577. Trumbull's opinion was challenged by Senators Carpenter and Edmunds, but Carpenter would later use the same (winning) argument in the Slaughterhouse cases.

tested by war, there was the foundation for making true equality a "deferred commitment." A study of five legal thinkers and their encounters with the constitutional problems of the Civil War era may encourage a better understanding of the American devotion to law-protected liberty which inhibited a commitment to law-protected equality.

Francis Lieber I:
Nationalism, the Instrument of Order

The possibility of Negro freedom arose not when white Americans deplored slavery, but when they feared for their own nationhood. This is the most important fact to understand in discovering why the promises of emancipation were stillborn. Once it is understood, one can begin to sense the deep tragedy of Reconstruction—not a tragedy in the shallow sense that justice was vanquished by injustice, but a tragedy in a more profound sense: the very forces which made the struggle for equal justice possible were the sources of its defeat.

Decades of abolitionist oratory had done little directly to improve the condition of the slave. Impassioned speeches had generated an awareness of slavery's evils, but most Americans were not convinced that the cause of freedom for slaves transcended devotion to the Constitution and the Union. The abolitionist movement itself, divided over respect for these things and over the morality of violence, reflected a widespread societal ambivalence which mitigated direct attacks on human bondage.

But indirectly abolitionism had its way. It generated enough anti-slavery feeling in the North to frighten Southerners into the one act that would insure emancipation: secession, followed by war. In threatening the Union, secessionists endangered all that nationhood meant to northern citizens—future prosperity and growth, the maintenance of democracy in the world, and the endurance of a vital but delicate balance between liberty and order.

Faced with that threat, Northerners would move against slavery and provide the Negro with his freedom. But the linchpin of this effort was the inescapable connection between that freedom and the devotion to and understanding of nationalism held by fighters for the Union. White passion for nationhood was hope for the black; but should the link between his liberty and a secure Union be broken, that hope would end.

Francis Lieber was mid-nineteenth-century America's best-known and most vociferous nationalist. He reveled in the role. Again and again he would tell friends and acquaintances of his most vivid childhood memory: in October, 1806, Napoleon's armies marched into Berlin after crushing the Prussians at Jena. As their boots clapped against the cobblestones, eight-year-old Francis Lieber wept loudly. The sight from his second-story window humiliated him, and he could not stop crying, even when his father told him to be still lest the soldiers hear him. Finally his father dragged him from the window and slapped him. This stopped the tears but did not erase his recollection of that tragic day.[1]

But Lieber's nationalism ran deeper than mere recollection of this childhood incident. His youth was spent in a series of commitments to nationalist causes. He had risked (and almost lost) his life nine years later while fighting in the Waterloo campaign. He joined and taught in the ardently nationalistic gymnasium of Frederick Lewis Jahn, and throughout his life he remained profoundly interested in the creation of a united liberal Germany.

When the Prussian government turned reactionary, Lieber maintained his nationalism even as he became a target for the suspicions of the Prussian police. He joined other young men in literary efforts to strengthen support for liberal German nationalism. But these were halted by the police, and he was forced to seek other places to satisfy his concern for liberty and nationhood. Greece in 1821 supplied it. Joining other philhellenes, he went to help the Greeks overturn their Turkish master.

However, his Hellenic adventure proved as disappointing as his efforts on behalf of German liberal nationalism. At home reaction defeated him. In Greece quasi-anarchy dismayed him. He had expected to find Plutarch's heroes but discovered thieves, cowards,

---

1. Merle Curti, "Francis Lieber and Nationalism," 266–267; Frank Freidel, *Francis Lieber*, 24–29; Lewis R. Harley, *Francis Lieber: His Life and Political Philosophy* (New York, 1899), 2, 22–29.

and swindlers instead. Liberated Greeks thought freedom meant no more taxes and almost no government. Lieber understood that centuries of Turkish oppression generated such feelings, but he could not condone "the cowardice and incapacity of the Greeks [which] made them unfit to defend or free their country."[2]

Returning to Prussia, Lieber found himself still the subject of government suspicions. When he had an opportunity to come to the United States, he took it. He arrived full of hope over America's apparently successful combination of nationalism and liberty. He brought with him the lessons learned in the Old World—divided nations such as Germany were easy marks for foreign dominance; liberty depended upon the establishment of a secure nationhood.

Lieber began his new life in the North. He was hired to head the Boston Gymnasium and combined that job with vigorous literary and intellectual activity. He wrote an evaluation of a visitor's first encounter with his new country, edited the first edition of the *Encyclopedia Americana*, and wrote for the prestigious *North American Review*. When Alexis de Tocqueville came to America, Lieber met him and explained to the Frenchman many elements of American democracy. He worked avidly for prison reform after meeting Dorothea Dix. Lieber's growing reputation brought him invitations to dine with President Jackson and to meet Henry Clay. It also brought him the friendship of the young Charles Sumner, one of the few men in America with an ego to match Lieber's.[3]

Although he constantly sought permanent academic work in the North, he was unsuccessful and so accepted a professorship at South Carolina College in 1835. For eighteen years Lieber and his family lived in the South. He was not pleased with the long stay. Although the Liebers themselves owned three slaves, slavery and its passionate, irrational defenders angered him—and he was often bored by the intellectual isolation of Columbia. He spent summers in the North whenever possible, often leaving his family behind. He continually badgered northern friends to find him a job at a northern school. They were still unsuccessful when Lieber finally left South Caro-

2. *The Life and Letters of Francis Lieber*, ed. Thomas Sergeant Perry (Boston, 1882), 41; Freidel, *Lieber*, 31–33.
3. Freidel, *Lieber*, 50–110.

lina and moved to New York. Soon after arriving, however, he was hired by Columbia University; he taught there from 1857 until his death in 1872.[4]

The dominant force thoughout Lieber's varied and active life was nationalism. His European experiences were the foundation for this sentiment, and his American encounters amplified it. His foreign birth helped to intensify his American nationalism. Throughout his life Lieber encountered a nativism that threatened and occasionally deprived him of his ambitions; he felt with some justice that his foreign birth barred him from complete acceptance into Boston society. In the South he experienced overt attacks on his alien birth. When his *Political Ethics* was published in 1847, a Charleston paper praised it but lamented that a foreigner had written it. Entering his classroom one day, he found written on the blackboard, "Why should a German draw South Carolina salary in Columbia?" He made an adroit reply, but the barb still stung. He launched a series of attacks on nativism in the local papers. He pointed out the contributions to many modern nations made by foreigners: Columbus, the Genoese, enriched Spain; the Italian Napoleon enobled France; Gallatin and Hamilton had redeemed their foreign birth many fold.[5]

Yet he believed that the best possible step for any immigrant was assimilation into American society, if unthinking nativism allowed it. Lieber's struggle for assimilation brought him nativist scars, but his love for the nation grew, forged more strongly because gained so dearly. In the midst of the Civil War the German-become-American said it best. For him no casual relationship to an everpresent nationality was possible. He did not take the nation for granted: "I love her as a man loves the wedded wife of his choice," he said. "Besides, I have been nearly forty years in this country and have identified myself with America by the blood of my sons, by my sharing in her literature, teaching her sons, defending her institutions, suffering and joying with her. America is mine—my own."[6]

Lieber's love for the nation combined with his foreign birth to provide a unique opportunity for him to explain the necessary con-

4. *Ibid.*, 129–417.
5. *Ibid.*, 200–201, 231–233; Curti, "Lieber and Nationalism," 268–269.
6. Lieber to Martin Russell Thayer, Jan. 14, 1864, Lieber Papers. Curti, "Lieber and Nationalism," 281.

ditions of American institutional life. He had an original view of the legal institutions of the country, a view which for the first time in an American political treatise presented the structure of institutional liberty that underlay the U.S. Constitution. In all his works he pointed out that liberty in America was more than constitutional; it was institutional. It was more than a legal document which guaranteed rights; it was a pattern of institutions which gave those rights vitality. He wrote four major books and numerous pamphlets and articles to explain this fact to Americans. His major effort, *Civil Liberty and Self Government*, appeared in 1853. It was enlarged and republished in 1859, reprinted in 1869, revised and republished in 1874, and reprinted in 1875, 1877, 1880, 1881, 1883, 1890, and 1911. Two more editions were published in England and one in Germany. Combined with his *Political Ethics*, the work provided the young nation with valuable insights into the nature of its nationhood and the necessity for law and union.[7]

Lieber produced his most important writings and laid the groundwork for a career of thought at a time when serious concern prevailed for the rule of law in America. From the 1820s into the 1850s the leading figures of the legal profession succumbed to deep doubts about the compatibility of law and democracy. As early as 1821 Joseph Story had warned, "Our danger lies in the facility with which, under the popular cast of our institutions, honest but visionary legislators, and artful leaders may approach to sap the foundations of our government." By 1846 Massachusetts legal giant Rufus Choate was speaking of "the distemperatures to which an unreasoning liberty may grow . . . to regard *law* as no more nor less than just the will—the actual and present will—of the actual majority of the nation." That same year Georgia legalist James Jackson warned of belief in "the infallible mob" whose judgments about the law placed order in serious jeopardy.[8]

7. Freidel, *Lieber*, 265.
8. James Jackson, "Law and Lawyers. Is the Profession of the Advocate Consistent with Perfect Integrity?" *Knickerbocker Magazine*, XXVIII (Nov., 1846), 378; Rufus Choate. *The Position and Functions of the American Bar, As an Element of Conservatism in the State: An Address Delivered before the Law School in Cambridge, July 3, 1845*, in Perry Miller, ed., *The Legal Mind in America, from Independence to the Civil War* (Garden City, N.Y., 1962), 264; Joseph Story, *Address Delivered before the Members of the Suffolk Bar*, in Miller, ed., *Legal Mind*,

These warnings took place in an environment almost guaranteed to frighten apostles of established legal traditions. Transcendentalists were speaking of the need for Americans to reject "Europe's courtly muses" and seek their independence in realizing their unity with a divine Oversoul. This was hardly the sort of condition in which men would respect the external commands and restraints of established Anglo-American law. Henry James, Sr., had described American society in terms similarly destructive. "Democracy," he said, "is revolutionary, not formative. It is born of denial. It comes into existence in the way of denying established traditions. Its office is rather to destroy the old world than fully to reveal the new."[9]

Amidst such thought it was hardly surprising that man's specific relationship to law was described in ominous ways. James Fenimore Cooper created an enormously popular character in Natty Bumppo, who responded to a judge's lecture on the need to respect the law with these words: "Talk not to me of law. I've travelled these mountains when you were not a judge . . . I feel as if I had a right and a privilege to travel them again before I die." American folk hero Davy Crockett claimed that the heart of the common man was at least the equal of books and the learning of judges when it came to knowing what was just. Crockett boasted that he had "never read a page in a law book in all my life." He was not ashamed of this fact. He insisted that his decisions as a justice of the peace came from "common sense and honesty" and "relied on natural born sense and not law learning."[10]

This disdain for judges and the legal establishment grew from colonial custom and the experiences of the Revolution. It burgeoned quickly in reaction to the partisan use made of the bench and English common law during the Federalist era. Responding to the Federalist common law prosecutions of political opponents by judges like Samuel Chase, Jefferson and his supporters relied on

---

72. See the other selections in that volume for further documentation of the concern over the relationship between democracy and the law.

9. James quoted in R. W. B. Lewis, *The American Adam: Innocence, Tragedy, and Tradition in the Nineteenth Century* (Chicago, 1955), 13. See Lewis's chapter, "The Case against the Past," for a provocative discussion of intellectuals' interest in being rid of old restraints.

10. Perry Miller, *Life of the Mind in America*, 99–104. This paragraph and those that follow are based on Miller's analysis of prewar legal thought.

natural law. They glorified the wisdom of the people and the superiority of natural law as opposed to the tyrannical potential of common law in the hands of Federalist judges.[11]

The success of the Jeffersonian offensive, mirrored in the election of Andrew Jackson to the presidency, worried many American lawyers. They feared that new world conditions might foster unique opportunities for a repeat of the natural law–inspired French Revolution. They were concerned that a mixture of natural law rhetoric with burgeoning democracy would create a dangerous explosive. To counter this possibility, most of the nation's legal makeweights sought to defuse the potential explosive by insisting on legal traditions that were less susceptible to use by the irrational Bumppos and Crocketts of America.[12]

Joseph Story, James Kent, David Hoffman, and other legal thinkers countered the revolutionary potential of natural law by invoking America's common law heritage and linking it to natural law beliefs. By skillfully using comparative law, these men demonstrated the apparent identity between common and natural law. They proved to generations of American lawyers that the musty precedents of common law and the eternal verities of natural law were inseparable. Since the imperative foundation of every legal education was Blackstone, who insisted that "the law is the perfection of reason" while teaching common law, there was little escape from the conclusion that the common law was the indispensable foundation of a stable and growing society.[13]

11. Albert J. Beveridge, *The Life of John Marshall* (Boston, 1929), III, 26–49.

12. I have argued elsewhere that American society was not as disdainful of law as these jurists feared. In fact, the growth of democracy encouraged average Americans to participate in self-rule to such an extent that they believed themselves to be personally responsible for the rule of law and order. See "The American Civil War Considered as a Crisis in Law and Order," 1013–1034. For views of antebellum society that emphasize its instability, see David Donald, "An Excess of Democracy: The American Civil War and the Social Process," *Lincoln Reconsidered* (New York, 1956), 209–235; Rowland Berthoff, *An Unsettled People: Social Order and Disorder in American History* (New York, 1971); Stanley M. Elkins, *Slavery: A Problem in American Institutional and Intellectual Life* (Chicago, 1959), 27–37, 140–164.

13. Miller, *Life of the Mind in America*, 126–131; Boorstin, *The Americans*, 33–39; Roscoe Pound, *The Formative Era of American Law* (Boston, 1938), 104–107; *Life and Letters of Joseph Story*, ed. William W. Story (Boston, 1851), I, 297–300; Morgan D. Dowd, "Justice Joseph Story: A Study of the Legal Philoso-

Lieber shared the fears of these Jacksonian jurists. Like them, he was worried about the anarchistic potential of an expanding democracy and the misuse of natural-law thought in this country. He admired the goals of natural law, but he feared that the thinking on which it rested was too abstract to provide a useful foundation for liberty. The spectre of the French Revolution haunted Lieber, as it did James Kent and Joseph Story—perhaps more powerfully, for he had seen firsthand its tyrannous offspring, Napoleon. He knew that devotion to abstractions often led men "to commit the most tyrannical outrageous acts, not infrequently founded alone, and acknowledgedly so, on absolute expediency as preparatory for that perfect state to be founded upon absolute theory." He saw in Jackson's democracy potential tyranny of the majority, and in Jackson that potential single tyrant which mass tyranny inevitably evoked. The sentiment placed Lieber securely within the Whig establishment.[14]

He joined the intellectual effort to harness the real and imagined excesses of mass democracy. He enlisted in the regiment of conservatives who sought to keep the irrational masses from controlling the nation. One means was to bombard them and the country with theories. American jurisprudents had concentrated on using the common law to weaken the natural law foundations of democratic thought. Lieber's contribution was to demonstrate the fallacies in the social contract ideas espoused by proponents of natural law—to suggest that governments and societies were not as easily made and unmade as the idea of a social contract might suggest. He argued eloquently, convincingly, and at times exhaustively that liberty was more than a credo of natural law; it was the result of centuries of growth. These centuries had seen the formation of institutions which gave liberty meaning in experience, not simply in theory. These institutions were liberty's imperative sinews.

Lieber defined an institution in his best Germanic prose: "A sys-

phy of a Jeffersonian Judge," *Vanderbilt Law Review*, XVIII (March, 1965), 643–662.

14. Lieber, *Civil Liberty and Self Government*, 285–294; Francis Lieber, *Manual of Political Ethics* (Philadelphia, 1881), I, 68–69; Benjamin F. Wright, *American Interpretations of Natural Law* (Cambridge, 1931), 261–266; Bernard Edward Brown, *American Conservatives: The Political Thought of Francis Lieber and John W. Burgess* (New York, 1951), 40–44.

tem or body of usages, laws or regulations of extensive and recurring operation containing within itself an organism by which it effects its own further development. Its object is to generate, effect, regulate, or sanction a succession of acts, transactions or productions of a peculiar kind or class." To Lieber, institutions meant self-government. They were the means to restrain impulsiveness, to counter the whim of the moment with the wisdom of the past. They provided the buffer for the many shocks which a growing nation encountered. They allowed change to be gradual and orderly. Without them America and England would be like France, dashing erratically in search of phantoms, rushing from anarchy to despotism, never finding liberty. Institutions were "the garden of growing liberty"; in their soil men could develop the character which freedom required.

> Institutional self-government trains the mind and nourishes the character for a dependence upon law and a habit of liberty as well as of a law-abiding acknowledgement of authority. It educates for freedom. It cultivates civil dignity in all the partakers, and teaches them to respect the rights of others. It has thus a gentlemanly character. It brings home palpable liberty to all, and gives consciousness of freedom, rights, and corresponding obligation such as no other system does. It is the only government which is really government of self as well as by self.[15]

Civil Liberty catalogued institutions which kept liberty secure in America. Lieber extolled the three-part division of the federal government as a beneficial obstruction to democratic absolutism. He lauded the party system for providing the opposition to government so necessary to preserving liberty. He admired a bicameral legislature and insisted that the right to initiate legislation belonged there, and not with the executive. The French Assembly lacked this power; the result, Lieber remarked, was not a legislative corps but a "legislative corpse." However, he insisted that American legislators not be simply the tools of the populace. The aspect of the legislative system which he emphasized was that in which the representatives were not just "deputies with simple powers of attorney," but independent agents legislating for the nation as a whole.[16]

15. Lieber, *Civil Liberty*, 304, 329.
16. *Ibid.*, 153–157, 183–186, 203.

But for Lieber "the jewel of Anglican liberty" was the independent judiciary. Judges were the middle men "between the pure philosophers and the pure men of government." They applied the principles of common law to American society; by resting each decision on an enduring series of precedents, their judgments were "natural, legitimate, and safe." It was in courts, not in legislative halls, that "great alterations in the course and administration of justice" were made "sparingly and by degrees." Popular attacks on an independent judiciary were the stuff that made despotism. They came from men who "wish for a paternal government, a monarch who may rule untrammeled by fundamental law, according to the fatherly desires of his heart."[17]

Lieber joined the opposition to a growing Jacksonian tendency to make the office of judge elective, and hence more immediately responsive to popular will. In 1853 he warned that "elective judges are a departure from substantial civil liberty." As the movement continued despite this warning, in 1859 Lieber added the argument that "a judiciary elected by the people seems to be universally and unqualifiedly considered a serious failure." His position placed him in a growing company of jurisprudents who were making opposition to the election of judges the last bastion against the increasing democratization of the nation.[18]

Like his fellow legal thinkers, Lieber was seriously worried that democracy would create a disrespect for legal institutions. He was worried that the common future-mindedness of Americans would leave them without roots and bereft of order. As an antidote to this dangerous ahistorical love of natural law theories, therefore, Lieber offered a usable past. Liberty did not demand an escape from tradition; progress was not the repudiation of history. "A truth of the weightiest import it remains that liberty and steady progress require the principle of precedent on all spheres," he insisted. "It is one of the roots with which the tree of liberty fastens in the soil of real life, and through which it receives the sap of fresh existence."[19]

17. Quoted in Miller, *Life of the Mind*, 105; Lieber, *Civil Liberty*, 218, 167. In 1938 Roscoe Pound would say, "Our chief lawmaking agency is judicial empiricism." *Formative Era*, 124.

18. Lieber, *Civil Liberty*, 229; Miller, *Life of the Mind*, 233.

19. Lieber, *Civil Liberty*, 213.

Lieber evoked here the "mystic chords of memory" which Lincoln would try to strike to save the Union. He asked his readers to accept the need for law and stability. Perhaps this and similar arguments would later help produce the response which saved the Union. Perhaps fear of the excesses of democracy sensitized legal thinkers like Lieber to the dangers of disunion. Certainly Lieber's commitment to stability and restraint did not indicate a commitment to governmental impotence or to that paralyzing constitutionalism which threatened to immobilize the nation during the secession winter. He believed that the foundations of liberty and government went deeper than written documents. In addition to demanding respect for law, the argument for liberty which Lieber made demanded respect for action. "We cannot hope for liberty in a pervading negation," he wrote. "We must find it in comprehensive action." Again, "The guarantee of liberty cannot be sought in mere opposition to government or in a mere negation of power."[20]

Living in an America whose dominant concern seemed to be with ending restraints, Lieber was especially sensitive to the idea of government by negation. His understanding of the formation and purposes of nationhood and his Whig sentiments made such ideas intolerable. He believed that nationhood was an organic creation which grew from the social conditions into which men were born. Neither the society nor the nation was contracted; rather, each evolved. One of the basic roots of nationalism was the possession of property. Such possession was indispensable to true individuality. It gave one a feeling of being something, of belonging to something. It provided him with the chance to see his humanity reflected in his relationship to it. It rescued him from a sense of being an indistinguishable part of the vague generality of mankind. Private possession was a crucial part of this process, but membership in a nation might serve the same function. In addition, a nation could serve the vital purpose of protecting his private holdings.

The creation of an individual nation came from the shared experiences of a group of people. The nature of these experiences might be cultural, ethnological, or political. In America nationhood rested on the political environment, an experience of the people with

20. *Ibid.*, 366, 148–149, 370; Miller, *Life of the Mind*, 230, 238; Basler, ed., *Collected Works of Lincoln*, IV, 271.

institutionalized self-government. In addition to providing a bond of unity, this talent for self-rule gave America a special mission in the world: other nations might learn from it the true foundation of civil liberty. Lincoln would later echo this concept in the Gettysburg Address and in his reference to the United States as "the last best hope on earth."[21]

Lieber understood the nature of American nationalism with true clarity. In a country of such vast size and variety of climate and ways of life, one thing linked almost all white Americans—the experience of self-rule. There existed here the continuing opportunity to create state and territorial constitutions, town charters, community laws. Even if only on election day, Americans could feel that they were involved in the process of governing themselves, and for many people the experience was even more involving. In a nation of small towns, citizens were often involved in the actual process of governing as councilmen, mayors, constables, and judges. Americans were also united by their devotion to the ideals of individualism, democracy, and liberty, but they experienced these ideals and hence gave them reality when they participated in the institutionalized self-government which Lieber described.[22]

Had he considered more carefully the consequences of his insight, the German-American theorist might have calmed his fears of Jacksonian democrats. The experiences in self-government which he described gave Americans of all classes a personal interest in maintaining the rule of law. Law in this nation was seldom imposed from outside; it was self-generated. Law and order and government in America were *cosa nostra*—our thing. An ordered community was secured not just by Whig conservatives, but by Jacksonian "radicals" as well. This would be proven conclusively in 1861 when small-town democrats filled northern regiments to fight for the Union.[23]

---

21. Curti, "Francis Lieber and Nationalism," 271–275; Brown, *American Conservatives*, 37–43, 64–68; Freidel, *Francis Lieber*, 151–163, 266–274.

22. Merle Curti, *The Roots of American Loyalty* (New York, 1946), 47; Grodzins, *The Loyal and the Disloyal*, 29; Potter, *The South and the Sectional Conflict*, 48, all suggest the idea that loyalty to the nation rested on devotion to local experience.

23. Paludan, "The American Civil War Considered as a Crisis in Law and Order," 1013–1034.

However blinding his fears, Lieber's awareness of the nature of our national experience was acute. He was especially sensitive to the irony of American unity—the very institutional self-government which, united, might also divide.

Lieber recognized that institutions of self-government, so necessary as the protectors of liberty and the foundation of nationhood, might also prove a danger to the nation. This danger arose from the basic fact of American federalism. Lieber admired local self-government very much, but he realized how potentially dangerous this institution was. Its danger lay in its potential for stifling action in the service of its own selfish needs: "One of the dangers of a strongly institutional self-government is that the tendency of localizing may prevail over the equally necessary principle of union, and that thus a disintegrative sejunction may take place."

Men might love their local institutions more than they loved the nation which made them possible. They might seek to impede measures necessary for the good of the whole. He was thinking especially of Calhoun's concurrent majority theory and the ability of a minority, under this theory, to veto measures it opposed. Lieber warned that such veto power "would simply amount to dismembering . . . would produce multitudinous antagonism . . . would be falling back into the medieval state of narrow chartered independencies."[24]

Devotion to local institutions was intolerable if it interfered with the life of the nation, for such devotion violated the basic principle of life: change. Lieber opposed any institutional idolatry which allowed local inaction to paralyze the whole political body. "The battering ram," he said, must be vigorously used against any institution that was "plainly hostile to a new state of things." He was reluctant to overturn institutions too quickly, but if they did not "greatly aid in the best progress of which society is capable," if they did not allow "changes which lie in the very principles of continuity and conservatism themselves," then they had to be destroyed.[25]

This response to Calhoun's ideas suggested, at least theoretically, tyrannical possibilities in Lieber's nationalism. His passion for nationhood was strong. He never forgot his German heritage, never

24. Lieber, *Civil Liberty*, 292, 320, 343, 366.
25. *Ibid.*, 302.

forgot his European nationalism, never ceased hoping for the unity which Germany would not achieve until a year before his death. He believed that excessive localism interfered with a greater destiny for a nation, and that the destiny of America was a great one. Impediments to nationalism always evoked his wrath and subtly suggested what he would have denied—that the goal of nationhood was important enough to justify illiberal means to achieve it. But this is not to say that every conceivable illiberal means was tolerable. He rejoiced at first when Germany was unified but was saddened at the dominance of iron in the new German nation.

While Lieber was a nationalist, he was not a centralist; the difference was important to him. "Centralization," he said, "is the convergence of all rays of power into one central point; nationalism is the diffusion of the same life blood through a system of arteries, throughout a body politic, indeed it is the growing of a body politic as such, morally and thoroughly cemented out of a mass otherwise uncemented." He insisted on the hypocrisy of those state sovereignty advocates who claimed to be fighting for liberty while seeking to preserve slavery. The equation of nationalism and centralism, Lieber believed, was a straw man used by state sovereignty advocates, nullifiers, and secessionists to disguise the illiberal nature of their goals.

His nationalism was liberal, not totalitarian. The erosion of liberalism implicit in his criticism of the local government excesses which actually occurred in the Civil War came only subtly and under the pressure of a fight for nationhood that was also a fight against a form of tyranny. Faced with a fight for union, Lieber would reject some of his liberal tenets. But he also would reject union and nationhood if the price of a unified nation were to be the corruption of liberty.[26]

In 1854 the time to make such decisions had not yet arrived. Then the major enemy seemed to be potential anarchy; democratic absolutism and *Civil Liberty* formed a well-reasoned antidote. The institutional self-government which Lieber advocated protected the individual while it encouraged popular devotion to and participation

26. Curti, "Francis Lieber and Nationalism," 271; Freidel, *Lieber*, 416–417; Francis Lieber, "What Is Our Constitution," *Miscellaneous Writings of Francis Lieber*, ed. Daniel C. Gilman (Philadelphia, 1880), II, 119.

in government. It limited power by guiding it into channels necessary for national survival. The result he had in mind was a nation where liberty grew as the nation itself flourished—a nation alive to change, awake to the need for stability, and aware that its life and strength were inextricably linked to its nationhood. "A weak government," he wrote, "is a negation of liberty; it cannot furnish us with a guaranteeing power, nor can it procure supremacy for public will. In other spheres it may be true that license is exaggerated liberty but in politics there can be nothing more unlike liberty than anarchy."[27]

Lieber's work was widely applauded by the nation's conservatives. Justice Story deeply admired his earlier efforts, and even southern state sovereignty theorist Beverley Tucker was pleased. New York Chancellor James Kent belied his conservatism with an outburst that Lieber treasured. "I love your books," Kent exclaimed. "I love you, you are so sound, so conservative, you are so very safe." *Civil Liberty* was well received in the South, despite its nationalist sentiments and thinly veiled attack on state sovereignty. Southern leaders were cheered by what the book apparently told them.[28]

For a long time many Southerners had had doubts about this handsome foreigner who was teaching their sons history and government from his platform at South Carolina College. Lieber's earlier writings in the *Encyclopedia Americana*, his association with men like Sumner, and his open hostility to secessionist sentiment had inspired worry. But now they thought they were hearing something that needed to be said. The South Carolina Court of Appeals added *Civil Liberty* to the list of works that prospective lawyers were required to read. The University of Virginia introduced the book as a law text. The *Southern Quarterly Review* welcomed the work with an effusion of thanks: "In these days of Communism, Spiritualism, Fourierism, Negrophilism . . . Odism, Odylefluids, Mesmerisms, and Millenarianisms, it is comforting to meet a book full of good, sound, wholesome principles, entirely free of all that abominable

27. Lieber, *Civil Liberty*, 302.
28. Lieber to Matilda Lieber, Sept. 6, 1841; Frank Freidel, "Francis Lieber, Charles Sumner, and Slavery," *Journal of Southern History*, IX (Feb., 1943), 76–77.

political and philanthropic cant . . . which now threatens to undermine all the old and most valued institutions, moral and political,
of civilized life."[29]

There was further consolation for conservatives in Lieber's attitude toward abolitionism. For a long time his devotion to order
and institutions made him a foe of the emancipation movement. He
was disturbed by the anti-institutional natural rights sentiments
which abolitionists often displayed. He hated slavery as they did,
but his hate was balanced by a respect for order. Until the late 1850s
he did not believe that abolitionist excesses were likely to end
human bondage; they were more likely to promote anarchy at worst,
and at least a disrespect for government and order throughout the
nation. As a South Carolina resident and slaveowner, Lieber felt that
critics of slavery were too often ignorant of the institution's complexity. He had studied it with his usual thoroughness, keeping
large scrapbooks, collecting statistics from prisons where blacks and
whites shared the same environment. His conclusion was that in
inherent capacities the races were basically equal. But this did not
cause him to adopt the attitude of Sumner. Lieber believed that, "although many [Negroes] were capable of the responsibility of political equality, it would be meaningless without social equality and
that surely would not follow."[30]

The theorist agreed with his friend Sumner that slavery was a
"nasty, dirty, selfish institution." He called it "eminently a state of
human degradation." He appealed to Calhoun to use his great influence to help end or at least ameliorate it. He even adopted pure
natural-law rhetoric in crying out to the southern statesman, "It
is not the North that is against you. It is mankind, it is the world, it
is civilization, it is history, it is reason, it is God, that is against slavery." Yet in 1850, when Sumner wrote of his unflinching determination to kill the pending compromise, Lieber was upset. He could
only agree with a friend that extremists North and South were
equally demented and that "a great insane hospital is the only fit
place for Toombs and Co., and in an adjoining apartment ought to

29. Quoted in Freidel, *Lieber*, 279–280.

30. *Ibid.*, 235; Francis Lieber, *The Stranger in America* (London, 1835), II,
188–210; Elkins, *Slavery*, 27–37; Aileen S. Kraditor, "A Note on Elkins and
the Abolitionists," *Civil War History*, XIII (Dec., 1967), 330–339.

be shut up Charles Sumner . . . [Wendell] Phillips and the other partners in this philanthropic concern."[31]

Although he deplored slavery, Lieber's opposition fell short of abolitionist outrage. They wanted to end the institution; he was satisfied to mend it. He hoped to make slavery less a relationship between men and property and more between men and men. Abolitionists thought it a sin likely to be perpetuated by amelioration, and no less a sin if it were carried out mildly. Lieber's solution to the problem of slavery was that of many northern moderates: he wanted the institution to evolve along humanitarian lines that would respect the fact that the slave was human, not animal, property. He suggested to Calhoun the possibility of more lenient slave codes modeled on those of other nations. He suggested that slave marriage be legalized, that slaves be allowed to own property, that they be permitted to work in their free time to buy themselves, that they be given land to work after a certain number of years' service, and that slave testimony be permitted in courts. He warned Southerners that those who supported a rigid, unchanging institution were doing the South great harm. If Dixie did not modify slavery with the advance of civilization, then violent change was a sure result. He reasoned here as he had in advocating common law principles against his view of natural law theories. The former allowed change and growth; the latter encouraged rigidity, then chaos.[32]

In the South important theorists shared Lieber's distrust of America's natural law heritage. They were especially hostile to the use of it by abolitionists. After 1832 Southerners, fearing the results of bitter abolitionist attacks, struggled mightily to be free from those aspects of national history which were inimical to their interests. The Declaration of Independence posed a major problem, and Dixie thinkers worked hard to develop interpretations of the document which would square their opposition to natural law egalitarianism with a desire historically to legitimize their proslavery position. A Charleston publicist produced the following bit of "twistory." Read properly, the Declaration meant that "all men in their national or

31. Perry, ed., *Life and Letters of Francis Lieber*, 228–230; Freidel, *Lieber*, 250.
32. Perry, ed., *Life and Letters*, 228–237; Freidel, *Lieber*, 240–241; Donald G. Mathews, "Abolitionists on Slavery: The Critique behind the Social Movement," *Journal of Southern History*, XXXIII (May, 1967), 163–182.

state capacity, are equally entitled, and equally at liberty, to rid themselves of oppression, and act for themselves, a right which as individual citizens they did not possess and could not exercise as against the established government." George Fitzhugh discovered that the abstractions of the Declaration and the Virginia Bill of Rights were "at war with all government, all subordination, all order." Similarly, Calhoun sought to destroy the natural rights theory which had become the heart of Jacksonianism. Like Lieber, he asserted that government was the result not of contract but of necessity. He was equally hostile to the anarchy which he believed northern perfectionism and natural rights devotion generated. Thus dominant southern thought shared philosophical enemies with Lieber. Similar fears and theories might be expected to produce harmony of sentiment between conservatives North and South.[33]

Slavery destroyed such a possibility. The frightened desire to protect their local institutions against change wrenched anti-natural law arguments from Calhoun, Fitzhugh, and others. Dismayed by growing anti-slavery sentiment and increasing northern political influence, southern theorists grabbed frantically for arguments to keep the future they feared from coming. They caught hold of feudalism, racism, and, most important for Lieber and other legal thinkers, the insistence that slavery should follow the flag.[34]

Lieber's studies had moderated his racism. His European liberalism was sufficient armor against feudalism. As the South constructed its feudal romances, he was likely to see, not spires rising heavenward, but massive imprisoning fortresses armed against change. Calhoun's thought was similar to Lieber's, emphasizing as it did the benefits of local self-government, but southern thought took a turn that was anathema to most northern jurists. Instead of maintaining a strict states' rights view, Southerners began to insist that slavery receive the active protection of the federal government. As an outgrowth of this sentiment, the Democratic government began to use national

33. Merrill Peterson, *The Jefferson Image in the American Mind* (New York, 1960), 162; George Fitzhugh, *Sociology for the South* (Richmond, 1854), 175; Vernon Parrington, *Main Currents in American Thought* (New York, 1930), II, 80–82.

34. Wright, *American Interpretations of Natural Law*, 268–274; Louis Hartz, *The Liberal Tradition in America* (New York, 1955), 145–176.

power to aid slavery interests. As understandable as such action was, it had important consequences for many northern thinkers. They began to be more alarmed by proslavery action than by abolition rhetoric.

Such alarm would lead them into an important new position. They would become not the defenders of an order in which slavery had its legal place, but protectors of an order which slavery seemed to be attacking. Slavery was never a proper candidate for inclusion in the national identity. At best it was something that most Americans lived with and thought about as little as they could. It was a necessary part of the constitutional compromise that made Union possible. Since they wanted their own local governments to be respected, most Northerners were willing to respect the southern desire to maintain slavery in the South. By insisting that slavery was the South's (and not the nation's) institution, Northerners probably numbed their responsibility for it even as they espoused the nations' legal traditions. But when frightened Southerners supported the abolitionist contention that slavery was a national matter, they unleashed the wrath of the guilty even as they threatened an innovation in constitutional government.

This innovation itself received the brunt of the response of northern lawyers. Their anger revealed a fact crucial for the emancipation of the Negro: many of the natural northern supporters of the South had become that section's antagonists. Men who had argued that the Constitution protected slavery where it was and that order demanded restraint in suggesting change now turned on the South. They removed the shield of law and order from the South and turned it into a sword for attackers of slavery. This was the moment when the possibility of ending slavery began to dawn. No longer would respect for order, Union, and the Constitution protect it.

In Lieber's case, the path that led him from his 1850 position that the Union was more important than the death of slavery, to his assertion a decade later that "the Union is not my end or my God," is not precise. The record offers a series of outbursts against southern actions—a growing outrage that the North should always yield to secessionist blackmail. But it also suggests what it does not specifically declare: that Lieber's faith in the institutions of the country was weakening due to the form of sectional conflict. Each institution of government was being strangled by an outreaching slave power. As each apparently yielded its autonomy, Lieber's outrage and sorrow grew. Finally he would be willing to admit that a union and the law and institutions it represented which had fallen under the control of slaveholders was not worth preserving. Too long had the South held the Union hostage to protect slavery. As the 1850s moved toward their explosive conclusion, Lieber and others came to feel that the hostage had itself become tainted. The conclusion grew that the death of the hostage might not be too great a price for the death of such a corrupting captor.[35]

The Kansas-Nebraska Act and the Kansas crisis provoked Lieber and many other legal thinkers to reconsider their positions on slavery, the law, and the Union. Seeking southern support for his bill to organize the Kansas-Nebraska territories, Senator Stephen Douglas wrote into the measure a repeal of the 1820 Missouri Compromise. The earlier measure had divided the territory of the nation into slave and free sections at latitude 36°30′. Douglas apparently believed that the Missouri Compromise had been abrogated by subsequent congressional action after the Mexican War. But to many Northerners the measure seemed to unchain slavery from its southern home and portend its escape into lands that white men believed safe from slavery and Negroes.[36]

Lieber responded to the bill with deep anger. It seemed to him unnecessary and immensely dangerous. In a nation already insecure because of potential democratic natural law excesses and southern secessionist threats, the last thing that was needed was to reopen the territorial issue. Yet there it was, a "nefarious . . . mischievous bantling . . . begotten in wickedness." He was angry at Douglas for introducing the measure and at northern democrats for supporting it, but he saved his greatest outrage for the stupidity of the South. The only true safety that the section had, in a world increasingly hostile to slavery, was a positive, immovable barrier against anti-

35. Lieber to Daniel Webster, June 6, 1850, quoted in Freidel, *Lieber*, 253; Lieber to Samuel A. Allibone, January 16, 1860, Lieber Papers.

36. Roy F. Nichols, "The Kansas-Nebraska Act: A Century of Historiography," *Mississippi Valley Historical Review*, XLIII (Sept., 1956), 187–212; Eugene Berwanger, *The Frontier against Slavery* (Urbana, 1967).

slavery inroads. The Missouri Compromise line was that barrier, he argued, and its destruction would frighten Northerners who were not antislavery to at least become anti-South. Yet with almost animal stupidity southern extremists had flown to the measure "as moths to the candle. It will recoil on that very South." he warned, "with fearful violence."[37]

Throughout 1855 and 1856 Lieber's letters revealed a growing sense of tragedy and dismay over incompetence North and South. The nation seemed bent on destroying itself. In addition to encouraging intersectional turmoil, this fact had profound personal consequences for the theorist. His eldest son had remained in South Carolina when the Liebers moved North. The young man was totally convinced of the rightness of southern secessionist sentiment. Lieber's growing sorrow over the sectional crisis was mirrored in letters to his son. By September he felt deep sadness indeed—so much that he wrote, "Let us resolve to remain closely attached to our deaths. . . . Let us my son, then, love one another, and hope for the time when the light of truth will no longer be obscured to our sight. . . . May God protect you." This son would fight for the Confederacy and die in the Battle of Williamsburg.[38]

Lieber's increasing anxiety for the Union, his anger over incidents in Kansas, and his outrage at the caning of Sumner by Preston Brooks led him to a strange position by the fall of 1856. During the election he was angry at both parties for their disunionist aspects; however, he hoped and then believed that the Republican candidate, John C. Fremont, would be elected. He thought this result would help resolve the crisis. How the election of a sectional candidate running on an antislavery platform would have eased tensions is difficult to understand; perhaps Lieber believed that the prospect

37. Lieber to Mrs. George Tichnor, March 18, 1854; to G. S. Hillard, Feb., 1854, and May 26, 1854. Quoted in Perry, ed., *Life and Letters*, 267–273. Reacting to the Kansas-Nebraska bill Emerson said, "The fugitive slave law did much to open the eyes of men, and now the Kansas Nebraska Bill leaves us staring." Horace Greeley wrote, "Pierce and Douglas have made more abolitionists in three months than Garrison and Phillips could have made in half a century." Quoted in Raymond G. Gettell, *History of American Political Thought* (New York, 1928), 334.
38. To Oscar Lieber, Sept. 6, 1856. Quoted in Perry, ed., *Life and Letters*, 289.

of a president unwilling to yield to disunion threats would end those threats.[39]

Whatever his reasoning, his hopes for Fremont's election were dashed. The voters chose James Buchanan, the one predominantly national candidate on the ballot. Their choice showed a devotion to the Union that Lieber would have applauded earlier, but by this time the price was too high. He believed in liberty and Union, the one dependent upon the other, but Buchanan's election seemed to reveal a willingness to buy Union by sacrificing liberty. He wrote bitterly to a friend that his belief in institutional self-government had received a deep wound, and that national unity was too much to hope for.

> Now I see the Union will not last. The North will be obliged to sever itself. The victory of Buchanan, the victory of southern bully-ism, the acknowledgement of Northern men that right or wrong, they yield because the South threatens to secede, will enflame and inflate proslavery to such enormity, and tyranny over the Free States, and madden it in its ungodly course of extending slavery within the United States, and into neighboring countries. . . . Civilization herself will avert her face and weep . . . you, I, every man that has muscle enough left to heave his breast will call out, "Let us part, come what may."[40]

The electoral institutions of the country had apparently fallen victim to slavery's corrupting hand. A minority of slaveholders had elected a president. When a foreign friend insisted that Buchanan's election showed that the nation's majority had tyrannical instincts, Lieber said no, insisting that it was not the majority which had acted. With the aid of cowardly northern politicians, the 350,000 slaveowners who ruled the South were able to coerce and rule the nation. Institutions, not democracy, had failed. This was strange respect for American democrats from a man whose chief fear had been democratic absolutism, but Lieber's attention was focused on a spreading malaise which threatened the very structure of government itself.[41]

Shortly after the electoral process had failed him, the Supreme Court demonstrated that judicial institutions could also be debased.

39. Freidel, *Lieber*, 289–290.
40. To Hillard, Oct. 23, 1856. Quoted in Perry, ed., *Life and Letters*, 290.
41. To Councillor Mittermaier, Nov. 28, 1857. Quoted *ibid*.

The Court's *Dred Scott* holding that Negroes had no citizenship rights which white men needed to respect jarred the theorist. Chief Justice Taney's opinion was "illegal, unjurisdicial, immoral and disgraceful." He satirized the decision in the *Atlantic Monthly* for March, 1859. He applied Taney's logic to a justification for cannibalism and showed that "roasting one's equals" was as firmly grounded in logic and justice as the Court's conclusion that a human being was a thing, not a man.[42]

When the Virginia Supreme Court upheld the *Dred Scott* decision by saying that a slave had no civil rights, Lieber was provoked to cold fury. The decision was "the foulest spot in the whole history of law—against common sense, nature and even possibility; against hundreds of decisions of southern courts, against English law, and the law of all modern Christian nations, against the codes of Middle Ages, against Civil Law, against the law of Athens . . . Mohametan Law . . . the Chinese Code. It is a decision that cries to the high heavens for signal punishment."[43]

The nation's institutional health was not good. In the White House sat a man who toadied to southern slavocrats. On the bench were men who ignored all legal history to serve slavery. The electoral process had been befouled by sectional blackmail. The national legislature, a congressman friend told Lieber, was practically an armed camp. This institutional sickness, spreading like an epidemic through all the vital institutions of self-government, was intolerable to him. Ominously, at the death of John Brown the theorist saw nobility. "He died like a man," Lieber observed, "and Virginia fretted like a woman." A month later, in January, 1860, Lieber had forgotten his earlier balanced view that both sides contributed stupidity and irresponsibility to the growing conflict. He observed now how remarkable it was that southern disunionists were petted and promoted by the government while Northerners "who simply think that slavery is exceptional and must be treated as such (as the world has thought now nearly two thousand years)

---

42. Francis Lieber, "A Plea for the Fijians; Or, Can Nothing Be Said in Favor of Roasting One's Equals," *Atlantic Monthly*, III (March, 1859), 342–350.

43. To Hillard, Oct. 14, 1858. Quoted in Perry, ed., *Life and Letters*, 304. The Virginia case is *Williamson* v. *Coalter*, 14 *Grattan* 394. Presiding Judge Allen said that the slave was "a nonentity so far as respects civil capacities" (397).

are first called Disunionists, and because disunionists, traitors."[44]

By late 1860 it was obvious to him that the two sections had become two nations. The recollection of Greek fighting Greek came to him, with images of the Peloponnesian war. He began to wonder, as did many other persons in the North, whether a general flow of blood might not be needed to wash the nation clean. In July he wrote, "What we Americans stand in need of is a daily whipping." When other nations in the past had reached a situation similar to that of the rapidly disuniting states of America "defying right, morality, and justice . . . God in his mercy has sometimes condescended to smite them."[45]

44. James Hammond to Lieber, April 19, 1860; Lieber to Samuel Tyler, Jan. 16, 1860. Quoted in Perry, ed., *Life and Letters*, 310, 305.
45. To S. A. Allibone, July 12, 1860; to Oscar Lieber, Fall, 1860, quoted in Perry, ed., *Life and Letters*, 315-316; George M. Fredrickson, *The Inner Civil War* (New York, 1965), 36-50.

Francis Lieber II:
Equality as a Weapon of War

Lieber's wish came true. The guns at Sumter announced that the nation would receive the purgation which he had asked for. But they also announced that the time had come for important legal and constitutional questions to be asked and answered. How much of this war could be fought within the traditional lineaments of American law? How much of the Constitution was applicable to wartime conditions? To what extent would traditional American respect for the Constitution limit the possibility of reacting to wartime needs? These were the general questions which the war posed, and secession was the first and most forceful interrogation. It inspired not only a conflict of arms, but also a race to see which party to the disunion struggle could claim the sanctification of the nation's legal past.

Southern orators sought to make secession not a violation of the law, but law's fulfillment. When Jefferson Davis accepted the presidency of the Confederacy, he evoked both the Declaration of Independence and the Constitution in an attempt to legalize revolt. Ignoring the ominous possibilities should black men apply his words to themselves, Davis argued that governments rest on the consent of the governed, and the Constitution "undeniably recognizes in the people the right to resume authority delegated for the purposes of government." Who was the true exponent of the American legal tradition? Not the North: "The Constitution formed by our forefathers is that of these Confederate states. In their exposition of it and in the judicial construction it has received, we have a light which reveals its true meaning."[1]

1. Frank Moore, ed., *Rebellion Record* (New York, 1862), Documents section, pp. 31–32.

Davis's words marked a national devotion to the Constitution and the rule of law which even disunion could not erase. The marked similarity between the Confederacy's constitution and that of the Union was further evidence of the same feeling in the South. That the sentiment was shared in the North is shown by the efforts of almost every responsible northern figure to make acts necessitated by war constitutional and to make the war for the Union a war for the rule of law. This debate was not, as one historian calls it, "fascinating but essentially irrelevant." The early days of the secession crisis were a time of battle, even though few shots were fired. A battle raged over the minds of Americans, with both North and South seeking to enlist men who respected the constitutional traditions of the nation. Had southern arguments gone unchallenged, it is likely that Union war efforts would have failed.[2]

Feeling the need to provide legal justification for a struggle against secession, in April, 1861, Lieber published a pamphlet which sold out ten days after the fall of Sumter. In it he summarized most of the well-known anti-secession arguments and added some of his own. The pamphlet contained an article written in 1850 against South Carolina disunion sentiment, in addition to Lieber's more recent thoughts.

In 1850 he had emphasized constitutional arguments in an effort to appeal to those men who might be frightened by northern actions. He suggested sympathy for a besieged South and pleaded with his worried neighbors in South Carolina to consider the safety they enjoyed under the existing constitution and laws. He insisted that secession was not a right guaranteed by the Constitution, that the principle of self-destruction was certainly not written into a nation-building charter. But the emphasis was on the safety and order which the Union provided. Men who wished to be free of this union, he argued, "seem to forget that the good which the Union, with her Supreme Court, or any other vast and lasting institution bestows

2. Stampp, *The Era of Reconstruction*, 25. James G. Randall says, "In the practical and vital sense the most serious question in 1860–61 was not the constitutionality, but the wisdom of secession. To affirm that secession was constitutionally possible was not the same as believing that it was prudent or desirable" (*Constitutional Problems under Lincoln*, 24). This statement overlooks the fact that a belief in the constitutionality of secession or in its revolutionary nature had practical consequences in motivating the will to fight.

upon men consists as much in the prevention of evil as in showering benefits into our laps." To avow secession was to apply the French theory of excessive individual rights and personal sovereignty to the states. To accept the right of secession was to accept the right of revolution; indeed, it was to invite, demand, revolution every fifty years or less. Society would be in continual chaos. Attempted secession would unleash war and provoke the destruction of liberty-protecting institutions. "No great institution," he wrote, "and least of all a country has ever broken up or can break up in peace, and without a struggle commensurate to its own magnitude . . . when vehement passion dashes down a noble mirror no one can hope to gather a dozen well-formed looking glasses from the ground."[3]

A decade later, as he watched that shattering take place, Lieber no longer spoke of written documents or the restraining power of institutions. He had seen how slavery could corrupt both. He still saw the Union as a force for order, but now the law he spoke of was broader than the specific limitations of the Philadelphia document. He had never believed that a constitutional superstructure was the protector of liberty or the ultimate foundation of government or society. Now, responding to what many viewed as the failure of the Constitution, Lieber spoke of the more fundamental sources of these. He would ultimately come to speak even of the uses of natural law for preserving the Union and order.[4]

In his 1861 discussion Lieber turned from arguments which emphasized the restraining nature of institutions and looked again to history. To promote union sentiment and the nationalism to which he was devoted, he traced the organic growth of both throughout American history. The settlement of the New World by one people, the Albany Plan of Union, the Stamp Act Congress, the Continental Congress, the formation of a national army, the Declaration of Independence, Washington's tireless efforts at creating an indivisible nation, the Constitution itself, all proved that the nation could never really divide. This call to memory was matched by a call to hope. The modern type of government, he insisted, was not the petty sovereignty but "the national polity . . . the organic

3. Francis Lieber, "What Is Our Constitution," *Miscellaneous Writings*, ed. Gilman, II, 128, 134, 127.
4. Brown, *American Conservatives*, 35; Lieber, *Civil Liberty*, 346.

union of national and local self government." This form of government "is . . . imposed upon our race, as the great problem to be solved and the great blessing to be obtained. It is sovereign to all else. It is the will of our Maker—the Maker of History."

In place of a call for simple stability, Lieber now asserted something more than written constitutions and contracts. The eternal verities of natural law appeared more frequently in his thought. He spoke of "instinctive social cohesion, [the] conscious longing and revealing tendency of a people to form a nation, to make the minor organization subservient to the great end of modern polity." He spoke of a contract that meant more than mere words, of a Union that was like a marriage, emphatically more than the stated terms of the written marriage contract. He spoke of "true public spirit and expanding patriotism . . . these," he insisted, "have their plenary rights too."[5]

This was fine as a nationalist rallying cry. It did generally place pro-Union sentiment within the framework of constitutional tradition and history. The constitutionalism of the earlier 1851 argument and the romantic outburst spawned by the secession crisis beautifully blended the dominant reasons for fighting this war. An intriguing indication of pervading constitutionalism in the North is the fact that the earlier argument received greater approbation than did the more recent one. Generally the pamphlet presented a point of view which Americans had heard in another form at Lincoln's inaugural. It emphasized important truths, but only hinted at answers to the question of the relationship between law, the Constitution, and civil war. Editorials throughout the North were calling for the enforcement of the laws, while southern states passed secession ordinances and shot national soldiers. Lincoln had promised faithfully to execute the laws of the nation in all of the states. But the question remained, what form of the law, interpreted in what way? Was the government to be held strictly to the letter of the Constitution in reaction to secession and rebellion? Would it remain, as many viewed it, the willing captive of a constitution whose form had helped precipitate the crisis?[6]

5. Lieber, "What Is Our Constitution," 14.
6. Arthur Bestor, "The American Civil War as a Constitutional Crisis," 327–

These decisions' implications for the Negro were vast. The more closely one adhered to the old Constitution, the more he would be likely to find himself supporting the legal traditions of a constitution which recognized and protected slavery. One might even banish slavery from the Constitution and still be faced with difficult questions of how constitutionally to justify measures required to guarantee the freedom so easily granted. American constitutional law retained for the states the power to protect personal liberty or to deny it. The Bill of Rights stopped the federal (not the state) government from violating individual rights. Acceptance of the Constitution brought the advantage of an immensely popular banner to fight under, but it also carried with it constitutional inhibitions to be managed.

Abandonment of the Constitution suggested the possibility of a new direction in nation-state relations—the possibility of providing citizens with the amount of protection which was necessary, not just that amount which could be constitutionally justified. It suggested that the war might produce a revolution.

Unlike any of the other subjects of this study, Lieber reacted to the legal questions of the Civil War by rejecting the Constitution as a guide: "The whole rebellion is beyond the Constitution. The Constitution was not made for such a state of things." Perhaps his foreign birth accounts for his lack of the usual veneration for the Philadelphia document; similar feelings were expressed by English-born E. L. Godkin. At any rate, Lieber felt that the best solution to the needs of war was to free his adopted nation from what he often viewed as "mere constitutionalism." In this wartime effort there were echoes of his earlier impatience with "mere theory" and his respect for hard evidence rather than speculation. In unprecedented times he preferred facts to constitutional preconceptions. Yet he also saw that he could not simply disavow the rule of law, and so he set forth an ideology that permitted innovation while it found security in legal tradition.[7]

352; Basler, ed., *Collected Works of Lincoln*, IV, 265; Howard Cecil Perkins, ed., *Northern Editorials on Secession* (New York, 1942), I, 202–237.

7. To Thayer, Feb. 3, 1864; E. L. Godkin, "The Constitution and Its Defects," *North American Review*, XCIX (July, 1864), 117–145.

Arguing for the preservation of the Union, Lieber believed that the Constitution could not serve as a guide. And so he evoked, again and again, the spirit of natural law. Ironically, this opponent of natural law's revolutionary potential could and did cite natural law to support a reaction to revolution. Believing that the Constitution had not prepared the nation for such a crisis, but left with the necessity of legalizing the war and its conduct, Lieber asserted what were to him commonsense and basic principles. The legal foundation of a nation was not its constitution, he argued, but its right to survive, and any law or constitution which restricted this right was contrary to reason. Specific constitutional shackles which inhibited necessary acts of war were dangerous foolishness.

During a war this basic right of survival was vastly more important than documents which described a nation's governmental structure. "I am one of those who believe in their innermost soul that first and above all *our country must be saved*," he wrote in the midst of the conflict. In 1853 he had asserted that civil liberty could not exist without a nation to protect it. Ten years later, with the life of the nation at sake, he restated the principle more forcefully. "The country—the nation is the preexisting condition of the Constitution itself, and to thwart the salvation of the country in the Constitution is very much as though a Catholic priest were losing time on some points of canon law when the overwhelming question is to save the soul from perdition."[8]

Lieber was a vigorous foe of men like Joel Parker, whose constitutional qualms led them to oppose some war measures. He was the mortal enemy of Copperhead orators, whose passion for the Constitution led them to seek the preservation of domestic liberties in a renunciation of the fight for union. He could not tolerate such a destructive use of the document. If it did not specifically declare that the nation had the right to survive, it was because its authors thought the point was obvious. If the Constitution did not provide a complete statement of how the nation was to react to all the conditions of civil war, it was because the framers of the charter had not envisioned civil war in America. But to allow disunion and potential anarchy simply because those men lacked sorcerers' predictive talents was insanity.

8. To Thayer, Dec. 29, 1863.

When, after 1862, the Democratic party wrote militant constitutionalism into its platforms, Lieber's nationalism became Republican
partisanship. In *Civil Liberty* he had extolled the virtues of political
opposition as vital to the preservation of liberty. But when political
quarrels involved questions of national survival, he quickly forgot
what he had written. The Democratic party became the party of
disunity, if not treason. Democrats were "wholly shameless like a
streetwalker. They boast of being lickspittles of the South and
have become as infamous as the Byzantines who preferred the Turks
and the utter ruin of their country and generation so that they
could injure their opponents within Byzantium." He felt that
slavery and state sovereignty had caused the war, and that the
Democratic party was tarred with both. Even after Appomattox
his hatred continued, and he described party leadership with the
phrase, "Satan is their legitimate prince."[9]

Such comments showed a willingness to overlook numerous
Democrats who were as dedicated to winning the war as he was,
and whose opposition to Republican rule was not necessarily disloyal. But in this fight for nationhood Lieber was willing to overlook
many things. His unwillingness to be bound by the Constitution
was matched by his disdain for other restrictive words—even when
the words were his own. In *Civil Liberty* he had written that the
power to suspend the privilege of the writ of habeas corpus obviously belonged to Congress, not to the President. But in the
early days of the war it was Lincoln who acted most vigorously to
save the nation. The President had inspired confidence in the government and in the nation's ability to preserve itself. Lincoln's suspension of the writ was essential for the preservation of safety
behind Union lines. Lieber approved his course and quicky encountered the expected cry of inconsistency. "A treatise on naviga-
tion," he replied, "is not written for a time of shipwreck." The
nation had to be saved. Without the nation there could be no liberty.
He was glad to be able to change his mind.[10]

9. To Thayer, July 19, 1868, Aug. 25, 1864. In *No Party Now but All for
Country* (New York, 1864), Lieber went so far as to suggest that even if there
were no law to overtake him, any man who even indirectly aided the enemy was
a traitor.

10. Freidel, *Lieber*, 213; Lieber, *Civil Liberty*, 111.

Lieber's support for the draft, which included the drafting of a conscription bill for Congress, also brought him criticism for changing his views. This time Ohio Congressman S. S. Cox cited Lieber against Lieber. The theorist denied this charge, asserting that his earlier remarks related to peacetime conscription and could not reasonably be cited as arguments against raising an army to fight a war for survival. If critics of conscription had another idea as to how the necessary troops could be raised, he would be delighted to hear it. Until they proposed one, he would consider their continual harping on constitutionalism in times of crisis as close to treason.[11]

Such militancy and partisanship were part of Lieber's offensive against a constitutional devotion which he feared would destroy the ability of the nation to fight for its own survival. He was seldom afraid that the government would advance too far beyond the Constitution, often worried that it would not go far enough. Despite Lincoln's vast expansion of the powers of the presidency, Lieber still thought him too respectful of constitutional restraints and too hesitant in demanding the most vigorous prosecution of the war. It was with reluctance that he supported Lincoln's renomination in 1864.[12]

Lieber's hesitant support revealed a basic difference between the two men. Although Lincoln had remarked to the professor about the similarity of their views, he was much more aware of the political realities in the wartime North. The President understood the power of constitutionalism in the nation. He recognized that constitutional concern was a fact of life to be dealt with, not simply a dangerous inconvenience to be deplored. Lincoln was guided by a vision of what a unified nation might be: the world's truest example of the blessings of self-government. But he knew that the war tested the existing constitutional institutions, as well as the ability to survive. Lieber's constitutional concern was minimal, his vision of the value of nationhood immense.

Attacked, nationhood was exalted to the level on which Lieber basically understood it—as a rather mystical thing, ordained by God, the wave of the future. At that level, of course, the road to national

11. To Thayer, Dec., 1868; Jan. 2, 1864.
12. Freidel, *Lieber*, 349–352.

salvation was open to almost any possibility which logic could devise. Having appealed to the eternal principles of natural law, Lieber might have found justification for the complete abandonment of the prevailing legal order. He might simply have declared that law is silent in the midst of war. Amidst the clash of iron and the flow of blood, it would have been understandable if Lieber had forgotten legal argument. He did not.

That he did not revealed a latent failure in the opportunities of the war. Lieber's aconstitutional attitude suggested the possibility that the Negro might gain his freedom in a legal environment that could secure equality. It suggested that traditional constitutional restrictions on federal action might be war casualties, and that legal impediments would no longer justify inaction where liberty was concerned. Albion Tourgee, soldier and antislavery advocate, suggested this hope. "For one, I don't care a rag for 'the Union as it was,' " he wrote. "I want and fight for the Union better than it was. Before this is accomplished we must have a fundamental thorough and complete revolution and renovation."[13] Lieber's insistence on the inadequacy of the Constitution seemed to nourish such ambitions. In his passion for saving the nation he insisted that constitutional limitations should be ignored in the service of higher purposes; one of those purposes was the end of slavery.

Early in the war large numbers of slaves escaped into Union lines. Since the announced purpose of the war was to keep the Southern states within the Union and uphold the Constitution, their presence raised embarrassing questions. Under the Constitution, the escapees were property of their masters. However, they were obviously unwilling property, and their absence from farms and plantations deprived the rebels of needed labor for their war effort. Common sense would have settled the problem in a minute, but the war raised more than questions of common sense; it raised constitutional questions with major implications for the way people lived. Federal action against slavery raised the spectre of a national right to change the domestic institutions of states—something that the Constitution forbade. Loyal slave states were especially sensitive on this matter,

---

13. Quoted in Otto Olsen, *Carpetbagger's Crusade: The Life of Albion Winegar Tourgee* (Baltimore, 1965), 24–25.

but even in states which had no slaves there was hostility. Fearing public response, for months the administration avoided a decision on the status of escaping slaves.

Lieber deplored the government's hesitancy. When Sumner asked for advice on the status of the fugitives, the theorist poured it forth as usual. Cutting through the constitutional question of states' rights in a civil war, he insisted that the war be viewed as an international war. This gave the southern states no claim to constitutional rights or privileges—they were simply a foreign enemy. The Union government owed them nothing and might use any method for securing their defeat. Only state municipal law allowed men to be called property, he observed. Natural law, the foundation for international law, did not recognize slavery. Which law should be applied? The answer was obvious. Surely no one could reasonably contend that one belligerent should enforce the municipal law of another. In cases of escaping slaves, therefore, the law of nature applied. "Those who commenced the Rebellion ought to have reflected upon this. It is too late to talk—*in the midst of war*—of rights made or guaranteed by municipal or constitutional law."[14]

Many abolitionists made this sort of argument. They saw the war as a chance to strike off the constitutional shackles which legitimized slavery. They welcomed the conflict as one in which men might choose natural law and liberty over the words of the Philadelphia document. Many even argued that the Constitution itself would permit such choices under the war powers doctrine which permitted any measure to protect the nation.[15]

That Lieber and the abolitionists shared a belief in such a liberated legal environment seemed to portend an alliance between them. During the war an unofficial one did occur, as the theorist welcomed all arguments which justified the fight for the Union. But those who read his works carefully would discover reasons to doubt his commitment to equality even as he demanded emancipation. Freedom for the slaves was a weapon in his nationalist arsenal, not an end in itself. It was a way to guarantee a legal order which would

14. To Sumner, Dec. 19, 1861. Quoted in Perry, ed., *Life and Letters*, 322–323; Freidel, *Lieber*, 318–319.

15. McPherson, *Struggle for Equality*, 66; William Whiting, *War Powers under the Constitution of the United States* (Boston, 1871).

offer the Negro very little of what he required beyond freedom.

Throughout the war Lieber demonstrated his devotion to an established legal order, even as he spoke of unprecedented legal circumstances and argued the irrelevance of the Constitution. His pamphleteering has already been mentioned; he also sought the assistance of other writers in legitimizing policies which war made necessary. For example, when questions arose over the authority of the President to suspend the privilege of the writ, Lieber obtained the most able defense of the action's constitutionality. He encouraged the deeply respected Philadelphia attorney Horace Binney to provide a justification for Lincoln's actions which placed them within the legal traditions of both England and America. Binney's effort received widespread attention and approval.[16]

Lieber himself was also showing legal compunctions. At first his respect for a free press made him reluctant to support army efforts to stifle opposition newspapers. He was worried about the legality of confiscation, and in 1862 he cautioned Sumner against drafting too sweeping a confiscation measure. And when he authored General Orders 100, he revealed clearly the way in which his aconstitutional liberalism was an instrument of his firm conservatism.

Lieber wrote General Orders 100 at the request of the army to provide a guidebook for troops in the field. He had come to the attention of Chief of Staff Henry W. Halleck due to an article he had written on prisoner exchange and because of his Columbia lectures on the laws of war. The question of the legal status of guerrillas, the uniformed enemy, and an army of occupation all demanded some form of regulation, and Halleck thought that Lieber's experience prepared him to provide it. The professor accepted the responsibility and so helped to provide legal justifications for actions on which traditional American law was all but silent. He helped make acceptable law out of imperative military necessity. He did so by once again using natural law ideals.[17]

16. Horace Binney, *The Privilege of the Writ of Habeas Corpus* (Philadelphia, 1862). Binney acknowledged his debt to Lieber in the preface to this pamphlet. Although he said that the question of suspension was essentially political and not legal, Binney went to great length to show that the action of the President fell within the Constitution. See Binney to Lieber, July 29, Oct. 26, 1861.

17. Brainard Dyer, "Francis Lieber and the American Civil War," *Huntington Library Quarterly*, II (July, 1939), 449–465. Pound, *Formative Era*, 12–24, argues

The code itself was a blend of high morality, pragmatism, and concern for law, built on a nationalist foundation. It was, as Elihu Root later called it, an attempt to impose "the restraint of rules of right conduct, upon man at his worst, in the extreme exercise of force." There was humanity in the code, a recognition that common decency required actions which strict reverence for law would oppose. Thus the adoption of regular rules of war in this rebellion might have been precluded by the fact that laws of war generally apply only to wars between nations, and the Union government claimed not to recognize the rebel government. But if soldiers were to be guided by something other than feelings of revenge and the necessities of the moment, some legal order had to be brought to the conflict. Therefore Lieber argued that the existence of this code in no way implied such recognition. It imposed the humanitarian obligation that men at war never forget that they were "moral human beings, responsible to one another and to God."[18]

The code revealed Lieber's conservatism in its emphasis on property rights. "The United States," he wrote, must "acknowledge and protect, in hostile countries occupied by them . . . strictly private property. . . . Offenses to the contrary shall be rigorously punished." Public property was subject to confiscation, but, with the exception of slaves, private property was to remain practically undisturbed. Such an attitude is not surprising, considering Lieber's belief that nationalism and private property were tightly linked. However, it would have severe consequences in Reconstruction days, when many of the most radical men concluded that only the confiscation and redistribution of private estates would provide a secure foundation for equality.[19]

On the subject of slavery Lieber wrote into his code his earlier arguments to Sumner about the status of escaping slaves. Since slavery depended on municipal law, and since southern municipal law did not apply to the Union army, natural law principles would

---

that in the nineteenth century natural law provided some stability for legal change.

18. "Instructions for the Government of Armies of the United States in the Field," *Official Records of the War of the Rebellion* (Washington, 1869), ser. III, III, 150, 163.

19. *Ibid.*, 152; Freidel, *Lieber*, 337; McPherson, *The Struggle for Equality*, 407–416.

apply here, as they did in international law. Under that law there was no distinction as to color. Therefore all men falling into Union hands were to be treated as free men. They were never to be enslaved again, and "the former owner or state can have . . . no belligerent lien or claim of service."[20]

Lieber's point that a free slave could never be returned to slavery was relevant to the time. Many Northerners wondered whether the Emancipation Proclamation, issued as a war measure, freed slaves forever or only for the duration of the war. Lieber's argument helped establish the ideal of permanent freedom in law, at least for some slaves. It was a useful precedent for future emancipation questions.[21]

In using law to buttress actions of military necessity, Lieber performed a conservative function. He helped preserve the idea that the war was a war against revolution. However, his use of natural law and his silence on the Constitution led southern critics of the code to call it a legal cloak for brutality. Nevertheless, law had replaced private judgment as a guide for the conduct of armies, and this was a considerable advance over previous conditions. The whole code wove together in conscise, convincing terms the outstanding elements of Lieber's thought—humanity, respect for law, and love for the nation. If General Orders 100 could be criticized for justifying severe military measures, such as those of Sherman in Georgia, Lieber would probably have replied by pointing to the code's insistence that actions always be guided by moral conscience. He would certainly have insisted that "to save the country is paramount to all other considerations." In providing a legal framework for that salvation, Lieber had symbolized the efforts of legal minds in the war era.[22]

As he viewed the nation in 1864, Lieber was pleased. The war was proving to be the bane of state sovereignty. "What are the things settled at this period of our struggle?" he asked a friend. The major settlement was this: "The people are conscious that they constitute and ought to constitute a nation, with a God appointed country, the integrity of which they will not and must not give up, cost what it

20. "Instructions for Armies," *Official Records*, 152.
21. Randall, *Constitutional Problems under Lincoln*, 380–385.
22. "Instructions for Armies," *Official Records*, 149; Freidel, *Lieber*, 337–341.

may." The thought of his divided homeland was with him daily, and he rejoiced that the Civil War, bloody though it was, was denying the United States the horrible opportunity to emulate a weak and divided Germany. He reminded fellow German-Americans in 1864 that the choice between Lincoln and McClellan was between the petty sovereignty of their homeland and the wealth and liberty of a united nation. He said very little about the effect of the war on the Negro.[23]

With Lincoln's election and the continued inexorable pressure of Union armies, the war ground to a close. It was time to reflect on the evils which had compelled the conflict, and to insure in law what had been won on the battlefield. During the fighting Lieber had been most cavalier in dismissing the Constitution as inadequate to the needs of the hour. But, after the war ended, he saw the importance of constitutionalizing changes. In early 1865 he offered a series of amendments to effect this purpose. These amendments were founded in his belief that "the heat of a civil war of such magnitude [had] ripened thought and characteristics which may have been in a state of incipiency before."[24]

The war may have wrought changes in the nation's thought, but it had not changed the thought of Francis Lieber. Conflict had allowed the nation to experience the nationalism which was at the core of his thought. It remained to be seen to what extent Americans would accept ideas which they had often distrusted before the war. Lieber's proposed amendments differed little from his earlier beliefs. Laws must evolve with the times. Petty sovereignty destroyed law and national growth. Slavery was the malignancy which had militarized state sovereignty. Both had to die, since both endangered the republic. He set forth again his nationalist ideas. He marched Washington, Hamilton, and Madison in bristling phalanx against state sovereignty dogmatism. He unrolled pages of history to demonstrate the deep roots of American nationhood. We were a nation,

23. To Thayer, Feb. 3, 1864. Quoted in Perry, ed., *Life and Letters*, 340; Curti, "Lieber and Nationalism," 268; Freidel, *Lieber*, 352; Francis Lieber, *Lincoln or McClellan?* (New York, 1864). This pamphlet was printed in Dutch and German as well as English.

24. Francis Lieber, "Amendments of the Constitution Submitted to the Consideration of the American People," *Miscellaneous Writings*, ed. Gilman, II, 147–149.

he insisted. It was time for our Constitution to say so more clearly.[25]

Lieber's amendments were efforts to constitutionalize his nationalism. He wanted an amendment to declare that natives of the country and naturalized citizens owed "plenary allegiance to the government of the United States and are entitled to and shall receive its full protection at home and abroad." He wanted to make treason a more easily punished crime by adding to the constitutional definition the idea that treason also consisted of "assisting in forceable attempts to separate states and territories from the United States or asking foreign aid with the intention of separation."

Lieber saw slavery as "originated in unhallowed greed . . . hostile to civilization and to the longevity of nations . . . deciduous institution . . . a cancer . . . maligant virus . . . perverting and estranging statesmanship and morals"; he thought it had to be destroyed by constitutional amendment. The rebellion, begun for the purpose of perpetuating and extending human bondage, now offered the chance to extinguish it forever. Lieber wanted to redeem the shame of the founders who had blushed to include the word slavery in the Constitution. "We claim it as a right to mention now, for the first time the word slavery in the Constitution," he said, "in order to abolish it."[26]

Lieber also wanted freedmen to have their civil rights guaranteed by the Constitution. He felt, as did Congress and nearly all Americans, that humanity and logic both demanded legal rights for the newly freed slaves. Therefore he offered in expanded form those old conditions for ameliorating slavery which he had suggested to Calhoun two decades before. Reacting to the fact that Negroes were denied full participation in state courts, Lieber sought to constitutionalize civil rights and make them subject to federal protection. His amendment to this effect was markedly similar to the first section of the subsequent Fourteenth Amendment in the attempt to make the freedmen national citizens:

The free inhabitants of each of the states, territories, districts, or places within the limits of the United States, either born free within

25. *Ibid.*, 150–152, 157–160.
26. *Ibid.*, 169–171, 177–178.

the same, or born in slavery within the same and since made or declared free, and all other inhabitants who are duly naturalized according to the laws of the United States, shall be deemed citizens of the United States and without any exception of color, race or region, shall be entitled to the privileges of citizens, as well in courts of jurisdiction as elsewhere.[27]

Lieber also predicted future congressional action in a proposal that a state's congressional representation be based on the number of voters rather than the number of residents. This was an obvious effort to encourage southern states to admit Negroes to the ballot. In a slightly changed form, this proposal also appeared in the Fourteenth Amendment. Both measures left the control of suffrage in the hands of the states, thus rejecting radical egalitarians' urgings that the federal government directly control suffrage.[28]

Such restraint by congressmen was predictable. They were sworn to uphold the Constitution, and they operated in an environment which encouraged respect for it. Lieber's disdain for excessive constitutionalism suggested the possibility of more sweeping measures, however, and less respect for federalism. But for men like Lieber, who sought a stable society in the war era, the necessities of Reconstruction were complex and potentially contradictory.

Lieber was prepared by his prewar beliefs to welcome the war. It was a chance to destroy state sovereignty, one of the most dangerous elements in a society whose democratic tendencies were frighteningly divisive. It was also an opportunity to strike down the slavery which had proved so inimical to those institutions of self-government which restrained democratic absolutism.

Slavery died in the war. But standing in the way of a complete reunion and the restoration of order was a South still proud of its traditions and still frightened by the potential of an unregulated population which had been held in slavery for over two hundred years. The obvious solution to such recalcitrance was the creation in the South of a dominant unionist element comprised of freedmen. Doing so would not only provide the Republican party with political power; it would also satisfy the demands of simple jus-

27. *Ibid.*, 179; Freidel, *Lieber*, 378.
28. "Amendments," *Miscellaneous Writings*, ed. Gilman, 179.

tice. It would repay the wartime sacrifices of thousands of black soldiers and would satisfy the sincere moral convictions of most Northerners.

But there was no sure stability in this course, for two reasons. In the first place, intransigent southern hostility to equality measures raised the spectre of a protracted conflict—a cold war prolonging the recent turmoil indefinitely. A continued struggle for equality threatened hopes that a more vigorous nationalism would be the result of the war. While the struggle for equality gained force from its association with the war, the memory of that bloody conflict may also have retarded the struggle.

In the second place, the makeup of that southern unionist element was deeply troubling. The freedmen were of that same poor, ignorant class that jurists had feared before Sumter. The prospect of expanded suffrage raised again the ominous prospect of a nation ruled by masses ignorant of the true foundations of law and liberty. Both the racist expectation that blacks would fail and the immeasurable scars of slavery, which provided evidence to confirm these expectations, gave Northerners reason to believe that continuing the Reconstruction struggle with the tools at hand would be unprofitable.

Lieber's prewar fears were aroused by moves for equality. Although he supported the congressional program, he showed an increasing reluctance to support it to its extreme logical conclusion. That reluctance corresponded to his growing distaste for the excesses of democracy and for a burgeoning mass of ignorant voters. Already disgusted with the way in which New York's Irish immigrants used their suffrage rights, he feared further debasement of the right to vote. When his son Norman wrote him about the ignorance of southern Negroes, Lieber thought enough of the information to pass it on to a close friend, Congressman Martin Russell Thayer, suggesting the dangers of unrestricted voting rights. He asked the 1867 New York constitutional convention to consider introducing a literacy requirement into the state voting regulations, hoping thereby to improve the quality of the ballot. An ardent devotee of liberty, Lieber never equated it with equality or democracy. "Democracy," he told Sumner, "has *never been for freedom.*"

A ballot in the hand of a former slave was no pleasant sight to this Jacksonian legal expert.[29]

Lieber also understood that belief in the inferiority of Negroes was widespread. "The poor white all the Union over wants to kick the Negro," he observed, "all democratic hypocrisy and cant to the contrary notwithstanding." He was increasingly worried that excessive zeal for black ballots would inspire a popular reaction, and that voters would oust from office the more nationalistic Republicans and replace them with state sovereignty Democrats. He repeatedly warned Sumner against pushing too hard on the suffrage question. It was impolitic to do so, he insisted; and besides, there were some states where blacks outnumbered whites and "in the course of the animated politics of a free country every distinction whatever becomes party distinction. Would you side in such a case with blacks?" Racism was indeed widespread. Despite his scrapbooks demonstrating basic racial equality and his antislavery theories, it infected Lieber himself.[30]

The theorist's fundamental passion was nationalism. He was reluctant to have it weakened by concern for side issues. He was afraid that, in their concern for equality, men like Sumner and Stevens would lose sight of the true prize of the war—the opportunity to settle forever the nature of the Union. However, when Reconstruction questions linked the condition of the Negro with the integrity of the nation, Lieber was a militant radical. He was vigorously opposed to the Black Codes, seeing in them the reimposition of the old slave system. He rejoiced at the passage of the Civil Rights bill, recognizing that simple enunciations of national citizenship were not enough to protect the freedmen and that specific legislation protecting their rights was imperative.

He was especially sensitive to any assertion by the South of what it called its rights. When southern states did not immediately yield to congressional conditions of readmission, the angry author suggested that one or two of the recalcitrant states be territorialized as

29. To Thayer, Oct., 1867; *Miscellaneous Writings*, ed. Gilman, II, 215–216; to Sumner, April 8, 1868. W. R. Brock notes in passing the fear of majority rule among Reconstruction Republicans (*An American Crisis*, 265).

30. To Sumner, Oct. 22, 1865; to Thayer, Nov. 20, 1867; Freidel, *Lieber*, 377–378.

examples to the others. As southern obstinance continued, Lieber began to lose all patience. He told Sumner that 50,000 troops should be kept in Dixie to keep Southerners from reviving their treasonous cause. When he thought of the best man for President, since he abominated the southern sympathizer Johnson, he thought of Secretary of War Stanton. The "southerners hate him so delightfully," he wrote gleefully, "it makes one's mouth water."[31]

Yet this radical militance did not shake him from his nationalist concentration. As Reconstruction became more and more vigorous in 1867, Lieber began to move away from his wartime friendship with Sumner. The radical egalitarianism of the Massachusetts senator and his cohorts was creating a situation which would undo the nationalism forged in the war. By late fall of 1867 Lieber was corresponding more frequently with moderates. He wrote to Thayer that he was concerned that radical men would "run the cart into such a mire that we shall be able to extricate it only by sacrificing a good deal of our best baggage."[32]

Observing the ongoing process of Reconstruction, Lieber began to echo his prewar fears. Congressional activity bothered him, and there were also disturbing signs outside Congress that the war had not induced that single-minded devotion to nationhood which Lieber epitomized. President Andrew Johnson was combining personal vulgarity with respect for southern rights in a combination that made him Lieber's favorite enemy. The theorist had been disgusted first of all by reports that Johnson had been drunk at the inaugural. He grew more bitter as the President demonstrated his state sovereignty sentiment. For a time Lieber restrained himself from supporting calls for impeachment, but finally he had had enough. Johnson, he believed, had "vulgarized" the nation with his stump philippics and his blatant southern sympathies. Worst of all for Lieber's sense of law and order, the actions of the Tennessean were denigrating the executive office and encouraging desperate opposition measures. He began to wonder if America, having already demonstrated for the first time the example of a great nation disbanding its army after war, would not offer another example,

31. To Thayer, Dec. 10, 1866; Aug. 19, 1867; March 8, 1868; to Sumner, Nov. 17, 1865; Feb. 7, 1866; to Hallack, April 15, 1865.
32. To Thayer, Oct. 11, 1867; Nov. 30, 1867; Freidel, *Lieber*, 379–380.

this time a bloody one. Would the nation now have to enact the spectacle of the military defending the people against an aggressive executive? "The time fast approaches," he wrote Sumner, "when the governors of Mass., N.Y., and Penn., will be obliged to hold their pens ready to sign at any moment calls for the armed loyalty to sweep down on Maryland and Washington."[33]

By the end of 1867 hatred for the chief executive's state sovereignty sympathies and fear of the violent consequences had made Lieber into a vigorous supporter of impeachment. He did not agree with those who felt that removal of the President would show the world the weakness of American government and law. On the contrary, it would demonstrate that a stalemate between the two active forces of the government need not lead to violence. Far from being a revolutionary coup, Lieber considered impeachment a constitutional alternative to one.[34]

When Johnson was not convicted, Lieber was sad. The President had deserved it as no other man had. He was "the fellest of things . . . impassioned reasoning without a pure heart," a man of "indestructible impudence." "I literally loathe and despise him," he confessed to Thayer. "That is the meaning of my L.L.D." Johnson's incompetent theorizing on the Constitution had promoted petty localism. It had succored an ideology inimical to nationalism, and hence deadly to liberty.[35]

Lieber felt that the Reconstruction Supreme Court had become similarly tainted. When the Court overthrew the military conviction of one Milligan for conspiring to organize pro-Confederate forces in Indiana and approved the petitions of former rebels Garland and Cummings to return unpunished to their prewar professions, he believed that it had overstepped the boundary demanded by the Constitution and prudence. He was especially worried about the *Milligan* decision, which seemed to suggest that any congressional measures in the South would be unconstitutional. "What is to become of our four years struggle and final victory if the Supreme

33. To Thayer, Dec. 2, Aug. 31, 1867; to Sumner, Aug. 28, Feb., 1867; William A. Russ, "Was There Danger of a Second Civil War during Reconstruction?" *Mississippi Valley Historical Review*, XXV (June, 1938), 39–58.
34. To Thayer, March 14, 1867; March 7, 1868.
35. To Thayer, Dec. 2, 1867; March 2, July 11, 1868.

Court unravels our toilsome web?" he wondered. He believed that the "unravelling process of the court [was] disintegrating and denationalizing." In the past he had written of the judiciary as the "jewel of Anglican liberty"; now he was not so sure. After all, he explained to Sumner, when he wrote those words he did not contemplate "a rebellion—a territorial mutiny, laying beyond the scope of the great Constitution, being decided upon by written law and letter lawyers."

Lieber disliked the judge's actions on two antithetical counts. First, he believed they paid too much attention to fine points of constitutionality, rather than to the crucial necessity of nationhood. He was always suspicious of men who tried to hide in constitutional phrases. Second, Lieber believed that the Court was expanding its role. Instead of confining itself to specific cases and to the strict legal questions at issue therein, it was trying to make policy as well. The Court, of course, always does both, and Lieber was extremely unhappy because the Court did not appear to be making the policy he wished it to make. Still, he sensed an expansion of judicial function which other observers would also recognize. He did not have a solution to this court imperialism but asked the noted educator A. D. White if "the intolerable nuisance" of judicial review might not "be diminished at least?"[36]

His distaste for the actions of the Court mirrored a growing discontent over the condition of politics, government, and law in America. Personally, the last years of Lieber's life were satisfying. He was internationally known and widely respected in the United States. One newspaper called him "a publicist . . . of more authority than any other man in this country." He probably agreed with this estimate. He had always ranked his works alongside those of Tocqueville, Grotius, and Montesquieu. But personal satisfaction was not reflected in his views of the state of the nation. "I believe, you know in the recuperative power of modern nations," he observed to his old friend Thayer, "and hope we shall recuperate, for the present we are going down, sliding daily."[37]

Perhaps underlying Lieber's malaise was his immense disappointment at the condition of Bismarck's united Germany. The theorist's

36. To A. D. White, Feb. 24, 1867; to Sumner, April 15, 1867.
37. To Thayer, May 24, 1868; Freidel, *Lieber*, 413-417.

dreams for a unified liberal nation diminished with each dispatch from his homeland. In America as well, the triumph of nationalism was becoming less glorious. Lieber supported Grant both in 1868 and in 1872, but he did not find much joy in the Grant era. Corruption and materialism seemed signs of a society gone wrong and of institutional self-government sick or dying.

The newspapers were filled with stories of venality and crime. He saw increasing indications that the detestable democratic theory of the French was corrupting American politics. "In such times," he lamented to Thayer, "if a man . . . did not believe in God, he would fly to Buddhism—seeking peace in *Nihilism*—at least I would." He was most troubled and saddened because the legal institutions of the country seemed corrupted by the pervasive avarice of the age. "The evil we have to contend with and to guard against," he wrote, "is that our *Law* degenerates into mere attorney apprenticeship and practice, and the *jurist* be forgotten. Already now he is little valued. The money-making attorney . . . is sought after. A sad hour for our country, *wholly* dependent upon Law."[38]

The law that he referred to was "a *Common Law*, ie. an independently evolved and evolving *National* Law (for that is the meaning of Lex Communis), with principles of Self Government, such as adhered to our colonists, like paste to the bookbinder's apron." The study of this law was "a great topic . . . a most noble and ample one." But in the Reconstruction years men seemed less and less interested in it, and the national institutions which preserved self-government seemed corrupted. Generally saddened by the whole legal environment, Lieber was especially dismayed by the lack of commitment to nationalism at the level of purity he demanded. He took out his frustration on a presidency and a judiciary engaged in supporting what was to him the most evil of causes—southern rights against nationalist necessities.[39]

He had hoped that the war had settled this conflict by destroying in one blow both state sovereignty and slavery, that poisoner of self-government. Certainly his own fight against such things had been a passionate one. He had ignored some of his early fears and rejected some of his earlier beliefs to serve the Union cause. He had enlisted

38. To Thayer, Sept. 7, 1868; Nov. 1, 1869.
39. To Thayer, Nov. 1, 1869.

even natural law, with all of its dangerous potential, in the service of that cause, adding the force of law to the fight against secession and its law-destroying consequences.

Yet his use of natural law, as well as the reasons for hostility to the Court and President, both pointed to a single cause, noble in itself but dangerous in potential consequences for human rights. Lieber's passion for nationalism blinded him to the innate value of the struggle for equality, separated from the cause of nationalism. Although he despised slavery, he had restrained attacks on it until antislavery sentiment could also be prounion sentiment, or until it became clear to him that only with slavery dead could there be a union which protected liberty. When Lieber used natural law, therefore, it was for two major purposes: first, to replace a Constitution proven inadequate with a legal guide so necessary in a nation fighting for union and law; second, to attack a slavery that had provoked disunion and hence threatened to destroy the nation and its liberty-protecting institutions. He evoked natural law for the same purpose for which he had evoked common law before the war—to protect law and union. But he did not adopt the logical consequence of this natural law rhetoric; he was ready to espouse the eternal sources of freedom when it became clear that slavery endangered nationhood. To carry to its logical conclusion the belief that all men were created equal would have required a single-minded devotion to equality—which of course meant exalting equality above nationhood, given the temperament of the times. Lieber loved equality for his own purposes, not for the black man. He thus came to ignore the basic purpose of natural-law thought—the protection of the rights of men.[40]

In the Jacksonian period Lieber had feared that the power of ignorant masses might overthrow law and order. In the war years and during Reconstruction he retained the idea that liberty depended on law, and law upon union. He was unable to separate the cause of liberty from the cause of union. He wavered from this belief only once, when the corrupting hand of slavery imperiled the

40. When Lieber discussed the Declaration of Independence, for example, he emphasized the way in which it revealed national unity, not its fundamental message of equal rights. To Sumner, August 25, 1867; "Notes on the History and Development of Constitutions," Lieber Papers.

institutions which were the sinews of nationhood. But the war offered a chance to purge this corruption and to insure a secure nationalism. After the war he was frightened once more by ignorant masses and was willing to moderate advocacy of human rights if such advocacy interfered with hopes for such a nation. Perhaps there were others who proposed the human rights legislation of Reconstruction for the benefit of the Union, and only secondarily for the benefit of the freedmen. They may have been more devoted to the law and order which the Union provided than they were to guaranteeing liberty. But if they were enough like Lieber to think this way, they probably also believed that in fighting for one they were fighting for the other. Lieber settled for Union and law.

Joel Parker I:
The Constitution—The Symbol of Order

Where Francis Lieber at least promised the destruction of the covenant which justified and preserved inequality, Joel Parker promised nothing. Lieber sought to go beyond mere constitutionalism whenever necessary to save liberty and union. Parker was a custodian of that Constitution and could envision no liberty or union without it. There was no hope for the Negro in Parker's thought; instead, there was a bedrock respect for the legal tradition which Northerners had fought and died for. From him they could learn of the Philadelphia document's adequacy for all circumstances, and the necessity of preserving it whatever the challenge.

Not all of them learned the lesson precisely. Most Americans accepted deviations from constitutional traditions in the service of saving the nation. They understood the necessity of destroying slavery whatever the traditional legal sanctions for it. They tolerated suspension of civil liberty in the war crisis. They welcomed the energy shown by Lincoln during the war, even if that energy pushed him beyond established precedent. But if they could not recite Parker's catechism flawlessly, they could and did retain the spirit that underlay it; they learned to respect and retain without major change the traditional constitutional system—the system which described the white man's union and helped secure the Negroes' chains.

Joel Parker's life was New England based. He was born in Jaffrey, New Hampshire, in 1795, attended Groton and entered Dartmouth in 1809 as a sophomore. Graduating at seventeen, he studied law and was admitted to the state bar in 1817. In 1821 and for about eighteen months thereafter he tried the life of a western lawyer in

Ohio. He was not satisfied being away from home and returned to New Hampshire at the end of 1822; he never again left New England.[1]

Parker practiced law from 1822 until 1833, during which time he served one undistinguished term in the state legislature. In 1833, at the age of thirty-eight, he was appointed to the state supreme court; five years later he became its chief justice. For ten years he distinguished himself in that post, earning a national reputation and attracting the attention of Harvard Law School, which in 1848 offered him the position of Royall Professor. After much thought he accepted, and for twenty years he taught law to men who would later influence the course of legal history in the United States.

During his years at Harvard, Parker taught four future Supreme Court justices: Horace Gray, Melville Fuller, Henry B. Brown, and Oliver Wendell Holmes, Jr. He taught twenty-nine federal circuit and district court judges, forty-four members of state supreme courts, twenty-five law school professors, five governors, four senators, five cabinet officers, ten noted legal authors, and five presidents of the American Bar Association. Among his students were the outstanding New Hampshire chief justice Charles Doe, and legal teachers and authors Francis Wayland, James B. Thayer, John Lathrop, John Chipman Gray, Benjamin V. Abbott, and Christopher Landell. Robert Todd Lincoln attended his courses during the Civil War. These men learned much of their constitutional law from Joel Parker.[2]

All of the students who met him were impressed. His lectures, though very demanding, were well attended. Occasionally he would lose the class and sail off alone into some esoteric realm, but the best students revered him and even the worst were awed. "By the students of the Law School," one pupil noted, "Judge Parker was generally looked upon as the deep repository of all legal knowledge." Another observed, "No one could be in his presence without feeling the stimulus to noble and high endeavor."[3]

1. George S. Hale, "Joel Parker," *American Law Review*, X (Jan., 1876), 235–269.
2. *Centennial History of the Harvard Law School, 1817–1917* (Cambridge, 1918), 379–401.
3. Hale, "Joel Parker," 260–266; Howe, *Justice Oliver Wendell Holmes, The*

He would enter the classroom quietly and with dignity, ignore the applause that by custom welcomed lecturers at Harvard, place his hat beside him, and without elaborate introduction begin to speak. "He handled the law in a scientific spirit," an observer recalled, "without emphasis, not without dry humor, and had ever a luminous method of exposition which grew more luminous as the subjects grew more abstruse." Parker's goal in lecturing was to show that the law was a complete and homogenous organism, with all its parts linked and capable of being understood in the dry light of reason. Like most of the era's legal establishment, he was suspicious of pure natural law and preferred the more conservative common law. His approach to common law suggested, however, that trained minds could find true principles of justice through an understanding of the intricacies of particular cases. Legal principles were Parker's passion. As he lectured to defend them from what he believed were dangerous heresies, the aloof, scientifically rational lecturer faded from view and the enflamed advocate appeared. It struck one student that such discussions "took the shape of almost personal combats. Judge Parker fought for principles of law as other men fight for life, or family, or for nation."[4]

Parker had developed his combativeness in an arena considerably less cloistered than that which Harvard provided. The courts of New Hampshire were known for the roughness with which lawyers treated witnesses and each other. Questions to ordinary witnesses were not limited to matters before the court, and hostile witnesses could expect to be targets for sarcasm, ridicule, and contempt. Charles Doe, the great New Hampshire jurist of the late nineteenth century, remembered vividly that he had seen "in his five years practice women and children and even men so controlled by the overbearing and coercing manner of some lawyers on cross

---

Shaping Years, 184–186. Reid, *Chief Justice*, 47, observes that, together with faculty colleague Theophilus Parsons, Parker exerted great influence on the students. "It is difficult to name two other men with equal opportunity to influence the American legal profession during the second half of the last century. . . . They were privileged to mold a generation of lawmakers, a generation of legislators, and a generation of judges."

4. Hale, "Joel Parker," 261; George W. Smalley, *Anglo-American Memories* (London, 1911), 26.

examination, that in an effort to bring truth to light they brought falsehood in its stead." It was the sort of environment where passionate advocacy was as indispensable to success as knowledge of the law.[5]

The purposes for which Parker fought also had their foundations in his New Hampshire experience. He began his public career in the 1820s and 1830s, when the state was absorbed in violent quarreling that signaled the rise of Jacksonianism in the state. Led by Isaac Hill, a future member of Jackson's kitchen cabinet, the Democrats moved against the economic establishment of the state and the Congregational church, as a fitting follow-up to taking control of Dartmouth College from the hands of former Federalists and giving it to the popular opposition. These efforts naturally shook the state's conservatives, but the rhetoric which espoused them was even more frightening. Hill's newspaper continually attacked the rich in the name of the people, stirred up old hatreds by reciting stories of debtors' prisons, and stooped to such character assassination as reporting that, when he was ambassador to Russia, John Quincy Adams had been a procurer for the czar.[6]

Parker supported banking measures, was a strong Congregationalist, and maintained a lifelong devotion to Dartmouth, the college he had left four years before the Democrats took it over. He was no friend of democracy; as Jackson's star rose, Parker's conservatism gained militance. Like other jurists of the nation, he was worried and angry about the potential for disorder posed by the rise of the masses. His attitude rested partly on snobbery, but it was fed by troubling incidents throughout society. Parker became chief justice of New Hampshire in 1838, an especially troubling year. The post-Jackson depression brought widespread suffering and discontent. It also encouraged the expression of violent hostility against an increasingly militant abolitionism. Convulsive incidents abounded. In Vicksburg, Mississippi, a mass lynching had occurred. In Baltimore bank directors had been besieged by a mob for hours. Near Bunker Hill an orphanage was burned to the ground. In St. Louis a mob

5. Reid, *Chief Justice*, 86.
6. *Ibid.*, 16–25; Glyndon Van Deusen, *The Jacksonian Era, 1828–48* (New York, 1959), 33.

dragged a prisoner from jail and burned him to death. Across the river in Illinois a court of law had joined in the lawlessness and indicted two men for defending their own property against a gang of vigilantes. In the words of that court, the two men were indicted because they had "unlawfully, riotously, routously, and in a violent and tumultuous manner, defended and resisted an attempt . . . to break up and destroy a printing press." These were the events which attracted Parker's attention as they had captured the eye of a young Illinois attorney named Lincoln.[7]

Parker's response revealed the expected concern about such threats to order and property, but highlighting his reaction was his attention to the actions of that Illinois court. He apparently felt that disorder was about what you could expect from unruly democrats, but for a court of law to endorse their riotous activity was especially unnerving. If courts became corrupted, then society's only hope for stability—its legal institutions—would fail, and contempt for the established principles of law and order would destroy free government. Then would follow despotism of the most dangerous sort— that of the masses. Speaking from the bench, Parker called upon government authorities throughout the nation to make punishment for lawlessness swift, sure, and severe. He prayed that public opinion would condemn it with equal vigor. He prayed for such a popular reaction, but he had his doubts.[8]

Expanding democracy did not inspire Parker with faith in the masses. The most obvious sign of his skepticism was his reluctance to respect the prerogatives of juries. An 1842 case in New Hampshire raised the question of whether juries should decide questions of law as well as questions of fact in criminal cases. Should they determine the meaning of a law and its constitutionality, as well as the question of whether or not the unlawful act had been committed by the defendant? At issue was the peculiar expertise of the trained legal expert, as opposed to a general acceptance of the common man's sense of justice. It was a question about which even judges

7. Joel Parker, *A Charge to the Grand Jury upon the Importance of Maintaining the Supremacy of the Laws* (Concord, N.H., 1838); Basler, ed., *Collected Works of Lincoln*, I, 108–115.
8. Parker, *Charge to the Grand Jury*.

quarreled, but Parker had no doubt as to the proper conclusion. He decided against the jury's right to deal with questions of law in criminal cases.[9]

The decision reflected an obvious bias against mass democracy, but it was also the product of a legitimate concern about the rights of the accused. Where judges decided the law, the defendant, if convicted, might claim that the rulings of the trial judge or the judge's interpretation of the law in question were in error. He could appeal to a higher court on this basis. If sustained, another trial and another possibility for acquittal would be granted to him. But if the jury decided both law and facts, it would be impossible to determine what interpretation of the law had been used in coming to a verdict. No one could know if an error in law had occurred. The defendant's chance for review by a higher court would vanish.[10]

It was impressive rhetoric to claim, as John P. Hale did in arguing for the jury's right, that the question pitted "the friends of free government, popular rights, etc.," against supporters of "legitimacy, aristocracy, etc." But this assertion begged the question of justice, as Parker quickly noted in replying. He conceded that judges might have autocratic tendencies, but he found that danger minimal in a nation as free as the United States. Here, he observed, "there is much more reason to fear that judges, as well as juries, may be swayed by popular feeling, sometimes dignified by the name of public opinion, to make an example of him who happens to be an object of popular suspicion and prejudice." The interpretation of law in the hands of men trained to place legal principles above popular passion was the best security against such injustice.[11]

Parker felt so strongly about this question that he abandoned the non-partisan nature of the judicial office and engaged in a pamphlet war with Hale while an appeal on the case was pending before his own court. Hale's attack on the dignity of law and the judiciary compelled response, he explained. Left unchallenged, such assertions endangered the nation's vital structure of ordered liberty. Hence

9. *Pierce* v. *The State*, 13 *New Hampshire* 536; Mark De Wolfe Howe, "Juries as Judges of Criminal Law," *Harvard Law Review*, LII (Feb., 1939), 582–616.

10. Howe, "Juries as Judges," 582–585; Levy, *Law of the Commonwealth and Chief Justice Shaw*, 290–295.

11. *Pierce* v. *The State*, 540–541, 568–571.

some response, even of such an extraordinary nature, was imperative. This peculiar conduct most clearly revealed Parker's fear of democracy, his respect for the existing order, and his recognition that justice did not necessarily reside in the will of the masses. This latter understanding gave special force to his defense of the legal establishment against democrats' growing conviction that they were competent to interpret their own laws.[12]

Parker was not just a frightened reactionary; he was capable of liberal views. The 1834 case of *Britton* v. *Turner* reveals this well. A worker had contracted to do a certain job for his employer. He finished only part of the work, and the employer refused to pay him. Ruling precedent in other states overwhelmingly supported the idea that the worker deserved no pay, but Parker defied that precedent. He ruled that the man should be paid at least for the work completed. Such a rule, he argued, eliminated the possibility that an employer might defraud a worker by firing him just before the completion of a task. Outside New Hampshire the decision was criticized as dangerous to the inviolability of contracts, but that state's lawyers and courts accepted it as both just and reasonable. As evidence of the decision's worth, *Britton* v. *Turner* is still required reading for most first-year law students.[13]

Parker himself pioneered an innovation in the legal process of New Hampshire when in 1832 he introduced a bill to give full equity power to the state supreme court. The measure proposed a radical change in the state legal system and received widespread opposition, but finally it passed. Shortly thereafter Parker was elevated to the supreme court, where he could administer the reform he had urged. He did so ably. The reform showed his willingness to change the legal environment but did not reveal any democratic instincts.

The nature of the opposition to the measure demonstrated the ex-

12. John P. Hale, *Trial by Jury, Remarks on the Attempt by Chief Justice Parker to Usurp the Prerogative of the Jury in Criminal Cases* (Exeter, N.H., 1842); Parker's pamphlet mentioned pp. 10–11. Parker would later say that "the selection of jurors is generally made with a view to their impressibility, their humanity, and their want of capacity to estimate the force of a connected chain of reasoning." *Daniel Webster as a Jurist* (Cambridge, 1853), 57.

13. 6 *New Hampshire Reports* 481; *Centennial History of Harvard Law School*, 244; Reid, *Chief Justice*, 48–49.

tent of Parker's liberalism. In the main, opponents were democrats
frightened by the nature of equity proceedings.[14] Equity law rests
on English traditions which offered relief for persons not protected
under common law. It deals with legal instruments like injunctions,
trusts, charities, and with technically legal but actually unfair practices, and mistakes or accidents which require relief from contract
requirements. Almost no one objected to such goals. But in the
practice of equity courts there was much that democrats and common law lawyers feared. In such courts there are no juries; the
judge is in full control and has complete responsibility for executing
the law and examining witnesses. He may demand evidence from
both sides and may even compel testimony that is self-incriminating.
In short, the judge may reach whatever conclusion seems just to
him without the interference of community sentiment. The law is
in the hands of knowledgeable men, not subject to the vagaries of
popular will. Parker's espousal of equity was a clear symbol of the
dimensions of his liberalism. It was legal, not egalitarian.[15]

His devotion to a law which maintained ordered liberty made
Parker a foe of most other legal reforms, in addition to an opponent
of Jacksonian democracy. He believed that the prewar movement
to codify and thus simplify American law was hostile to ancient
forms and hence a "device of ignorance." A jurist who sought to
achieve prominence by advocating fast and wide-ranging reforms
was "a very dangerous and mischievous animal." Parker believed
that precipitous change (especially change in law) was the enemy
of society. Law was not imposed on society; it grew out of the
social order and hence was inextricably woven together with it. To
change the law too quickly was to threaten more than written laws.
"A great change cannot be affected in one part without corresponding changes in others, or a disturbance in the harmony of the
system." Vital to order, imperative for liberty, American legal
traditions had to be preserved and protected. Respect for the established legal order had to be engendered in the population. Without

14. Robert Stillman Batchellor, "The Development of the Courts of New Hampshire," *The New England States*, ed. William T. Davis (Boston, 1897), IV, 2295–
2311.

15. Edwin B. Gager, "Equity, 1701–1901," *Two Centuries Growth of American
Law, 1701–1901* (New York, 1901), 115–152; Pound, *Formative Era*, 154–157; Miller,
Life of the Mind, 172–176.

it, uncertainty would be followed by disturbance, disturbance by majoritarian tyranny, and tyranny certainly by the end of liberty. These were attitudes which Lieber would have joyfully applauded.[16]

As he encountered the sectional crisis, this intense devotion to the restraints of law guided Parker's actions and judgments. Indignation over slavery did not move him as much as it did Lieber. Parker's capacity for outrage was generally reserved for legal principles, not for black people. The Union was a special object of admiration. It was the bulwark of American law, and without it there would be dissolution of order and an erosion of legal sinews. Disunion meant that there might be no more rule of law. Therefore Parker supported early efforts at compromise. He accepted the Compromise of 1850 as a means to preserve the Union even though he objected to the Fugitive Slave Act (on legal, not moral grounds). He even stopped his subscription to a religious newspaper which had vilified the compromise and its supporters. Although he disliked the fact that fugitive slaves were denied trials to determine their status, Parker still felt that the overall measure was constitutional and thus demanded defense by men who respected law.

However, his support of compromise was not unequivocal. As long as both North and South indicated their respect for law, or as long as one side or the other did not completely ignore legal principles, Parker would back efforts to keep the sections joined. But events in Kansas soon suggested that he would have to change his views. Although he was more conservative than Lieber, the Kansas-Nebraska bill and the subsequent violence in Jayhawk territory indicated to Parker, as to Lieber, that Southerners who spoke so eloquently about liberty and constitutional rights would trample both to perpetuate slavery and to force it on free citizens. More important, events in Kansas revealed that governmental institutions, designed to protect equal justice and promote liberty, could become shields for violence and the tools of tyranny.

The Kansas question had begun when Senator Stephen Douglas of Illinois introduced a bill to organize the Kansas and Nebraska territory. The measure incorporated the idea of popular or squatter

16. Parker, *Daniel Webster as a Jurist*, 64; Parker, *Charge to the Grand Jury*, 5–7, 17–21; Howe, *Holmes: The Shaping Years*, 191.

sovereignty, whereby the question of slavery would be resolved by the settlers themselves. The bill also repealed the Missouri Compromise by opening up lands north of 36°30′ to slave settlement.

The passage of the measure opened new lands for settlement, and this magnet pulled to the territory thousands of people eager for farms of their own. For many of these people the issue of free soil was tangential to the question of property. However, they became involved in this issue whether they wanted to or not when newspapers and legislators in the East and militants in the West proclaimed Kansas as the testing ground of whether popular sovereignty would bring victory for free or slave territory. Pro- and antislavery groups rushed to Kansas to gain control of the territorial government. By the time the first election for territorial legislature was held, freesoilers seem to have had a majority— but proslavery elements from Missouri rushed into the state and succeeded in electing a proslavery legislature. When this body met, it wrote laws which punished antislavery speech and activity and which required an oath for all officeholders. Freesoilers responded by establishing their own legislature and their own constitution which excluded both slavery and Negroes from the territory.

In Washington President Pierce faced a difficult choice. It was widely known that the Kansas elections had been carried by fraud and intimidation on the proslavery side. Yet these elections had been called and recognized by the legally appointed authority in the territory, Governor Andrew Reeder. Whatever the degree of fraud in the elections, they at least had Reeder's sanction. In contrast stood the freesoil government in Topeka. Although it probably expressed the sentiments of the majority of the people insofar as slavery was concerned, its legality was most dubious. Freesoilers had simply decided to call their own election and then produced a government which they insisted was legal. Faced with such options, Pierce followed the decision of the territorial governor and chose the fraudulently elected but "legal" government. Congress accepted this choice.[17]

17. Of course, the legality of the election carried by the proslavery forces was also dubious. The Kansas-Nebraska bill stated that the only persons eligible to vote would be white males twenty-one and over who were "actual residents of the territory." None of the Missourians could meet this qualification. Although Gov-

Whatever might be done in Washington, however, Kansas settlers were determined to take charge of their own fate. Armed
men on both sides, threats of violence, murders, and reprisals produced the inevitable result in such a volatile place. Civil war broke
out. Easterners sent guns to freesoil settlers; proslavery forces from
Missouri joined with colleagues in Kansas. In May, 1856, the freesoil
town of Lawrence was attacked; one man was killed, two antislavery newspapers were put out of business, and homes and buildings were burned. John Brown replied to this violence on the night
of May 24 with the murder of five proslavery colonists. Freesoilers
generally deplored the act, but it inflamed the conflict even more.
By December, 1856, losses in "Bleeding Kansas" totaled approximately two hundred killed and two million dollars' worth of property destroyed. The northern reaction to the Kansas crisis was a
political revolution. The slavery question had helped destroy the
Whigs; now the consequences of possible slavery expansion into
Kansas helped create the Republican party. Men who cared little
about the fate of slaves were aroused by the Kansas situation. They
created a political party that, two years after its birth, would win
1,335,264 popular votes (as opposed to 1,838,169 for the winning
Democrats). Eleven of the sixteen free states would vote Republican in 1856.[18]

Parker took part in this revolution. A Whig since the party's
birth, he took to the platform in October, 1856, to lecture former
colleagues on the "True Issue and the Duty of the Whigs." The

---

ernor Reeder did cast out a few returns and demanded new elections in these cases,
he nevertheless accepted the vast majority of the returns, apparently because he
was threatened with violence. United States, 33rd Cong., 1st sess., *Senate Misc.
Documents* #72, July 21, 1854 (Kansas-Nebraska bill); Roy F. Nichols, *Franklin
Pierce* (Philadelphia, 1958), 410; Leverett Wilson Spring, *Kansas: The Prelude
to the War for the Union* (Boston, 1885), 50–52. Pierce insisted that he could not,
as President, involve himself in the election process. "Imputed irregularities in
the election had in Kansas, like occasional irregularities of the same description
in the States, are beyond the sphere of action of the Executive." *Message from
the President of the United States to the Two Houses of Congress at the Commencement of the Third Session of the Thirty-fourth Congress* (Washington,
1856), 12, 14.

18. Allan Nevins, *Ordeal of the Union* (New York, 1947), II, 380–450; James
A. Rawley, *Race and Politics: "Bleeding Kansas" and the Coming of the Civil
War* (Philadelphia, 1969), 133–134, 158–162; Nichols, *Franklin Pierce*, 407–445.

lecture was an extended argument designed to show that the Republican banner of anti-expansionism could be carried by former Whigs without fear of repudiating Whig precedents. Both Webster and Clay had spoken against expansion, he told his listeners, and debates in the constitutional convention and in Congress at the time of the Louisiana Purchase supported such opposition. Although the Republicans were not without fault, they were the most respectable inheritors of Whig principles.

That Parker should become a Republican is hardly noteworthy. His reasons for this choice are interesting, however. As the major party closest to abolition principles, the Republicans were described by contemporaries as disturbers of the peace. In the eyes of Democratic leaders like Pierce and Buchanan, the growth of this new sectional party sanctioned the disruptive tactics of abolition and signaled the doom of the Union. As a man deeply concerned with the preservation of order, Parker at first glance would appear to belong in the party of the status quo. But he saw the greater threat to order in the actions of the southern-dominated Democratic party; Kansas was the exemplar of that threat.[19]

Parker recognized in Kansas the evil results of law perverted in the service of slavery. He saw evidence of such perversion in the territory's proslavery laws. They made it a crime for men to speak openly against slavery, and they denied antislavery men the right to vote. If a man was convicted of opposing slavery, he was subject to imprisonment at hard labor for two years; he might be made to work on the public highways with a ball and chain clamped to his ankle. All this for having spoken openly for human freedom.[20]

Reacting to this "usurpation and oppression," freesoilers had tried the only nonviolent alternative: they had formed their own constitution and asked to be admitted to the Union under it. But this lawful resistance, Parker said, had met with vilification and

19. See Pierce, *Message*, 1–3. Buchanan referred to the Republican party as the "Black Republicans" and feared that the party's success would destroy the Union. Philip Shriver Klein, *President James Buchanan* (University Park, Pa., 1962), 257, 366.

20. Joel Parker, *The True Issue and the Duty of the Whigs* (Cambridge, 1865), 5–9; Charles Warren, *History of the Harvard Law School* (New York, 1908), II, 210–211.

violence in Kansas, and legal sophistry there and in Washington. This attempt to form a free government was attacked as treason in Kansas. "A refusal to be gagged was insurrection," Parker continued, "asking to be admitted into the Union as peaceable citizens, desirous of escaping from oppression, was treason against the peace and dignity of the United States."[21]

He admitted that violence in Kansas was not a proslavery monopoly. However, he believed that freesoil militance had occurred only after peaceable opposition was met with force. The proslavery men of Atchison, Buford, Titus, and Emory had made even piracy respectable by attacking, murdering, and plundering freesoil settlements—under the banner of law and order, of upholding the "true government" of Kansas. They justified their brigandage by calling themselves a militia. After that, freesoilers took up arms. Only after the law had been twisted to punish peaceful, constitutional resistance, only after liberty under law had been made a farce, had violence become a recourse.

Parker had seen in Kansas what other legal theorists such as Lieber had seen: the failure of America's political and legal institutions to cope with the slavery expansion controversy. Under the guise of law had come oppression. Behind the facade of legality had come vigilantism. Masked by a call for law and order, men who urged freedom were sent to jail, and the legal authorities of the territory threatened to keep them there, with support from Washington. It had been said, Parker observed, that what was happening in Kansas was civil war. He had thought that civil war was the worst possible calamity. But bad as it was, he now understood that there was something worse—law which was designed to protect liberty but employed to destroy it. He was so outraged at the activities of proslavery forces that in this discussion of Kansas violence he did not even mention the five murders in Ossawatomie.[22]

Similar sentiment motivated Parker's reaction to the *Dred Scott* decision. Again, an institution believed to be a bulwark for order was succumbing to the mounting crisis. In this case, instead of politics absorbing the image of law and then debasing it, the law itself

21. Parker, *True Issue*, 11.
22. *Ibid.*, 11–14.

descended into the political arena. The Supreme Court abandoned its wise posture of judicial aloofness and attempted to decide the country's most passionate political issue.

The Court's action ignored Parker's treasured, instinctive dichotomy between the elevated heights of law and the squalid domain of politics. Joining a chorus of legal argument, Parker explained his opposition to the decision. First of all, it was simply unwarranted by the Constitution. The power to "make all needful rules and regulations respecting the territory or other property belonging to the United States" was explicitly given to Congress. When the Court ignored this provision, it was engaging in "sheer usurpation of powers of Congress." The decision was also, in Parker's opinion, "a gross perversion of legal principles." Taney's argument that Negroes had never been national citizens was refuted easily, and, given southern agreement to the Northwest Ordinance and Missouri Compromise, one could argue that the idea that Congress might not legislate against slavery in the territories was a recent proslavery innovation of John C. Calhoun. Parker even claimed, rather extravagantly, that the Constitution recognized slaves not as property but as persons. Therefore congressional action against slavery could not deprive a man of his property and did not violate the Fifth Amendment, as Taney claimed it did. The whole opinion, Parker believed, was an attempt to disguise political opinion in the mantle of constitutional truth.[23]

23. Joel Parker, *Personal Liberty Laws and Slavery in the Territories* (Boston, 1861), 58, 89–94. The question of the legality and method of congressional legislation for the territories was a complex one in terms of constitutional argument, though historically the case was clearer. In fact, Congress had legislated slavery both in and out of territories up to 1820 with little objection from either section. Slavery was excluded by congressional action from the Old Northwest and permitted in the Old Southwest. It had been permitted south of 36°30′ and prohibited north of that line. John C. Calhoun argued from 1847 on that Congress was only the agent of the states and had to execute their will in legislating for the territories. Since slavery was legitimized by the Constitution, Congress could not exclude it without violating its role as the congressional agent of slave as well as free states. In addition, there was the argument of Lewis Cass and later Stephen Douglas that Congress should allow the people of the territory to govern themselves insofar as slavery was concerned. Trial of the Cass-Douglas position resulted in "Bleeding Kansas." The Calhoun theory came close to adoption by the Supreme Court in the *Dred Scott* decision. Parker's position seems to have history and the intention of the Constitution's framers behind it; now it is the law of the land. Andrew C. Mc-

In itself this effort was deplorable, but in its consequences it was frightful. It contributed to disunion. Many honest Southerners were given the idea that their position was constitutional and that opposition to it was not mere politics but an unlawful attack on the Constitution. "If disunion takes place," Parker predicted, "it will be occasioned, in some measure at least, by this unhallowed interference of the Supreme Court with the great political question of the day." The decision led Southerners to believe that the Republican party was not simply engaged in the usual struggle for power but was "attempting to deprive them of a constitutional and legal right."[24]

Parker had sensed a crucial fact. In trying to settle a political argument, the Court had instead increased the argument's passion. It had told one member of a potentially deadly national conflict that his opinion was not merely strong political argument—it was constitutional truth. In addition, the Court had chosen sides in favor of human bondage and against an opinion and a section whose strength was increasing daily. The decision was a constitutional crime—but worse than that, it was a political blunder. It lost the Court the support of many of its most able and non-partisan defenders, and it demonstrated how profound a threat slavery was to the rule of law in America.[25]

Disillusioned with the legal health of the nation, Parker began to see individual acts of violence by Southerners as larger constitutional issues. When Preston Brooks attacked Charles Sumner on the Senate floor, the Harvard teacher saw it as an attack on freedom of speech and other constitutional privileges. He joined Longfellow, Jared Sparks, Henry Dana, and faculty colleague Theophilus Parsons on the platform at a protest meeting against what Parker called a "felon blow . . . of . . . painful significance." They met there in

---

Laughlin, *A Constitutional History of the United States* (New York, 1935), 512–521, contains the clearest exposition of various constitutional arguments. *Simms* v. *Simms*, 175 *US* 162, 168 (1899); *Binns* v. *United States*, 194 *US* 486, 491, (1904); *Dred Scott* v. *Sandford*, 19 *Howard* 448–451.

24. Parker, *Personal Liberty Laws*, 58–59.

25. *Ibid.*, 59–62; Alfred H. Kelly and Winfred Harbison, *The American Constitution* (New York, 1963), 390–391; Kutler, *Judicial Power and Reconstruction Politics*, 8–10. Kutler correctly suggests that the Supreme Court as an institution retained respect even though the *Dred Scott* decision was widely condemned.

Cambridge, Parker told the crowd, not simply to express indignation over a private criminal act. They were there "as the exponents of an unalterable and unconquerable determination to assert and maintain the supremacy of the law . . . at whatever costs and at all hazards." His deep anger pushed him into a rare personal comment. "I am, perhaps, known to most of you as a peaceable citizen," he said, "reasonably conservative, devotedly attached to the Constitution, and much too advanced in life for gasconade; but under the circumstances, I may be pardoned for saying that some of my father's blood was shed on Bunker Hill, at the commencement of one revolution, and that there is a little more of the same sort left, if it shall prove necessary, for the beginning of another."[26]

Parker was hardly an abolitionist. Except for his espousal of equity, he was not even a reformer. Yet here was the sound of a determination to fight being born in a man never known for what he himself called "an immoderate desire for agitation." His words had deep meaning for future events. They were significant enough to reach across the Atlantic, where the *Edinburgh Review* reported them and observed, "Deeply indeed, must the independent spirit of New England have been stirred when such words can be wrung from such a man in such a place. The violence of the South, significant as it is, is much less significant than the slow, intenser wrath of the North."[27]

Parker's words were brave, extracted in a moment of revulsion at the victory of violence over law and a bit overblown for a man of sixty-three. In calmer moments he was still willing to try to end the causes of revolution. Though bitter at the South, Parker still saw that northern actions often provoked southern hostility. Northern personal liberty laws were especially guilty on this score.

The Massachusetts personal liberty law was notably challenging. Passed in 1855, it reflected the outraged conscience of the state after the capture of Anthony Burns and was practically a point-by-point contradiction of the federal fugitive slave laws. It permitted judges and justices of the peace to issue writs of habeas corpus to suspected fugitive slaves. Those who claimed that an individual was a fugitive

26. Parker, *True Issue*, 90; *Centennial History of Harvard Law School*, 249; Warren, *History of the Harvard Law School*, II, 209.
27. *Edinburgh Review*, Oct., 1856, quoted in Hale, "Parker," 258.

slave had the full burden of proof on them, and they could not testify in the subsequent trial. Confessions by the alleged slave were not admissible evidence, and two witnesses to the slave status were required for proof. Prison sentences of one to five years and fines of one to five thousand dollars awaited anyone who attempted to remove a fugitive slave from Massachusetts without a trial. State officials and judges were forbidden to assist in executing the federal fugitive slave laws of 1793 and 1850, and the prisons and jails of the state could not be used to detain suspected or even convicted fugitive slaves.[28]

This law was a blatant violation of a federal law and of Article Four, Section Two of the Constitution. Men who were already fearful about the prospect of disunion were rightly frightened by it. Parker joined the legal elite of Massachusetts in signing an address to the state legislature for the repeal of the Bay State's personal liberty laws. He wrote a series of articles in the *Boston Journal* during the secession winter, pleading for repeal. The laws were completely unconstitutional, he insisted, and they encouraged disunion sentiment. If Massachusetts and those other northern states which had them did not repeal these statutes, more moderate northern states might actually support the South in its contention that northern lawbreakers were responsible for intersectional tension. He pointed out that southern actions were already dangerous enough to the Union and required no further encouragement.[29]

What troubled him most about the whole personal liberty law question was the way in which the North was adopting the dissolutive methods of the South. Both South Carolina and Massachusetts were insisting that the national government was "a kind of foreign jurisdiction ... against which we are to erect bars of prohibition, by the interposition of antagonistic state authority." The tragic result of this action was that "state organs, which have been regarded as elements of stability and strength to a Republican Union have become elements of weakness and disaster." The continued exercise of state interposition would produce not just a Union divided into

28. *Acts and Resolves Passed by the General Court of Massachusetts in the year 1855*; *Statutes at Large*, IX, 462.

29. Parker, *Personal Liberty Laws*, 24–25; Warren, *History of the Harvard Law School*, II, 263–264; *Memoir of Benjamin Robbins Curtis*, ed. Curtis, I, 335.

a North and a South, but a Union dividing into smaller and smaller parts, with order vanishing in the process. Speaking in December, 1860, William Seward expressed the same sentiment: "Dissolve this American Union and there is not one state that can stand without renewing perpetually the process of secession until we are brought to the condition of the states of Central America—pitiful states, unable to stand alone. No, gentlemen, republican states are like the sheaves in the harvest field. Put them up singly, and every gust blows them down; stack them together and they defy all the winds of heaven."[30]

Parker's fear of the potential anarchy in disunion placed the prospect of force behind his pleas for compromise. While admitting that northern actions were at fault for the sectional antagonism over personal liberty laws, he still believed that the South had instigated the crisis. If compromise failed to appease the seceding southern states, then "those who love the Union, and desire its continuance, may as well accept the alternative, whatever that shall prove to be, at this time, as at any other."[31]

The alternative sounded from Charleston harbor. The South was ready to preserve its right to secede with the force of arms. It was also quick to assert that its effort had the blessing of the true U.S. Constitution. The assertion was both a rallying cry for secessionists and a potential narcotic for northern warriors.[32]

Southern constitutional claims were echoed by northern rebuttals. Not content simply to assert the right of survival, most northern thinkers responded to the South with their own constitutional arguments. Newspapers and journals carried a large amount of legal argument over the right of secession. The President, congressmen, and jurists joined in the debate. All apparently sensed the importance of capturing for the Union-saving struggle to come the banner called "Constitution."[33]

30. Parker, *Personal Liberty Laws*, 47–50; *Rebellion Record*, ed. Frank Moore (New York, 1862), I, 6.
31. Parker, *Personal Liberty Laws*, p. 12.
32. Roy F. Nichols suggests that southern pro-secession pamphleteering was more than a propaganda device. "Misunderstanding the cultural nature of the federation, southern leaders thought they were dealing with a primarily legal controversy." *American Leviathan*, 186.
33. *Northern Editorials on Secession*, ed. Perkins, 202–237; Randall, *Constitu-*

Along with many other northern jurists, Parker joined in this effort to deny secessionists the blessings of legality. His argument was published almost concurrently with Lincoln's July 4 speech to Congress, which among other things refuted the right of secession. Indeed, it is possible, if the *North American Review* followed the modern practice of issuing periodicals a week or two before the printed date, that the President had the benefit of Parker's writings when he prepared his speech. It is equally possible, however, that both men drew on similar traditional arguments and that Lincoln had not read the professor's writings. Still, their points were markedly similar in many instances, as they moved to counter arguments that secession was justified by the Constitution. Both insisted that the people of the nation, not the states, had ratified the Constitution. Thus the southern claim that states had made and might now unmake the Union collapsed. Both men denied that any southern state (save Texas) had ever been sovereign, i.e., "a political community without a superior," in Lincoln's phrase. Thus the so-called sovereign right of secession was refuted. Both accepted the fact that states had rights, but both expressly denied that one of those rights might be the right to destroy the federal government. And both men pointed out that even under the most constrictive constitutional view possible, that of the Articles of the Confederation, the Union was perpetual.[34]

Beyond such points the arguments diverged. Lincoln emphasized the role that the common man was playing and would play in the struggle to come. The war was "essentially a peoples contest," he said, and in every northern town ordinary people were rushing to preserve a democratic government and the right of the people to work their will by ballots, not by secession and gunfire. "Our popular government has often been called an experiment," Lincoln noted. "Two points in it, our people have already settled—the successful establishing, and the successful administering of it. One still remains—its successful maintenance against a formidable attempt to overthrow it. It is now for them to demonstrate to the

---

tional *Problems under Lincoln*, 12–24; *Memoir of Benjamin Robbins Curtis*, ed. Curtis, I, 337–340; Basler, ed., *Collected Works of Lincoln*, IV, 265.

34. Joel Parker, "The Right of Secession," *North American Review*, XCIII (July, 1861), 212–244; Basler, ed., *Collected Works of Lincoln*, IV, 432–437.

world, that those who can carry an election, can also suppress a rebellion." He called the people to a fight for their government.[35]

Parker did not share Lincoln's vision of the war as a popular crusade for democratic government. To him it was fundamentally a struggle for the preservation of the rule of law. His argument thus stuck to legal-constitutional questions as he sought to undermine the value of secessionist constitutionalism. He added two notable arguments to those already presented. First, he demonstrated how the Constitution itself defied secessionist theorizing in the way that it gave powers to the federal government without permitting state interference in that exercise. There was no place in the nation's charter which stated that national functions were to be performed only at the pleasure of the states. On the contrary, the Constitution expressly said: "This Constitution and the laws of the United States which shall be made in pursuance thereof . . . shall be the supreme law of the land . . . anything in the constitution or laws of the State[s] to the contrary notwithstanding."[36]

Parker also struck at the southern assertion that the North had broken the nation-making contract first, thereby justifying an equal southern right. Using his expertise in contract matters, he pointed out that the laws which regulated private contracts did not permit one party to break the contract if there was a difference of opinion over what it meant. Both parties had the right to insist on compliance as they viewed it. Since the South did not accept a common arbiter, the only recourse was force. Southern theory did not justify a lawful, peaceful secession; it practically demanded a war of coercion.

Such arguments led Parker to his conclusion: the law did not justify the dismemberment of a nation. It demanded national unity, maintained if necessary by force. Secession was the opposite of constitutional; it was revolutionary. Southern arguments were sophistry. What was the true situation? It was this: a group of southern leaders had determined to secede. They had appropriated the common property of the nation, fired on an unarmed ship carrying supplies to a government-owned fort, attacked with seven

35. Basler, ed., *Collected Works of Lincoln,* IV, 438–441.
36. Article VI, sec. 2; Parker, "The Right of Secession," 223–228.

thousand men a fort manned by seventy, and then cried, "We want to be let alone." The preservation of law and order demanded that they not be let alone.[37]

Along with other anti-secession arguments, Parker's comments served to justify the Civil War. They helped "swell the chorus of Union" by adding to it those who were vitally concerned about the preservation of ordered liberty under the Constitution. But justifying going to war was a much simpler task than those which lay ahead—especially for a man like Parker, who had provided justifications that were firm but rather narrowly based.

As the war advanced, it would make unprecedented demands on the legal-constitutional structure. It would require some sustaining vision beyond mere legal precedent, a recognition that something more than the legal order and societal stability was at stake, that the nation stood for more than its established constitutional traditions. Lincoln called upon the spirit of democracy and the aspirations of the people to make their democratic experiment work. He would say at Gettysburg that the war was testing the viability of government of and by a people in search of a vision of equal liberty. Francis Lieber rested his justifications on the advance of the United States to a vital and powerful nationhood.

But Parker's vision was narrower. The precedents which he called upon to save the Union were fundamentally and almost exclusively legal-constitutional. He conceived of the Union in a limited sense as a legal entity, serving the purposes of stability and order. Given the protean nature of war, his position was likely to become more difficult as the conflict raised unprecedented questions. The first signs of difficulty were minor, however, and Parker responded effectively to them.

With the war less than a month old, Union soldiers in Maryland arrested a Confederate sympathizer named John Merryman and held him in prison in defiance of a writ of habeas corpus issued by the chief justice of the Supreme Court. Taney insisted that only Congress had the power to suspend the privilege of the writ, and that Lincoln's support for the defiance of his order was a long stride toward tyranny. The case raised the important question of the ex-

37. Parker, "The Right of Secession," 232–237.

tent to which the federal government might ignore peacetime
restraints in a time of civil war. The Chief Justice had suggested by
his actions in this case that peacetime precedents might inhibit the
ability of the government to maintain the Union. Naturally enough,
Lincoln rejected Taney's contentions, but he was aware of the
need to provide a legal rebuttal which justified his actions.

Lincoln replied to Taney's argument in his July 4, 1861, speech to
Congress. He emphasized the extreme dangers of the moment and
the overriding necessity of preserving the rule of law throughout
the nation. He implied that it might be necessary to overlook some
laws if they impeded the effort to save the union. Shall "all the laws
but one . . . go unexecuted and the government itself go to pieces,
lest that one be violated?" Lincoln claimed that he had not violated
even one law, but his implication was clear: he was concerned about
constitutional questions, but not so concerned that he would lose the
government to respect one law.[38]

This argument would have satisfied men with their eyes on the
struggle and not on the struggle's legitimacy. But Joel Parker was
not such a man. He recognized that the legality of the President's
actions deserved stronger buttressing than Lincoln had supplied. He
also understood the need to counter charges of men like former
Supreme Court Justice Benjamin Curtis and his brother George
Ticknor Curtis, a constitutional historian, that in a war for the rule
of law Taney's attention to legal principle was preferable to Lincoln's apparent willingness to decide which laws he would violate
and which ones he would respect.[39]

In October, 1861, Parker published his defense of Lincoln's action. He joined legal thinkers of radical temperament like Francis
Lieber and Harvard associate Theophilus Parsons and Congress's
outstanding constitutional lawyer, conservative Whig Reverdy
Johnson, in upholding executive suspension in areas of potential or
actual military action. Again Parker's emphasis was legal. He attacked Taney's reliance on English precedents by pointing out
major errors in the jurist's historical evidence. He revealed Taney's
inattention to relevant American precedents—notably *Luther* v.

38. Basler, ed., *Collected Works of Lincoln*, IV, 430.
39. Lorraine Williams, "Northern Intellectual Reaction to Military Rule during the Civil War," *Historian*, XXVII (May, 1965), 337–338.

Borden, where the Chief Justice had himself upheld a suspension of the privilege of the writ when martial law was declared.[40]

Parker's argument revealed that his legal focus did not blind him to reality, nor did it make him the arch-conservative that Taney was. He was sensitive to the jurist's devotion to law and liberty, but he believed that in this case Taney focused too much on the past. The latter was constructing an antiquated legal argument to meet rapidly changing conditions in the world of American law. He was admiring the past while the future, rapidly and dangerously becoming the present, went unattended. Parker held up the conditions of that present for Taney and others to view. He was surprised that the jurist had been able to ignore them. Insurrectionary mobs threatened the capital, setting fire to bridges in an attempt to isolate the city. The President had declared martial law. Yet Taney had ignored these things and decided that Merryman must be freed. But were army officers to await the pleasure of civil courts before arresting mobs and arsonists? Parker admitted that the military should always be subject to the civil power in time of peace—but this was not a time of peace, nor was the place of arrest a place of peace. Should a general engaged in suppressing an insurrection allow himself to be subject to civil arrest? Should the army stand idle while the general raised bond so he could command again? Taney's argument and his actions allowed all this to happen. To Parker the whole thing was dangerous, not simply foolish. Concede that Taney was right, and "the judicial power may be made quite effectual to overthrow the government in time of war."[41]

Parker did not feel that the Constitution protected its assailants in their efforts to destroy the Union. He did not believe, as Taney ap-

40. Joel Parker, "Habeas Corpus and Martial Law," *North American Review,* XCIII (Oct., 1861), 494–496, 480–482. On *Merryman,* see Walker Lewis, *Without Fear or Favor: A Biography of Chief Justice Roger Brook Taney* (Boston, 1965), 446–455; Charles W. Smith, Jr., *Roger Brook Taney: Jacksonian Jurist* (Chapel Hill, 1936), 185–195; Bernard Steiner, *Life of Roger Brook Taney, Chief Justice of the United States Supreme Court* (Baltimore, 1922), 490–500; Carl Brent Swisher, *Roger Brook Taney* (New York, 1935), 550–556. All of these works are favorable to the opinion of the Chief Justice. Surprisingly, none of them refers to contemporary criticism of it by jurists like Parker.

41. Parker, "Habeas Corpus," 480–486, 490. The modern consensus is that Taney was right, Lincoln wrong. See Bernard Schwartz, *The Reins of Power, A Constitutional History of the United States* (New York, 1963), 94.

parently did in 1861, that the nation would destroy its own liberty
by conducting a civil war. He certainly did not conclude, as Taney
did privately, that the dissolution of the Union was preferable to the
growth of a presidential dictatorship that would be spawned by
war. Parker believed that the Constitution could survive; it did
allow the nation to preserve itself, even in the event of a civil war.
The conduct of war was not a struggle between the Constitution
and war's necessities. "The constitutional right to make war or to
suppress insurrection," he insisted, "is necessarily *the paramount
constitutional right and power* . . . the principles we have endeavored to maintain are in accordance with the Constitution and
under the Constitution."[42]

Parker's arguments suggested a sweeping assertion of national
power. They might have justified almost any act committed under
the cover of military necessity. His statement that in time of "paramount military obligation . . . the military law must be held to super-
cede the civil" certainly suggested a rather broad grant of power
under the Constitution. But Parker was far too devoted to constitutional limitations to follow to their logical conclusion words extracted from him in the passion-filled post-Sumter days.

He believed that there were limits to the constitutionality of acts
of military necessity. But in 1861 he was not very clear on what
these limits were. The mounting crisis did not present all its possibilities and necessities in clear and logical form. Parker, like other
legal experts, was groping to discover what the limits of constitutionality might be. Each man was going to have to make his own
decision on that score, to decide when to accept the actions of the
government and when to shout a warning that the Constitution and
the nation were in jeopardy. In a society attempting to fight for law
under unprecedented conditions, such decisions were important.

In the same pamphlet that attacked the *Merryman* opinion,
Parker tried to clarify the limits of permissible actions under the
Constitution. After his sweeping assertion that war against insurrection was the paramount constitutional right, it is remarkable
that he drew his constitutional boundaries very close to peacetime
restrictions, approvingly quoting Roger Taney in the process. Al-

42. Parker, "Habeas Corpus," 517–518; his italics. Swisher, *Taney*, 456.

though he had attacked Taney for interpreting wartime conditions in terms of days of peace, Parker himself sought to cling to the prewar world as tightly as he possibly could.

He constricted the realm of martial law to the narrowest possible limits; it was legally permissible only in areas of actual military activities. In such areas civil courts could not consider any suit which might impair the efficiency of the army, yet civil suits might still be taken to such courts. Civil judges could preside over cases involving contracts or non-military trespass, for example. These courts were also justified in acting against military officers if the court decided that they acted outside the limits of their military duties. "If an arbitrary force is used," he declared, "having no connection with the exigency, or not within the possible scope of the necessity, the party guilty of it will be civilly responsible for his acts."[43]

Parker apparently had some doubt about the relationship between civil and military law in certain cases. He admitted that the military was sometimes the judge of what constituted true military necessity. But if this were true, how could courts decide whether an action resting on the often fuzzy line between military and civil process was justified or not? Parker did not answer this difficult question. Perhaps he realized that no general rule was possible in such a complex realm; perhaps he had not yet discovered an answer to this most intricate problem. Writing in 1861, it is likely that he was more interested in justifying action than in defining its legitimate range. He knew that a war for law could not be allowed to subvert civil justice, so he insisted, in rather general terms, that martial law could not be total. The immediate necessity was to demonstrate to Northerners that the hand of Mars might act in the service of law. Parker enjoined Union supporters to remember:

Peace and war cannot exist in the same place at the same time. Let us not murmur if we cannot have peace, with the arts of peace and the rights of peace, at the same time that we are obliged to have war, with the necessities of war and the powers of war. Let us be

43. Parker, "Habeas Corpus," 501. Parker cited *Luther* v. *Borden,* 7 *Howard* 1 (1849): "No more force can be used than is necessary to accomplish the object and if the power is exercised for the purposes of oppression, or any injury willfully done to person or property the party by whom and by whose order it is committed would undoubtedly be answerable."

thankful that it is so seldom that this constitutional martial law is over us, and when it is so, its operations are very limited as respects territory and its powers in regard to persons and property; and that, in this case, the private inconvenience and suffering are but as small dust of the balance when compared with the great public good to be obtained by the preservation of the constitutional government of the country.[44]

Such an exhortation was sufficient in the first days after Sumter, when Parker felt that the enemies of the Constitution were only in the South. But soon he realized that enemies to the national charter and the rule of law might also operate behind northern lines. A growing chorus of abolitionists began to see in the war the best possible chance to destroy slavery, and to place the victory of emancipation before the achievement of order as the goal of the war. They began clamoring for the government to use the war to end slavery. The fundamental source of Parker's opposition to secession was his fear of revolution. But abolitionists quickly discovered that the war might be a glorious revolution. Less than three weeks after Sumter, William Goodell proclaimed, "It has begun. It is in progress. . . . The Revolution must go on, to its completion—a *National Abolition of Slavery*." Moncure Conway echoed, "The revolution is on our side, and as soon as the nation feels that, and acts upon it, the strength of the South is gone. . . . WE ARE THE REVOLUTIONISTS."[45]

Before the war Parker had deplored the anarchist potential in such talk. He had condemned abolitionists for refusing to recognize that without law there could be no true freedom. But in the heat of war such counsels as abolitionists offered were more influential, and therefore to Parker more ominous. Fighting against slaveowners who had defied the law, the nation now seemed willing to listen not only to advocates of law but also to assailants of slavery. The Harvard professor feared that abolitionists would come to dominate Union councils, pervert the purpose, and dilute the energies of Union supporters. He moved to counter emancipation arguments while attacking secessionist rebel rhetoric. His was becoming a two-front war.

Under the pressure of this conflict, Parker began to see the neces-

44. Parker, "Habeas Corpus," 518.
45. Quoted in McPherson, *The Struggle for Equality*, 65–66.

sity for clarifying important points. What was the nature of the nation that was fighting? What was the status of the enemy? Most important, what actions taken against that enemy were permissible and would not endanger northern rule of law in the struggle for the rule of federal law? He was not alone in this questioning. In stimulating a massive constitutional inquiry, the war demanded more and more that Americans answer constitutional questions that had not even been adequately asked in prewar days.[46] It thus helped expand and raise the volume of constitutional debate. This phenomenon elicited Parker's comment that "innumerable speeches in Congress and out of Congress, within the last few years, may serve to show with what diligence, if not with what success, constitutional law has recently been studied."[47]

Ironically, the more constitutional concern expanded, the more dismayed Parker became. He was no more pleased with having every man be his own constitutional lawyer than he had been with having every jury member be his own judge. Hence, almost as if seeking to make the law more and more exclusive, he began to define narrowly the limits of constitutionality, to insist with increasing vigor upon the purity of legal doctrine as espoused by highly trained jurists, and to decry any constitutional doctrine which promised great changes in the federal system. The logic of these doctrines would lead to an inescapable conclusion: slavery and its traces should be preserved, in the name of constitutional liberty.

Most troubling to Parker was the fact that abolitionists began to wrap their dangerous doctrines in constitutional bunting. Seeking

46. A reviewer of George S. Williams's *The Constitution of the United States for Use of Schools and Academies* (Cambridge, 1861) observed, "The apparatus for studying our Constitution has improved more rapidly since the integrity of the Union was threatened than at any preceding period." *North American Review*, XCIV (Jan., 1862), 271. An obscure Kentucky lawyer noted also in 1862, "The American people are engaged in a great struggle in the course of which they begin to be, for the first time, thrown upon the serious discussion of the most fundamental and vital principles of enlightened and constitutional liberty." Robert L. Breck, *The Habeas Corpus and Martial Law* (Cincinnati, 1862), 10; quoted in Hyman, "Reconstruction and Political-Constitutional Institutions," *New Frontiers of American Reconstruction*, ed. Hyman, 14n. This latter article contains a discussion of the paucity of constitutional inquiry before Sumter and the stimulus to such inquiry provided by the war.

47. Parker, "Constitutional Law," 441.

to appease the constitutionalism of the American people, antislavery writers and speakers began to insist that slavery might be ended under the war powers of the Constitution. David Lee Child published a lengthy pamphlet in the late summer of 1861 entitled *The Rights and Duties of the United States Relative to Slavery under the Laws of War*. The American Anti-Slavery Society issued a cleverly edited pamphlet quoting non-abolitionists who asserted that the right to emancipate during war was a constitutional right.[48]

Parker moved quickly to refute these arguments, or at least to quarantine them. He did not deny that the war might result in the liberation of some southern bondsmen, perhaps a great many. But this fact did not justify a sweeping assertion that slavery throughout the South might therefore be swept away by government proclamation. Emancipation could take place legally only when the army occupied rebel territory, and then it would be only temporary. Practical necessity would force a commanding officer to recognize the freedom of fugitives escaping into his lines. But if the slaves did not escape permanently from those states where slavery was legal, then the reestablishment of peace would bring reestablishment of slavery. Only under martial law could slaves be freed by the Union government, and Parker had decided while discussing the Merryman arrest that martial law operated only in territory actually subject to army occupation. Until the time of such occupation, "proclamations for emancipation, from whatever source, will be of no avail." Parker insisted that the President and Congress "have no more authority to emancipate the slaves, than the writer of this article." Should either attempt to do so, it "would be a gross usurpation of power."[49]

Behind this anti-emancipation argument lay a theory of the nature of the Union and of the war which would prove a formidable barrier to more revolutionary proposals. Parker had a national reputation as an exceptionally able state judge and a growing influence

48. McPherson, *Struggle for Equality*, 66–67, 125–126; George B. Cheever, "The Slaves Are Free by Virtue of the Rebellion and the Government Is Bound to Protect Them," *New York Independent*, Jan. 16, 1862; Hyman, ed., *Radical Republicans and Reconstruction*, 25–70.

49. Joel Parker, "The Domestic and Foreign Relations of the United States," *North American Review*, XCIV (Jan., 1862), 234.

as a teacher. He was also an incisive logician, sure of his law, history, and analysis. Before the war he had fought a bitter legal battle with Joseph Story, the most prominent legal theorist of the post-Marshall period. He had dared to challenge Story over the legality of a section of the 1841 national bankruptcy act which Story himself had written. Parker presented his own position so well that after Story's death the Supreme Court upheld Parker's position.[50]

Parker's view of the war was that a conflict to maintain the rule of law in America through the Constitution had to be fought as closely as possible within the limits set by that document. The Constitution had established a nation of divided sovereignties. There were national functions with which states might not interfere, and there were state functions that might not be trespassed by the nation. Insurgents in the southern states had violated the Constitution by attempting to destroy a union that was perpetual, and by interfering with the legitimate functions of the federal government. The government was thus within its constitutional rights in waging war to stop such interference, and to stop secession.

Since secession was unlawful, the states were legally still within the Union until the federal government granted the fact of successful secession. Being still within the Union, the rebel states were still subject to its laws and could even claim the privileges of states in the Union. Individual rebels within these states might be punished for their acts of treason, but the states themselves could not be punished. The war was not between the states and the nation; it was between the rebels and the government. The act of secession, Parker said, was "legally powerless from the first . . . practically powerless at last." Therefore, political relations between the states and the nation remained unchanged; the Constitution and the laws

50. The cases in question were *Kittredge v. Warren*, 14 *New Hampshire* 509 (1843); *Kittredge v. Emerson*, 15 *New Hampshire* 227 (1844); *Ex parte Christy*, 3 *Howard* 292 (1844); *Peck v. Janess*, 19 *New Hampshire* 516 (1845); *Peck v. Janess*, 7 *Howard* 612. The confrontation is discussed in *Centennial History of Harvard Law School*, 245–246. Story's position is in Story, *Life and Letters of Joseph Story*, II, 509. Parker's self-confidence is well illustrated in the 1843 case *Hall v. Chaffee*, 14 *New Hampshire* 215. There Parker held that the very number of cases upholding a certain construction of a rule involving wills indicated the weakness of the rule. He believed that fewer cases and precedents would have been more convincing. He overturned the rule.

of the states remained unimpaired. The Constitution gave the right to suppress the rebellion. "But this neither increases the power of the United States over the State, so as to authorize a war of conquest, nor relieves the United States from the performance of their constitutional duties to the State and its citizens. Nor does it deprive the State of its State rights under the Constitution." [51]

These ideas were a logical extension of the position taken by the Union government as it wrestled with the question of the nature of the war. The question was as important as it was difficult, because it was the foundation for whatever legal sanction the Union-saving effort had. In addition, a position on the nature of the war determined the arsenal of lawful weapons available to the northern government. There were three possible descriptions of the war's legal nature. The first said that the war was an international war between two sovereign nations. The only law which covered the encounter between these two nations was international law, a rather permissive list of regulations based on humanitarian considerations and the necessities of international politics. The laws of one state did not apply to citizens of the other, and the domestic relationships within each could not be touched by the other unless and until one party conquered the other. The second option was to see the war as an insurrection. An insurrection is an armed, organized effort to overthrow a government or some of its laws. Members of an insurrection are subject to the laws of the existing government until they themselves become the government. The third option was to consider the Civil War as a rebellion, a larger and better-organized type of insurrection which under international law conveys the status of belligerent upon its members. The rebel government may claim all the belligerent rights in international law of a fully recognized state. It may be recognized by foreign governments, and it must be granted belligerent rights even by the parent government. However, the granting of such rights does not mean that the rebel organization must be recognized as a separate state. Even while recognizing the belligerent status of the rebels, an existing government may attempt to crush rebellion and insurrection, and it may punish its opponents for treason.

51. Parker, "Constitutional Law," 456, 462–463; "The Domestic and Foreign Relations of the United States," 196–199.

The broadest range of weaponry was at hand if the war was viewed as an international conflict. Then no constitution restricted the attempt to preserve the Union; the only restrictions were those imposed by the flexible limits of international law. The northern government could blockade enemy ports, confiscate enemy property (such as slaves), and make whatever laws it chose for the conquered territory. The advantages of such a view were clear, and abolitionists especially supported it. But in a war to preserve the rule of law, the advantages were not clear at all.

The Lincoln government rejected the idea that the Civil War was an international war. Indeed, it had to, or its right to continue the conflict would have vanished. Union leaders insisted that the war was being fought to preserve the constitutional union established and agreed to in 1789. Secession was an illegal attempt to overthrow that Constitution and to substitute coercion for elections as the means of changing governments. They refused to recognize the Confederate government as a legal or even a de facto government, and they called southern soldiers rebels, insurgents, and sometimes traitors.[52]

Events soon took hold of this logic and wrenched concessions to reality which undermined the administration's legal reasoning. The southern government was simply too powerful and too effective to be dealt with as anything but a belligerent power. When hostilities broke out, Lincoln proclaimed a blockade of the South. According to international law, that act was a virtual recognition of belligerent status. Under the original theory of the war southern sailors were pirates and could be put to death when captured. But the facts of war, the virtual certainty of reprisals for such acts, led the government to treat captives as prisoners of war. At first the government had protested that foreign governments seemed willing to recognize the belligerent status of the Confederacy, but soon these protests became mere formalities.[53]

These concessions to necessity did not in themselves create antagonism between Parker and the Lincoln government. Parker was sensitive to the need for the law to respond to the demands of

---

52. Randall, *Constitutional Problems under Lincoln*, 59–65.

53. *Ibid.*, 66–69; Quincy Wright, "The American Civil War," *The International Law of Civil War*, ed. Richard Falk (Baltimore, 1971), 45–46.

war, and he would support the Supreme Court decision in the *Prize* cases which justified many administration actions. But the danger of division was implicit in the fact of deviation from established legal principles. What would worry the professor would be the possibility (soon to become a reality) that one concession to necessity might produce an increasing tolerance for concession. He worried that it would grow easier to reject precedent and tradition with each new crisis, real or imagined. Soon men would reject the past with burgeoning thoughtlessness, and an accelerated move toward revolution would begin.

Even as he played the role of supporter of Lincoln's war against revolution, therefore, Parker was readying himself to assume the status of opponent. When the administration yielded to the necessities of the moment and to the urgings of its more radical supporters, he would find himself fighting on a broad front against theories and actions employed by the government to constitutionalize a war becoming a revolution. He would oppose the use of "war necessity" as an excuse for radical pro-Union actions. He would oppose widespread suspension of the privilege of the writ, Stanton's conduct of the War Department, and territorialization of conquered parts of the South. He would battle against the theories of men like War Department Solicitor William Whiting and the attacks on "mere constitutionalism" by radical emancipationist ministers. And he would become an intemperate critic of Abraham Lincoln for selling out a war against revolution. All the while Parker would remain a loyal unionist whose attacks on such radicalism would not repeal his hatred of secession.

In one sense it may be said that Parker had greater faith in the Constitution than any of these other men. His opposition to their desire to use radical measures against southern traitors and northern conspirators rested on his belief that such use of war powers was not only dangerous to liberty, but also unnecessary. Although he respected Lieber's prewar work, especially *Civil Liberty*, Parker reversed Lieber's wartime belief. He believed that the Constitution as it stood was adequate to provide for the survival of the Union. Parker's conservatism did not lead him to the opinion that the Union was doomed. On the contrary, in rebuttal to men who argued that only extraordinary war powers could save the nation, Parker pointed out how many weapons the Constitution, without war powers, provided against southern rebels. Disunionists were individually liable for their actions before federal courts. They might lose both life and property for their treason. Under the legitimate construction of the nation's charter, confiscation was permissible, the President could blockade southern ports, and West Virginia might be recognized as a new, loyal state. At one point he even suggested, without elaboration, that "an extraordinary remedy" might be required should there be too few loyal citizens to uphold a loyal state government. He had also indicated that a limited degree of emancipation was necessary, possible, and constitutional.[54]

"I believe that there is constitutional power to accomplish all that can be accomplished," Parker wrote. "Let that power be brought into exercise, and made effectual." He believed that northern traitors might be arraigned for conspiracy and then tried and punished, rather than being thrown into jail under arbitrary arrest. Instead of allowing soldiers to close newspapers with southern sympathies, let Congress make laws which punished giving comfort to the enemy. The Constitution was not endangered by legislative action against sedition; the difference between liberty and license of the press was well known, Parker insisted. In general, Congress could use its existing powers to preserve the Union. One day in class a student interrupted Parker's discussion of the privilege of the writ in wartime with a hypothetical instance that included a mass of treasonable acts, and asked if suspension of the writ behind the lines might be tolerated in such cases. "No sir," Parker snapped.

54. Parker, "Constitutional Law," 457, 463; "Domestic and Foreign Relations," 298. Randall, *Constitutional Problems under Lincoln*, 471–476, argues that in the matter of West Virginia the state of Virginia was not legally consulted; hence the loss of that state's western counties was unconstitutional under Article IV, section 3. Parker suggests the error of this view. Assuming that a state cannot legally secede, it follows that the state government still exists; it is the people of a state who are rebelling. Hence, if there is a loyal government in the state, it must be legitimate and capable of exercising the functions of a state, including that of acceding to its own partition. Randall seems to assume that the rebel government of Virginia was the state's only lawful government, a difficult position from which to argue the legitimacy of the war for the Union. Parker felt that the rebel government was no legal government at all. The true government was the loyal Pierrepont government, which did agree to the formation of West Virginia. The Supreme Court adopted Parker's view in *Virginia* v. *West Virginia*, 11 *Wallace* 39 (1870).

"I would not suspend the writ of habeas corpus, but I would suspend the [offender's] corpus." The professor believed that existing institutions provided the nation with adequate safety.[55]

Despite a Constitution which he found fully adequate to meet the dangers of rebellion, men still came forward and advanced the war powers doctrine. Worst of all, they insisted that the programs and policies which they championed were constitutional. Legislators like Charles Sumner and Kansas Congressman Michael F. Conway, executive advisors led by War Department Solicitor William Whiting, and a brigade of abolitionist ministers all urged revolution in the name of the nation's fundamental law. The controlling motive of all was to make the war for the Union a war to free the slaves. Should they be listened to, Parker's support for the Lincoln government and the flexibility of his constitutional thought would be sorely tested.

55. Joel Parker, *The War Powers of Congress, and of the President* (Cambridge, 1863), 59; *Centennial History of Harvard Law School*, 250.

Joel Parker II:
The War Becomes Revolution

As long as the prize of the war was only the Union and the stability and order it represented, Parker apparently felt on sure ground. He remained a supporter of the Lincoln administration and hoped to convince it to ignore the radical counsels of abolitionists. But soon Lincoln's need to secure international support, the minimal success of Union armies, and increasing pressure for a direct blow against slavery led him to issue the preliminary Emancipation Proclamation on September 22, 1862. The war which Parker had supported as counterrevolutionary now became potentially revolutionary. The President's action portended national interference in state institutions, the destruction of private property, an expansion of federal power far too extensive even for Parker's Whig sentiments. His fears of the tyrannical potential of national power were intensified even more when, seemingly as a means to suppress dissent over the proclamation, the administration expanded the potential domain of martial law to every corner of the nation. In another proclamation issued two days later, the government warned that "all persons discouraging volunteer enlistments, resisting militia drafts, or guilty of any disloyal practice, affording aid and comfort to Rebels against the authority of the United States shall be subject to martial law and liable to trial and punishment by Courts Martial or Military Commission."[1]

Angered and worried by these administration actions, Parker

1. Basler, ed., *Collected Works of Lincoln*, V, 436–437; James G. Randall and David Donald, *The Civil War and Reconstruction* (Lexington, Mass., 1969), 376–378. Randall and Donald do not connect the two proclamations, thus obscuring an important characteristic of opponents to emancipation.

joined in an outburst of criticism against Lincoln and his policies. He declared that the President was a monarch comparable to Napoleon III, the czar of Russia, or the sultan of Turkey. His government had become "absolute, irresponsible, uncontrollable . . . a perfect military despotism." Parker enlisted for extended service in the anti-Lincoln brigade and would fight there for the duration of the war. He entered Massachusetts politics by supporting an effort to have radical Senator Charles Sumner ousted by the state legislature. He began a barrage of anti-emancipation, anti-national power, though still pro-union, arguments that would continue until his death.[2]

The vast constitutional change implicit in the call for general emancipation had threatened Parker profoundly. Here indeed was a cry for revolution, and now the government had taken it up in the midst of a war to stop a revolution. He knew that war demanded some deviation from established precedent, but general emancipation projected not just a deviation from constitutional traditions, but a repudiation of them—a true revolution undermining the fundamental principle of the entire constitutional experience: local control of local institutions.

Parker was equipped by education, experience, and conviction to cope with constitutional questions such as those posed by secession and the arrest of John Merryman. He was equally prepared to argue that, without emancipation, the Constitution justified practically every aspect of the war for the Union. But his very strengths— knowledge of the nation's constitutional traditions, judicial experience, legal argument—were weaknesses confronting emancipation. For emancipation was revolutionary; it demanded profound, fundamental alteration of the constitutional system, a rejection of an elementary aspect of the very thing which Parker understood and treasured, and which he believed the nation fought for. Prewar assertions by abolitionists that the Constitution had to die to make liberty live and wartime announcements that revolution would

2. Parker, *The War Powers of Congress, and of the President*, 8–9, 27, 32–34; Benjamin R. Curtis, *Executive Power* (Boston, 1863); James G. Randall, *Lincoln the President* (New York, 1945), II, 174; Warren, *History of the Harvard Law School*, 277–278.

result from the conflict fortified Parker's opinion that emancipation was inimical to law.

A bitter clash portended between pro-emancipation figures and the Harvard legalist. Parker practically accused Charles Sumner of treason, and abolitionist divines publicly questioned Parker's loyalty. The professor's sensitivity to slavery was more than outweighed by his hypnotic fascination with traditional legal principles. The hatred of Sumner and his associates for slavery was hardly less single-minded.

The clash was more bitter on Parker's side because of his fundamental insecurity about his position. For all the talk about a Constitution fully adequate to cope with all the needs of war, once the question of emancipation was raised, a growing despair over the increasingly revolutionary nature of the conflict became evident. The feeling persists that Parker feared what lurked beyond any change in the document; that he believed that too severe a strain would destroy it; that, ironically (the words are Lieber's) "The Constitution was not made for such a state of things."

Certainly Parker had little use for the state of things proposed in the winter of 1862 by the solicitor of the War Department, former patent attorney William Whiting. Faced with the need to justify executive efforts to defeat the Confederacy, Whiting provided the War Department and the President with practically a blank check. With the approval of Lieber, Whiting argued that the government was not chained by any restrictive interpretation of the Constitution. It had complete power to preserve itself in any manner that it saw fit. Since Southerners had ignored the Constitution, they might not be protected by it. He advanced the general welfare provision of the preamble and asserted that it allowed almost unlimited government action. The only check was the power of the people to elect new officials. Whiting went on to claim broad powers for the government on the basis of many other constitutional provisions. The goal in most of these claims was emancipation. Congress, he said, might emancipate using its treaty powers. It could use the power of eminent domain for the same purpose; it could emancipate to secure domestic tranquility, to suppress insurrection, or to maintain a republican form of government. Whiting's catalogue of powers left the federal government virtually unrestrained.[3]

It was the sort of argument that Parker despised. It expanded power, diminished liberty, and glorified both actions as justified by the Constitution. Whiting's argument seemed to Parker a fabrication of the crisis of the moment, a repudiation of Anglo-American legal tradition and of the nation's constitutional traditions. "A tissue of miserable sophistry, bad law, and if possible, worse logic," the professor claimed; mere "Patent War Office Constitutional Law."

If the solicitor had read any American law at all, Parker suggested, he would have recognized that congressional power to promote the general welfare was extremely limited. John Randolph, James Madison, and Joseph Story had all defined it narrowly, Story confining it to the power of taxation. Had Whiting received better legal training, he might have known that the power of eminent domain was equally useless as sanctifier of war powers. Parker gave him a little lecture on the meaning of eminent domain as if chastising an inept pupil for forgetting proper legal terminology. Under the solicitor's reasoning, the government might decree that a man's property should be destroyed so that the public could have use of it. "The Government does not take an enemy for public use under the power to supply its necessities," the professor announced. "It never takes a nuisance for public use. What the Government destroys, of that character, to relieve the public from injury, threatened or suffered, it acts upon by an antagonistic power . . . that of

3. William Whiting, *The War Powers of the President and the President and the Legislative Powers of Congress in Relation to Rebellion, Treason, and Slavery* (Boston, 1862), 11–13 17–22, 27–29, 30–32; Randall, *Constitutional Problems under Lincoln*, 348–349. Harold M. Hyman, "Reconstruction and Political-Constitutional Institutions," 28–29, assesses the influence of Whiting on Lincoln and the War Department but does not criticize the questionable constitutional reasoning which led to Whiting's conclusions. In the summer of 1863, Whiting would set forth an opinion of the arresting power of provost marshals that defined even a civilian's refusal to answer questions about obstruction of the draft as an offense punishable by military arrest and trial. Thomas and Hyman, *Stanton*, 280–281. After the war another jurist of growing reputation would decry the tyrannous potential of Whiting's *War Powers under the Constitution*, which repeated his wartime arguments. Although an energetic supporter of the Lincoln administration, John Norton Pomeroy said that Whiting's theories "would make the Congress, and especially the Executive, the most hateful of despotisms, and would crush out all personal independence and civil liberty" ("Recent Works on the United States Government," *Nation*, XIII [Oct. 12, 1871], 242).

police." Apparently Parker derived some pleasure from such pedantic scolding.[4]

His rebuttal to Whiting concentrated on more substantial matters, however. Fundamental to the solicitor's argument was the insistence that the cause of the war was slavery, and that victory in the conflict would swiftly follow emancipation. To Parker too much revolution was implicit in such a course. It would lead to the destruction of property of loyal as well as disloyal Southerners, and it would imperil the states' control over their domestic institutions. Property rights and states' rights were both in danger—a dreadful thought for this former Jacksonian judge.

The war was already so troubling, not just in the toll of lives it took but in the societal upheaval it threatened. Parker abominated it. It was "an outrage upon civilization, a vast crime against humanity, an insurrection against free principles, and treason against liberty." The war shook "to its foundations the confidence of mankind in the capacity of the people to govern themselves."

Certainly the war shook Parker and worried him deeply. In his zeal to exorcise Whiting's assertions, he snatched at arguments that were hardly worthy of his learning. True to his abolitionist instincts, Whiting, he argued, had simply assumed that slavery had caused the war. The War Department official reasoned that, since slaveowners had endangered the Union, slavery might be destroyed to save the Union. But under such logic one could as easily prove that cotton-growing was a danger to the Union and had to be destroyed to save it. Parker thought a better case could be made for the divisive nature of cotton-growing than for that of slavery. After all, disunion had come only after cotton became monarch of the southern economy. Prior to that coronation, no serious threat to the Union had emerged, even though slavery had existed in the South.

No, the cause of the war was not slavery. The conflict was a power struggle. "Unholy passions . . . irresponsible ambition" clashed "in order to gratify a greed of gain, a lust for power, and a thirst for revenge." Frightened by diminishing power and prodded by northern extremists, Southerners used the pretexts of tariff, state sovereignty, and slavery to raise the banner of secession. Secession might therefore be crushed, union and order restored, without

4. Parker, *War Powers*, 9–10, 15–21, 32.

touching slavery. Parker's answer ignored twenty years of history, but it was a necessary concomitant of his fear that the war might become revolution.[5]

One of Whiting's more formidable justifications for emancipation was that the conditions of war had created an environment where international law might replace the nation's domestic constitution. Under the laws of international conflict, belligerents might legally destroy the war-making capacity of their enemies. No one could reasonably deny that slaves supplied the rebels with food, clothing, and ammunition. Therefore it appeared logical to Whiting and many others that emancipation was a legitimate tool of war.

This argument troubled Parker because he recognized the occasional necessity for the North to act as though engaged in international war, even as it claimed that the South was not a legitimate nation. As early as June, 1861, Parker had admitted that in some cases the insurrection might result in "what is properly denominated as a war without losing its character as an insurrection." The institution of a blockade, exchanges of prisoners, and treating captured rebels not as traitors but as prisoners of war all implied recognition of the Confederacy. In such cases "parties to [the] war have necessarily to a certain extent the political character of belligerents." Such necessary incidents did not, however, change the basic character of the war. It was still an insurrection, not an international conflict. When Richard Henry Dana, Jr., argued the *Prize* cases before the Supreme Court, he adopted this argument as the basis of his presentation, and won.[6]

Whiting contended, not only in these few necessary instances, but also in every encounter between the government and the rebels, that the law of nations might apply and that constitutional protection for slave property could be swept away. In reply, Parker insisted that the Constitution still applied to every case except those mentioned. Otherwise the whole legal foundation for the war against secession vanished. In addition, even assuming the just application of international law to this conflict, the very thing which Whiting desired so much, emancipation, would be denied him. No

---

5. *Ibid.*, 6–7.
6. *Prize* cases, 2 *Black* 635 (1863); Warren, *History of the Harvard Law School*, II, 275; Parker, "Domestic and Foreign Relations," 211–225.

sweeping proclamations might issue from Washington to free the slaves. It was a basic principle of international law that belligerents would not change each others' municipal law in the midst of war; only when actual occupation of territory took place could such laws be changed. An attempt to justify emancipation under international law was, therefore, simple foolishness.[7]

Parker's reply to Whiting was an occasionally strained but generally well-considered and useful rebuttal to what appeared to many as an ominous centralized power. By the summer of 1863 the number of arbitrary arrests had increased alarmingly as far as conservatives were concerned. The sentiment that they feared may be seen in the fact that in June, with the approval of Lincoln and Secretary of War Stanton, Whiting had defined the silence of civilians being questioned about conscription as a crime punishable by martial law. Incidents which gave substance to their fears included the suppression of anti-administration newspapers, especially the *Chicago Times*, in June and the arrest of Ohio Copperhead Clement Vallandigham for making a speech that same month. This latter event angered even Lincoln supporters George William Curtis and Horace Greeley. Curtis remarked that the "mistake of the government" was in "not trusting the people sufficiently." They had "quite sense enough to understand any amount of seditious nonsense, be it uttered ever so glibly." Greeley echoed that sentiment: "Freedom of speech and of the press are rights which like everything human have their limitations." But "the license of speech and of the press which men like Vallandigham indulge in, calls for no abridgment of either."[8] Those who feared government infringement of civil liber-

---

7. Parker, *War Powers*, 22. Parker's theory on international law and emancipation coincided with that held by at least one prominent abolitionist in 1861. In the summer of that year David Lee Child published *The Rights and Duties of the United States Relative to Slavery.* "Here is a principle of the laws of war, perfectly settled and unquestioned," Child wrote. "Conquerers have the right, *to the extent of their conquests*, to establish such government and laws as they see fit" (my italics). Quoted in McPherson, *Struggle for Equality*, 67–68.

8. Williams, "Northern Intellectual Reaction to Military Rule," 343; *Harper's Weekly*, VII (1863), 338; Society for the Diffusion of Political Knowledge, *The Constitution* (New York, 1863–64). This pamphlet contains speeches by the governor of New York, Horatio Seymour, future presidential candidate Samuel Tilden, historian George T. Curtis, and several congressmen denouncing the policy of the Lincoln government.

ties would have been more alarmed if they read a widely printed letter of Lincoln's written June 12 which contained these ominous words: "The man who stands by and says nothing when the peril of his government is discussed, cannot be misunderstood. If not hindered he is sure to help the enemy."[9]

In such an environment there is little wonder that conservatives like Parker spoke out. The war seemed to create an atmosphere of distrust and suspicion where opposition was seen as disloyalty, where the victory of the now revolutionary government and its policy was to be gained at the cost of northern liberties. Parker and his associates were overreacting, of course. Lincoln was no despot and had no intention of destroying liberty in order either to save the Union or to free the slaves. But even the President allowed his understandable fears to lead him to excesses. His antilibertarianism seemed to Parker and others symptomatic of a condition throughout northern society—a passion for results that made many men heedless of the nation's legal foundations, and made some of them willing to distort them for their own ends.

The aspect of the northern quarrel over constitutional principles which most troubled Parker was revealed in the winter of 1862. Two Cambridge preachers, Henry Dexter and Leonard Bacon, addressed the people of the town. They argued that the Emancipation Proclamation was a constitutional exercise of war powers and that the war's purpose was to reconquer lost territory for the United States; when that land was regained, it might be purged of slavery. Noting the opposition to the Proclamation by jurisprudents like Parker and former Supreme Court Justice Benjamin Curtis, the preachers argued that legal logic was a device used by these men to obscure the common sense of the matter—that higher law, simple justice, and the war powers of the government under the Constitution all justified emancipation. They suggested that opponents of the measure were disloyal.

It is hard to conceive of an argument better calculated to enrage Joel Parker. That it had been offered not by trained lawyers but by preachers simply added to his fury. "When a clergyman assumes to know more of Constitutional law than those who have spent

9. Basler, ed., *Collected Works of Lincoln*, VI, 265.

their lives in the investigation of its principles," he suggested maliciously, "he is apt to exhibit himself as an unmitigated ass . . . when he makes a political prostitute of himself, pandering to the lusts of a political party, he is entitled to no greater respect than—other persons who disregard their duties." The fact that Bacon and Dexter had "a D.D. attached to their names, [did] not disqualify them from being A.S.S., and mischief makers besides."

Parker hauled out his arguments against war powers again: a violation of the Constitution which President and Congress had sworn to uphold. The argument for territorialization got the predictable retort—since the states were not out of the Union, they maintained their status under the Constitution. Besides, the land owned by many southern states had never belonged to the United States anyway, and so could not be "reconquered" as the ministers suggested. "The ordinances of secession, the insurrection, the usurpation of State authority, and the war itself, all combined, have not changed the Constitution," he concluded.[10]

The most troubling thing about this ministerial attempt at constitutional argument was what it symbolized. Lieber had viewed the war as an opportunity to recast the nation's law without the corrosive impurities of slavery and state sovereignty. But Parker feared that the conflict might destroy traditional legal restraints like states' rights by adding doctrines more dangerous than any it destroyed. He feared that the efforts of Dexter and Bacon were "not only an offense against good manners but . . . an evil [which gave] rise to new and unfounded dogmas, to false reasonings and conclusions, and to loose Constitutional notions in the community, at a time when there should be no tampering with our constitutional rights and duties."[11]

He feared that the nation was becoming a place where the purity of the law was no longer respected, that the war had encouraged disdain for law in the North as well as the South. In shaking mankind's confidence in the capacity of people to govern themselves, the war made men doubt the Constitution's adequacy for coping with crisis.

10. Joel Parker, *Constitutional Law and Unconstitutional Divinity* (Cambridge, 1863), 1–6, 32, 40–41.
11. *Ibid.*, 6.

It had made them seek a new constitution under the guise of the old. It led them to say that everything they thought necessary was constitutional. This was especially the case with abolition. For a long time it had been admitted that slavery was a local institution of the states, in no way under federal control. Politicians who desired emancipation had been puzzled to find a plausible theory to justify it. Now the rebellion had supplied the theory—war powers. But the doctrine was a theory without constitutional foundation. Under it Americans were being asked to violate their oaths to defend the national charter, to make war on the rights of states, to destroy a portion of the sovereignty of the states. They were being asked to give up their rights as white men to protect the freedom of blacks, to sacrifice a tradition of ordered liberty to secure emancipation.

Would this sacrifice save the Union? On the contrary; Parker felt that it would probably help destroy it. One reason why the South had seceded was the belief that secession was necessary to protect its liberties. One reason why it could continue to fight was the widespread southern belief that the rebellion was to save the Constitution. Parker had tried to weaken the southern will to fight by demonstrating the unconstitutionality of secession. But now abolitionist sentiment was encouraging northern actions that affirmed rebel claims. The administration was following a policy which would encourage the southern belief that they fought for law and the true Constitution. Such a belief in the North had been sufficient to inspire millions to go to war, to sacrifice lives and fortunes. It could not fail to give equal inspiration to the South.[12]

Violation of the Constitution would have no less disastrous effects in the North. Men were not fighting for a revolution; they were fighting against one. The army was in the field to protect the Union, not to free the slaves. "A war for emancipation . . . in other words a war for revolution," Parker insisted, "cannot be supported, as such, by those who have sworn to support the Constitution . . . and if it is placed on that basis, there must be division at the North as well as between the North and the South." Such division in north-

12. Joel Parker, "The Character of the Rebellion and the Conduct of the War," *North American Review*, XCV (Oct., 1862), 522, 530–532; "Domestic and Foreign Relations," 233; *War Powers*, 14–15, 40.

ern opinion might well encourage northern states to link themselves with the South, if not in actuality, at least in sentiment.[13]

Election returns in the North often confirmed Parker's judgment. In 1862 reaction to the Emancipation Proclamation and to widespread arbitrary arrests led voters to return Democrats to power in many states. Throughout the war voters reflected their constitutional scruples by defeating many Union candidates and almost always keeping other elections close. Militant peace men like Clement Vallandigham, George Pendleton, William Allen, Fernando Wood, and others coupled their pacifism with warnings against unconstitutional usurpation, keeping the attention of large constituencies. The impact of this sort of agitation convinced Lincoln that he might lose in 1864, and it is likely that only military victory saved him.[14]

In April, 1862, Parker had written:

> In these days of difficulty and of trial, in which the stormy passions and illogical arguments of heated politicians obscure the principles of constitutional law, and the more insidious undercurrents of interested political aspirants are drifting us hard upon the breakers of disorganization, prudence ... may well admonish us to take a fresh observation of that political sun by the aid of which the ship of state must be steered, if we expect to attain the haven of constitutional peace.

Apparently large numbers of Americans were keeping their eyes where Parker wanted them. "If the present government is subverted, either by a secession of parts or by a usurpation of powers belonging to the States, who shall assure us that the process of disintegration, or usurpation, once begun will not end in the entire destruction of the republic?" Apparently others shared his sentiment. Fighting for law against secession, they were reluctant to give it up to what they feared might be usurpation.[15]

It is difficult to assess Parker's precise impact on the constitutional

13. Parker, *Constitutional Law and Unconstitutional Divinity*, 52; Parker, *War Powers*, 14–15.

14. Klement, *Copperheads in the Middle West*, 20–24; Kenneth Bernard, "Lincoln and Civil Liberties," *Abraham Lincoln Quarterly*, VI (June, 1951), 383.

15. Parker, *Constitutional Law*, 436–439.

debate during the war. His actions are clearer than his influence. He provided legal justification for the war for the Union and law. He demonstrated that the conflict might be fought by the government under the Constitution, and that the Confederacy was denied the moral and legal force of constitutional right. He also insisted that the Constitution, as it stood, was adequate to meet the exigencies of civil war; that claims by abolitionists and their allies that war powers were needed to give the document life were not well founded if the war was to keep its counterrevolutionary purpose. He maintained that legal powers granted by war applied only to battlefield areas. Where war did not rage, war powers could not exist.

Parker's view of war powers might have served the administration if the war had been confined to actual areas of battle, and if emancipation had not become crucial to winning the war. Believing otherwise, Lincoln lost Parker's support after the fall of 1862. Yet the President was sincerely concerned about the constitutionality of his acts, and he never took the position (insisted upon by Lieber) that the war was "five-hundred miles outside the Constitution." Lincoln was wise enough to see that the national charter was too much the object of national devotion to be ignored, especially when the purpose of the war was ostensibly to maintain the rule of law. Parker recognized this clearly and vocally.[16]

The impact of what Parker did is less easily discovered. His arguments provided a source from which active lawyers of the Civil War era might draw. His realistic analysis of the extent of belligerent rights in a vast insurrection later appeared in argument before the Supreme Court and was accepted as the official constitutional description of the war. His warnings against the dangerous outreach of martial law surfaced in postwar Court argument. Appearing for the victorious side in the *Milligan* case, David Dudley Field followed Parker closely on the necessity of the President being bound by the Constitution, and in rejecting Binney's justification for executive suspension of the privilege of the writ. The professor's dogged insistence that the states were indestructible parts of the Union, theoretically accepted by the Lincoln administration, also made

16. Randall, *Constitutional Problems under Lincoln*, 513–515; Randall, *Lincoln, the Liberal Statesman*, 132–133.

an appearance after the war in *Texas* v. *White*. The possibility that Parker's writings were called upon directly in any of these cases cannot be excluded. In any event, he had helped to keep the nation aware of the restraints of the Constitution, and thereby insured that constitutional concern would play a role in the determination of policy.[17]

It is possible that Parker's well-argued constitutionalism, and that of others like him, forced more radical men outside the government to constitutionalize their reform proposals. Reading the restrained interpretations of emancipation which came from the executive department, they became worried that the South would not surrender its slaves when it surrendered its arms. To counter such a possibility, abolitionists worked hard to make constitutional law of the military proclamation, to provide the legitimacy which Parker insisted that it lacked. They sent Congress enormous petitions, lobbied vigorously, and encouraged the passage of the Thirteenth Amendment. Parker grudgingly accepted the amendment, perhaps somewhat placated by a feeling that his efforts had made such legitimacy necessary.[18]

The most useful aspect of Parker's constitutionalizing, however, may have been to keep alive in the North the idea of a responsible opposition. As the professor understood, experienced, and feared, it was very easy to allow the passion of partisan politics to provoke cries of traitor against any opposition. Copperhead excesses suggested that such cries were facts. The Vallandighams and Woods walked very close to treason indeed; not so close as their opponents claimed, but close enough to engender the belief that there was only one loyal party, one loyal pattern of thought.[19]

17. *Prize* cases, 2 *Black* 635; *Ex parte Milligan*, 4 *Wallace* 2; *Texas* v. *White*, 7 *Wallace* 700; *Speeches and Arguments of David Dudley Field*, ed. A. P. Sprague (New York, 1884), I, 33–36, 80–86.

18. McPherson, *Struggle for Equality*, 125–127; Joel Parker, *The Three Powers of Government* (New York, 1869), 62; Godkin, "The Constitution and Its Defects," 117–145.

19. Bernard, "Lincoln and Civil Liberties," 384–385; Williams, "Northern Intellectual Reaction to Military Rule during the Civil War," 334–349; John Bigelow, *The Life of Samuel J. Tilden* (New York, 1895), I, 172, quotes Tilden's wise observation, "I am quite aware how difficult is the conduct of a constitutional opposition during the period of war; how necessary it is to guard against its degenerating into faction, and to keep its measures directed to attaining the utmost practical

Although Parker himself occasionally stooped to partisan incantations—such as calling Lincoln an oriental despot and inferring that Sumner aided southern treason—the generally high level of his argument suggested that opposition need not be treason, that during a war to secure the results of a free election politics need not end. One reason why Parker deplored the efforts of pulpit lawyers to attack constitutional arguments as treason was his fear that all legal discussion might be made to seem simply a clever device of egghead traitors, an attempt to use law to hypnotize and paralyze the war effort. But if law ever became merely the billingsgate of the marketplace, its ability to raise the level of politics would be gone and its power to restrain democracy ended. This fear motivated his insistence on severe legal logic, his strict attention to precise definition and analysis. A constitution which permitted everything was simply not a constitution.

For this reason he continued to be appalled that patently unconstitutional legislation was time and again stamped constitutional by its proponents. Parker opposed the revolution they thus encouraged for its effect on the national character and hence on law and liberty in the United States. He asked the troubling question, "If every dream is constitutional what does the Constitution protect us against?" He was dismayed that the war had spawned such a debasing of the Constitution's purity. He was angry that the conflict, caused by extremists for slavery and abolition, had bred not so much the destruction of law but law's perversion. It had not only substituted force for law; it had also made force take on the name of law. It was a perversion that had taken place both on the battlefield, where it might have been expected, and throughout American society as well. There is something to be said for a discussion with inherent rules and limitations, especially in times when unrestrained debate might have such ominous consequences. There is something to be said for a rigid respect for law in a potentially lawless environment. Parker said it.[20]

By the time the Civil War ended, most Northerners had advanced

---

good for the country at every varying stage of public affairs. I know also, that such an opposition is often the only means of preserving civil liberty or of conducting an existing war to a successful termination."

20. Joel Parker, *Revolution and Reconstruction* (New York, 1866), 41, 70–71.

beyond Parker's position. Four years of continual effort to save the Union, the growing influence of the federal government in the war effort, and the inescapable connection between saving the Union and emancipation produced an increasing willingness to tolerate the exercise of national power on behalf of equality. This is not to say that the war had transformed the United States into a centralized state—state sovereignty, not states' rights, was a casualty of the war.

Still, the experiences of the war produced a greater public acceptance of federal power and a recognition of the need for using national power to protect the only large and definitely loyal element in the South. To carry out its will, Congress would pass laws that established federal influence in areas not previously touched. It would produce two constitutional amendments, a civil rights bill that would be used in the 1960s and 1970s as an instrument to secure equality and would provide an unprecedented peacetime occupation of eleven states of the Union. Congress would also occasionally threaten the Supreme Court and would impeach the President of the United States. Although legislators stopped far short of the revolution proposed by their more radical associates, the times were hardly ordinary—and to men like Parker they were revolutionary indeed.

As he faced the problems of Reconstruction, Parker still felt the need to resist revolution. He believed that since he had helped inhibit the revolutionary potential of wartime measures, perhaps he could play a similar role after Appomattox. In his view there was certainly enough evidence that he would be needed. He looked around and saw a nation where the rights of states remained under siege, where the independence of judges, the division of power in the federal government, the sanctity of civil courts—in short, republican government and civil liberty—were in peril. Worse, the attackers were men who claimed that the Constitution blessed every attack, every campaign. They asked men to forget the legal havens of the past and, calling on war powers long after the war had ended, they demanded changes in the nation's law that would slowly strangle traditional freedom. "The Constitution," Parker rebutted, "recognizes no necessity . . . to destroy the rights which it solemnly guarantees."

As he had done during the war, the Harvard professor turned

again to demonstrate logical fallacy and perverse reasoning in the arguments of radical congressmen. When they used the war power doctrine to justify their proposals, Parker again countered with his wartime arguments denying that power, all the more vehemently because as far as he was concerned the war had been won. When his opponents elaborated the guarantee clause, the former judge expanded his earlier arguments. They said that congressional power to guarantee a republican form of government legitimized every Reconstruction measure until such a government, securing equal justice for all its citizens, existed. Parker replied, echoing Andrew Johnson, that this clause of the Constitution actually condemned Congress's actions. Republican government, government elected by the people and subject to their will, held office there. If the guarantee clause was so potent a force for protecting black men's rights, why had it not been used to reorganize the racial situations in northern states? Congressional actions, he insisted, were a repudiation of the guarantee of republican government. They imposed on Southerners a government which they would never have chosen themselves.[21]

Parker understood the congressional sentiment that national unity demanded the uninhibited exercise of federal law in the South. But again he found the Constitution as it stood adequate to the occasion. The 1787 document allowed federal courts to function, national laws to be enforced, executive decisions to be implemented. Legally these functions were not changed by the war; indeed, the war had been fought to guarantee their continued operation. The power of Congress to pass laws for the rebel states had only been obstructed, never invalidated. Congress could have passed binding legislation for those states, even in the midst of war, and it could still do so— even without representatives from those states being present in Congress. The President could carry out those laws now as well as during the war.[22]

This sounded like a broad concession of power to a Congress

21. *Ibid.*, 62–63. Congress was in fact using the guarantee clause for a new purpose, but this was the only alternative for men who wished to preserve states and yet make changes within them. William A. Dunning, *Essays on the Civil War and Reconstruction* (New York, 1904), 130–135.

22. Parker, *Revolution and Reconstruction*, 65–68.

whose designs Parker suspected. It was less restrictive than President Johnson's position that legislation for the South was unconstitutional without the presence of southern congressmen. Yet Parker conceded little more to Congress. As was often the case in this era, rhetoric outran reality. Parker was simply following the logical conclusion of his belief that the states had never legally seceded. His insistence that the Constitution remained unchanged by the war was the restrictive reservation that took force out of these apparently broad concessions. Therefore he condemned every piece of Reconstruction legislation as a usurpation by Congress.

Parker believed that congressional action ignored the nation's past and rejected fundamental truths about man which the framers had clearly understood. Reconstruction congressmen ignored the fact that the Constitution was basically a means of protecting the individual against centralized government—against man's inevitable misuse of power. As he condemned the evils of Reconstruction, Parker increasingly revealed the undertone of Puritanism in his thought. Combined with his legal training, there was little room for optimism about men. He believed that, given a chance, men would do evil; the purpose of law was to restrain them.[23]

Parker seriously doubted whether any efforts to reform the South would be successful. No legislation could possibly change men's hearts; no one could seriously believe that defeating southern armies would produce a miraculous conversion of southern sentiment. Unsuccessful rebels might recognize the defeat of their armies, but they would not change their basic beliefs about the abilities of black men. If over-optimistic legislators did not understand this, Parker said, the Constitution's authors had. The document did not compel loyalty; it inspired it.[24]

Cries for revenge and hopes for conversion were fine as political

23. Parker, *Three Powers of Government*, 6–12. In a lecture on Feb. 9, 1869, before the Massachusetts Historical Society, Parker argued that the Puritans' strictness did not restrict necessary liberty; it served, rather, to restrain potential troublemakers and to maintain an orderly society. *The First Charter and the Early Religious Legislation of Massachusetts* (Boston, 1869).

24. Parker, *Revolution and Reconstruction*, 68–69. For a recent statement of similar views on the possibilities of Reconstruction, see James E. Sefton, *The United States Army and Reconstruction, 1865–77* (Baton Rouge, 1967), 253.

oratory, Parker observed, but they had no connection with constitutional law. If congressmen hoped for legal guarantees against another rebellion, they would be sadly disappointed:

> The folly of such a position needs no exponent. No guarantees can
> possibly be given. Place the heel of military despotism upon the
> necks of the people of those States and you have only the greater
> probability that they will eventually attempt to cast off the oppres-
> sion. Exterminate the southern people, and fill their places with
> Yankees, emigrants from Massachusetts if you please,—and you will
> have only made assurance doubly sure, that if they deem themselves
> oppressed, you will have another rebellion, founded perhaps in a
> better reason . . . and more likely to be successful.[25]

Parker here misrepresented the motives of Reconstruction, either
for reasons of polemic or honest shortsightedness. The major goal of
Reconstruction was not to change hearts or produce a psychological
transformation of attitudes in Dixie. It was rather to protect freedmen from the all too frequently demonstrated fact that such changes
were impossible, that only positive legislation would provide protection for former slaves and their white sympathizers.

But the former Jacksonian jurist did not see law as a positive
force. It was protection against too precipitous change, not an im-
petus to change; not an instrument of power, but a shield against
power. Liberty was not something which government guaranteed;
it was something to be guaranteed against government. "We cannot
hope to find liberty in a pervading negation," Lieber wrote. Parker
believed that it could only safely be found there.

His Calvinism found outlet in his jurisprudence. Throughout the
Reconstruction era Parker continually exhorted men to remember
their basically evil nature and thus to retain law in its negative role.
He reminded his Harvard students

> that what men have been, men may be, and will be again. Let me
> say that ambition seeking power and place, unscrupulous in its mea-
> sures for the attainment of its objects, and regardless of conse-
> quences so that object is attained is as active and enterprising now
> as it has been in any period in the history of the world. Let me sug-
> gest that sophistry is none the less specious in the law than it is in

25. Parker, *Revolution and Reconstruction*, 70.

religion, where false prophets and false apostles deceive even the very elect. Let me warn you that the liberties of the country have no immunity from peril and wreck, and that there is no policy of insurance upon which indemnity can be sought when the loss shall have come.[26]

This negative view of men and the law, this fear of unrestrained power, made him more fearful of the perversion of law to partisan purposes. He had hated it in Alton, Illinois, and East St. Louis and Kansas before the war. He had hated it as the South seceded and when northern reformers cried "war powers." He hated it now. Law perverted was the tool of any demagogue. It protected no man's liberty against momentary passion; it was diluted and weak, no longer able to restrain. There could be no law when any man could call his momentary whim constitutional law.

Therefore, as much as he distrusted revolution, Parker expressed his willingness to accept it more readily if it was openly avowed as revolution. Though Thaddeus Stevens's policies were detestable, his honesty about them was preferable to the sophistry which came from Sumner and Whiting. Opposed to almost all postwar changes, Parker still conceded that a few actions which lay outside the Constitution might be necessary to restore order and satisfy justice. He was willing to allow the military trial of the assassination conspirators. He was pleased that slavery had died in the war, though he was still angry about the Emancipation Proclamation. But extraconstitutional measures had to be presented as such. To call them lawful endangered law and the Constitution. "If we want revolution, let us say we intend revolution," he wrote. "Attempting to shield . . . unauthorized measures under the pretense of constitutional authority [could] destroy the vitality of the Constitution, making it an instrument to serve the purpose of any party in power, by forced or sophistical construction . . . in that way it will become an engine of despotism, instead of the anchor sheet of freedom."[27]

This theoretical concession to revolution was seldom realized in fact; no meaningful piece of Reconstruction legislation received Parker's approval. The measures were too threatening to his vision of legitimate order. His arguments against congressional Recon-

26. Parker, *Three Powers of Government*, 35; Hale, "Joel Parker," 263.
27. Parker, *Revolution and Reconstruction*, 70–71.

struction were calls to the restraining force of law and to a construction of the Constitution which checked power. His *Three Powers
of Government* (1867) asked men to remember that concentration
of power had justly been feared by the founding fathers. The legitimate purpose of government was "not merely the administration of
public affairs and the enforcement of duties," but also "the imposi-
tion of restraints [and] the establishment and security of private
rights." These rights were in danger in a democracy as well as in a
monarchy if power were not divided. Without such division "there
is no civil liberty. Property, liberty and life itself are held at the
unchecked will of an irresponsible power." In the United States
power had wisely been divided both at the federal level and between
the federal and state governments. The power of each countered the
power of the other and kept Americans free.[28]

Parker failed to note in this argument that the divided powers
concept was well adapted to preserving the liberties that Americans
already had, but not to expanding those liberties equally to all
citizens. The existing system which he sought to maintain was not
easily an instrument of quick change, especially when any of its
parts opposed change. Only through a momentary rejection of the
national balance of powers would any Reconstruction legislation be
passed. And it would be through an inability to reject the checks of
federalism that this legislation would only be temporary. Parker had
nothing against the expansion of liberty; he simply mistook the existing means of preserving liberty for the end those means sought
to realize. He did not see how liberty was possible without the structure which presently preserved it. He was afraid that any structural
change would collapse the whole liberty-preserving system. He was
so afraid that even the actions of the essentially moderate Reconstruction Congress, actions most respectful of federalism, angered
him.[29]

Fearing change, Parker attacked its apostles. He thought congressional leaders spent far too much time making "flaming speeches
about the march of knowledge" and decrying "the labors of the
original framers of the fundamental laws of the States and the na-

28. Parker, *Three Powers of Government*, 2–5, 10–11.
29. On the problems inherent in the division of national powers during Reconstruction, see Brock, *An American Crisis*, 6–8, 250–273.

tion." The founders had believed that compromises over slavery were preferable to continued agitation and disunion. But the present leaders were endangering all the principles of civil liberty and order by arguing whether freedmen should immediately be given the vote. Did they not see, Parker queried, that emancipation had already brought misery, disease, and death to great numbers of former slaves? Did they now intend that it should bring a greater evil—the destruction of our form of government? If so, then slavery, as bad as it had been, would be exceeded in evil.[30]

In Parker's opinion, Congress seemed bent on such destruction. It appeared to respect none of the traditional restraints on its power. Unlawfully, it had ignored the two-house division of responsibility for seating its own members and had acted in unison to exclude southern states from representation. Unlawfully, Congress had tried to destroy the independence of civil courts by threatening imprisonment even for judges who called the Civil Rights Act unconstitutional. Unlawfully, Congress now made war on the President, not because he had violated the Constitution, but because he was insufficiently committed to radical political ambitions. During the war the President's actions had threatened usurpation. Now it was Congress, grabbing power wherever it could, threatening to end the finely balanced system which alone preserved liberty. It was denying the states a rightful place in the restored Union. Most ominously, Congress was trying to create a whole new constitution with the Fourteenth Amendment.

This "vicious constitutional notion" was "not . . . an amendment to the Constitution, but the destruction of it." The process of constitutional change had here been carried "to the prejudice of the fundamental principles which governed the relation of the United States to the several states on its original adoption." Under this new union consolidation would continue, gradually bringing all power into legislative hands, gradually withering the ability of the states to protect their citizens.[31]

---

30. Parker, *Three Powers of Government*, 12–15.

31. *Ibid.*, 13–15, 35; Joel Parker, *Origin of the United States: and the Status of the Southern States* (New York, 1869), 61–69. In commenting on the Civil Rights bill, Parker was referring to section two, which said that "any person who, under the color of any law, statute, ordinance, regulation, or custom, shall subject

This criticism of the amendment exposed the embattled advocate, not the objective professor. Parker was being profoundly anti-constitutional in his objections. The document itself provides for profound change in its structure if sufficient popular pressure for that change is demonstrated. In effect, the amending process was the instrument by which the framers allowed popular will to triumph over rigid constitutionalism. In the Reconstruction years popular will obviously demanded some constitutional recognition that all the citizens of a state deserved equal protection of the laws. Parker might have feared the sort of constitution which popular pressure could create, but he was not justified in calling it unconstitutional.

He was not sensitive to the general recognition that the freedmen required protection against their white neighbors. Willing to urge an awareness of reality on Chief Justice Taney in the *Merryman* case, Parker himself seemed blind to the atrocities, murders, lynchings—in short, the lack of law and order in the postwar South. He lacked the moral idealism and sense of humanity which animated abolitionists and motivated much Reconstruction reform. This does not mean that Parker lacked idealism. His was directed toward things rather than people, toward a theoretical rather than a particular reality, toward the law, not toward some black man's hardship. This attitude produced a callousness toward the sufferings of the freedmen. Elements of a severe Protestant ethic appeared repeatedly in his reactions to people's Reconstruction problems. He seemed to believe that men found their way in this world by themselves, and that their station depended on their own efforts. He once modified his respect for the efforts of the Good Samaritan by observing that the example should be followed "within the limits of prudence." One former student called Parker "the most manly man" he had ever met. This image holds—a disciplined, severe man, gracious with associates but devoted to legal principles whose survival he equated with the survival of society itself.[32]

---

or cause to be subjected, any inhabitant of any State or Territory to the deprivation of any right secured or protected by this act . . . shall be deemed guilty of a misdemeanor." This same section made John Bingham oppose the Bill. *Statutes at Large*, XIV, 27; *Congressional Globe*, 39th Cong., 1st sess., p. 1293.

32. Howe, *Holmes: The Shaping Years*, 184–186; Hale, "Joel Parker," 261–262, 266; Joel Parker, *An Address Delivered at the Centennial Celebration, in Jaffrey, August 20, 1873* (Winchendon, 1873), 20–21.

Parker had developed this devotion in the Jacksonian age, as expanding democracy had inspired fears of anarchy. Now at the end of his career he again revealed his apprehension about an excess of democracy. It was not just unchecked power in the hands of Congress that disturbed him, nor was it executive usurpation. His fears about a perverted law and a union which no longer restrained the dangerous uses of power had their foundation in Jacksonian fears. Unrestrained democracy encouraged a continual selfish scramble for gain, while the nation and law and order fell apart. No longer restrained by law, the mad scramble for office would continue, and constitutional sophistry would justify every selfish ambition. Parker's attacks on Reconstruction legislation always included attacks on the personal ambition of the legislators, on what he believed was their demagoguery.

After the war he shared a spreading fear that the nation was in danger from ignorant voters who apparently were turning politics and government into a "great barbeque." He once observed that the worst form of slavery was not the human bondage of black to white, but the slavery of a man to a political party. In such servitude ambition devoured every noble purpose. He saw this poisonous bondage spreading. He grew afraid that the Democratic party, which shared his post-Appomattox constitutional views, would "enter into a lively competition with the radical wing of the republican party, in the hope of once more obtaining the Presidency and treasurership of the company, and the power of appointing the engineers, conductors, ticket sellers, switchmen, lamplighters, etc." The source of this great race for spoils was a tragic decline in the quality of the electorate, a decline aided by the attempt of legislators to send to the polls "immense numbers of emancipated slaves . . . too ignorant to comprehend the nature and character of suffrage."[33]

Parker wanted to send into society a group of lawyers who shared

33. Joel Parker, *Three Dangers of the Republic* (New York, 1869), 77-78, 100. For widespread distrust of democracy see Brock, *American Crisis*, 265; John G. Sproat, *The Best Men: Liberal Reformers in the Gilded Age* (New York, 1968); Matthew T. Downey, "The Rebirth of Reform: A Study of Liberal Reform Movements" (Ph.D. dissertation, Princeton University, 1963), 37, 150, 382-385; John J. Clancey, "A Mugwump on Minorities," *Journal of Negro History*, LI (July, 1966), 174-192; Martin Duberman, *James Russell Lowell* (Boston, 1966), 227-234.

his fears. As he gave his last lecture at Harvard in 1868, he spoke of his apprehensions with the hope that his students might move to reverse the dangerous trend that he saw growing throughout the nation. He noted that European experience suggested the dangers facing the republic. Parker's most constant negative example was the dictatorship of Napoleon III which rested on the support of ignorant French peasants. Who could foresee the dangers in America when, stripped of constitutional checks and balances, the government fell into the hands of ambitious demagogues eager to use an ignorant electorate to increase their own influence? The recent actions of Congress had practically robbed Parker of hope. Perhaps the intelligent, educated people of the country would rise up and protect that now embattled Constitution which had been so worthy of defense before. He closed his notes. This was his final lecture, he told his listeners. He had just resigned. He was seventy-three years old and it was time to rest.[34]

Parker retired to his home in Cambridge. He lived the life of a respected citizen, an old man who had achieved prominence on the state bench and then at Harvard. His fame reached back to his birthplace in Jaffrey, New Hampshire. It was natural that the citizens of the town thought of him to speak of Jaffrey's history as the town celebrated its first centennial in 1873.

Seventy-eight-year-old Joel Parker had thought of pleading his age in order to avoid having to speak, but finally he consented to tell the little of the town's history that he knew. He traced its antiquity, noted that Jaffrey rested on granite deposits and that granite was reputedly formed at the earth's beginning. He told the story of the beaver pond whose depths further revealed the town's antiquity. He told about the early proprietors of land deeded by King James I, of the laying out of lots, the planning and building of roads, and the small, self-sufficient community formed by courageous men against the odds of a wilderness. They built a mill, organized the town on the basis of self-government, provided religious instruction, and established schools and laws.

The powers and privileges of the town were used, not buried in

34. Parker, *Three Dangers of the Republic*, 91–93, 107.

the earth. Jaffrey provided for its aged and poor, alleviated want
and destitution. It governed itself in meetings where full consideration was given to all measures, where discussion and opinions on all
matters flowed freely. The concerns of the town were those expressed in the Declaration of Independence and the Constitution.
"Nothing could have been better adapted to the execution of all
these purposes," he said, "than these 'little Democracies' as Tocqueville has called them."[35]

The formation of these communities produced a "brotherhood
promoting the welfare of each other and the community, establishing good order, social intercourse, and a kindly feeling toward
each other." The town secured the prosperity of the household and
provided its defense. "If any one who does not know would seek
an exemplification of the utility of the Town incorporations," Parker declared, "let him look at Jaffrey today, and study her history."
The "little democracies" were rightly cherished. It was because of
this town organization that the American Revolution did not create
"a state of disintegration." The town officers, elected by the people,
retained popular support. They continued to exercise the responsibilities they had accepted in the name of the king, but now in the
name of the people. "No other system could have so well supplied
civil government, under such circumstances," he observed.

As he considered the town's future, Parker's vision was on an ordered, quiet, stable society. He wanted to dedicate the next century
of Jaffrey's history to many things: to a religion which sustained the state "by the inculcation of truths which lie at the foundation of organized and orderly society," which did not engage in
doctrinal disputes over trifles, but which was "peaceable, gentle,
easy to be entreated." He wanted to dedicate the next century to
education and sound learning which had due regard for the nature
of things and "to the construction of mankind [instead of] manufacturing multitudes of projects for making the world different
from, and thus better than, that which God made."

The study of federal government best suited to this ordered community was one which did not teach that the United States were a

35. Parker, *Address Delivered at the Centennial Celebration*, 1–39.

nation before they were states, and that the Constitution was formed by the nation. He wanted to avoid that "sophistry" which would declare that the war powers, designed to preserve the liberties of the people, could be used to destroy them. He hoped that everyone would be taught that "the Constitution was adopted by the several people of the different States, whereby the peoples of those States became a Nation for the purposes manifested by it."

He hoped to dedicate the second municipal century to a prudent philanthropy and a lofty ambition; "not that ambition that seeks position by bribery, but that which eschews popularity for its own sake and seeks to attain 'noble ends by noble means.' We dedicate it to the wise and just exercise of all the political and municipal Rights conferred upon the Town; and to the faithful discharge of all corresponding duties."[36]

So commonplace in many of its sentiments, Parker's address still symbolized something of importance to the understanding of America in the Civil War era. As he spoke, Jaffrey was beginning its second century. The next day another town, perhaps two or three, would announce the beginning of a new one hundred years. It would be part of a common pattern mostly unnoticed outside the limits of those towns and cities, as unnoticed as previous centennial celebrations in many American towns of greater age.

Some celebrations would receive more attention than others. Declamations announcing a new day would sound more meaningful, more true. But only parts of the nation would be entering new centuries. For many, the passage of a hundred years would be insufficient to produce a new day. They would wait and later join their more advanced colleagues. The dividing line between new times and old was not precise; often it was not drawn when men announced it. Joel Parker was dedicating the second municipal century in terms of the first. He was hoping, as he had hoped in the midst of the war and Reconstruction, to use memory to free the nation from what he feared was a dark future. For him, a constitution which protected the "little democracies" and thus secured

36. *Ibid.*, 40–41. Lieber insisted throughout his life that there could be "No right without its duties. No duty without its rights." See Lieber to Thayer, Nov. 5, 1869.

existing rights had always been the imperative guide to the republic's future. Happily, but sadly too, there were many such men. Dedication to the nation's legal tradition had led them to fight successfully to save the Union. Unfortunately, it led also to a rejection of the means to gain the egalitarian spoils of that war. Perhaps it was enough to ask of Parker's generation that they had saved the Union.

Sidney George Fisher I:
Social Order and National Power

On a small farm a few miles outside Philadelphia, Sidney George Fisher, gentleman farmer and amateur political theorist, fought the Civil War. He never heard the sounds of battle or saw enemy soldiers. He occasionally noticed the young men in Union dress who went off to war, returned home, and left to fight again. He read the casualty lists and noted sadly the death of someone he had once known, and then returned home to his study to read and write. Fisher had his encounter with the conflicts of war, not on the battlefield, but in his study, or occasionally at family gatherings. Denied the chance to face combat, he nevertheless fought a constant battle over the legitimacy of ends and means in the war for the Union. He argued vigorously to convince not only his Copperhead relatives, but also the nation's reading public that a war for union and law could be fought within the confines of constitutional law and under the sanction of Anglo-Saxon legal tradition.[1]

Fisher was born in 1809 and died in 1871. By every outward sign he was a failure. He held no political office, no military commission. He tried to make his living by farming but failed completely. The small fortune he inherited when his father died was gradually dissipated, until at the close of his life he was forced to borrow money from his brother's children in order for his family to survive. His

1. Fisher's in-laws were vocal southern sympathizers, especially his father-in-law and brother-in-law, Charles Jared Ingersoll and Charles Ingersoll. The latter was arrested during the summer of 1862 and was later attacked by a mob of Union men for his Copperhead views. Sidney George Fisher, *A Philadelphia Perspective: The Diary of Sidney George Fisher*, ed. Nicholas Wainwright (Philadelphia, 1967), 433–437, 494–496, Aug. 25–Sept. 1, 1862; April 22–29, 1865. Hereafter this will be cited as *Diary*.

brother had loaned him large sums of money from time to time; thus
Fisher knew where to turn when in need.

The idea that he might turn to occupations other than gentleman
farmer seldom occurred to him, and when it did, he found ways
to rebuff it. He was an elitist without resources, an increasingly
impoverished American squire who, though trained as a lawyer, seldom practiced. He admired the potential nobility of the legal profession but thought that in his day lawyers were too frequently
ignoble men interested only in the pursuit of wealth. Fisher kept
his hands clean and his pockets empty. He was even disdainful
of his brother's occupation of businessman, though willing to accept
his money.

The Fisher family had been prominent in shipping but seems to
have gained a good portion of its status by marrying well. Sidney
married into the eminent Ingersoll family and thereby secured a
loose connection with Philadelphia society. The marriage reinforced his self-esteem and fortified his patrician instincts. "I always
feel socially superior to a man who is not a gentleman by *birth*," he
wrote, "and I never yet saw one who had *risen* to a higher position,
whose mind and character, as well as his manner did not show the
taint of his origin. . . . Although I have no great reason for boasting
on the subject, I have a right to consider that 'I am a gentleman,' tho
a poor one."[2]

Years would soften but never eliminate the edges of Fisher's
elitism. Indeed, it is this sense of his being a member of the American
nobility that is the key to understandng his legal-constitutional
thought. Fundamentally Fisher feared a disordered society, a world
where status and stability were endangered, the sort of economics
and politics which Andrew Jackson (Fisher called him "a concentrated mob") seemed to stand for. What worried him about such a
world was that those who would control it would lack the virtues
of the elite. Unaccustomed to power and wealth, these new men
would use both for their own advantage, not for the advantage of
the nation. They would arouse an essentially ignorant public opinion

2. *Diary*, iv; Fisher quoted in Nicholas Wainwright, "Sidney George Fisher—
The Personality of a Diarist," *Proceedings of the American Antiquarian Society*,
LXXII (April, 1962), 16.

to serve their own ambition. Their sense of responsibility would be personal, not molded by that sense of propriety and duty which guaranteed the proper conduct of the well-born. Words written in 1936 by social scientist Ralph Linton reflect Fisher's mood:

> The lack of a definite aristocratic culture which provides the members of [the] ruling group with common ideals and standards of behavior and thus integrates them into a conscious society is perhaps the most distinctive aspect of the modern condition. Exploiters and exploited have existed since the dawn of history, but the only parallel to the modern situation is that of Rome in the days of the late Republic. Here also power came to be vested in the hands of a group of self-made men who had no common standards and no feeling of responsibility to each other or to the state.[3]

Fisher's elitism was thus more than mere snobbery. It rested on respect for the sorts of attitudes that sent Massachusetts's Adamses, Virginia's Byrds, New York's Roosevelts, and Pennsylvania's Biddles into public service. It rested on an admiration for the noblesse oblige of his own class and a distaste for demagogic politics and for the economics of Dodge and Bragg. It made him incapable of trusting the standards, values, or conduct of the common people or businessmen made wealthy by an expanding economy. Such views led him to treasure his life as country gentleman and scholar and to be extraordinarily sensitive to any threats to the stability of the society or the nation.

Fisher avoided the crude worlds of politics and business. He left the tending of his farm to hired hands and spent his time writing, reading, and enjoying nature and life. "Every day is to me a divine and wonderous gift of enjoyment which I appreciate and realize," he wrote. "Pleasure flows to me and inundates my life in full streams, from nature, from books, from my own thoughts, from wife and child, from political and social events, from everything I see and hear and feel." Fisher's life was self-indulgent, but it provided the

3. Ralph Linton, *The Study of Man* (New York, 1936), 111 as quoted in E. Digby Blatzell, *Philadelphia Gentlemen: The Making of a National Upper Class* (New York, 1958), 61; see also 59–63. For Fisher's view of the value of upper class standards in securing honest and selfless state service, see his discussion of the career of Nicholas Biddle in *Diary*, 154–158, February 28, 1844.

chance to read widely and write continually. He liked to quote
Bacon: "Reading maketh a full man, writing an exact man."[4]

He wrote continually in public and in his diary about the events
of his age. From 1854 to 1860 he published an average of four articles each year for the *Philadelphia North American*. He wrote
two small books before the war (*The Law of the Territories* and
The Laws of Race as Connected with Slavery) which appeared
under his pen name "Cecil." During the war he published his most
important book, *The Trial of the Constitution*, and two major articles for the *North American Review*. After Appomattox he continued to contribute to this journal and also wrote for the newly
founded *Nation* magazine. The editor thought enough of Fisher's
reputation to include him in a list of contributors.

Lacking first-hand experience in the events of his age, Fisher had
the advantages of detachment and leisure, the opportunity to delin-
eate the meaning of the disunion crisis for the nation's constitutional
traditions. His observations were not always correct, but they were
often original. Frequently they were precisely on target, clearly revealing the essence of the question at issue. Under the demands of
the war era he discovered, as did Lincoln and other responsible
northern leaders, a vital Constitution responsive to the heartfelt
public insistence that the Union be saved. However, for Fisher the
Constitution yielded less easily to demands for emancipation and
equal rights. On this point his racism revealed a kinship with constitutional limitations and sorely tested the liberal views which
disunion had called forth.

Fisher's constitutional views reflect northern public opinion more
accurately than those of Lieber or Parker. Lieber's aconstitutional
liberalism ignored the pervasive northern insistence that the war was
for the Constitution as well as for the Union. It recognized but
made practically no concession to the linkage in the northern mind
of law, nationhood, and constitutionalism. Parker's passion for constitutional restraint in the midst of war may have been intellectually
defensible and logically consistent. But it was difficult to distinguish
from Copperhead oratory or Buchanan's paralyzing theories, even
for those willing to seek out distinctions. To Parker the Constitution

4. Wainwright, "Sidney George Fisher," 23.

meant only certain definite things. He understood its provisions and hence its limitations. Constitutionalism was not an emotional incantation; it was a theology whose clearly stated dogmas required strict obedience.

The average Northerner was neither a professor of constitutional law nor an immigrant ideologue. He was probably a man whose veneration for the Constitution was strong but uncomplicated by knowledge. He was most likely to demand reverence for the national charter while insisting on an interpretation of it that met any and every need. Fisher was the man for such a situation. While more knowledgeable than most men about the provisions of the Constitution, he was more concerned with the survival of the government it described than with rigidly literal interpretation. He was less concerned with what the Constitution said than with what it could be made to say. In a struggle which tested existing legal institutions' capacity to respond to crisis, this was an eminently useful view.

The essential agreement between most Northerners and Fisher as to the flexibility of the Constitution was not weakened by Fisher's elitism—in fact, it may be that his views paralleled theirs more closely because of it. He did not develop a scrupulous regard for constitutional limitations on national power because his admiration for those who properly exercised power led him to trust their judgment and their sense of noblesse oblige. They could be trusted to do what was necessary without being corrupted by the exercise of power. Most Northerners probably favored loose construction because they experienced the disunion crisis less in terms of its legality than in terms of its likely effect on the way they lived. They wanted the government to be relatively unrestrained in its fight to preserve the way of life that the Union represented.

This is not to say that either of them gave up the Constitution entirely. The government's contention that the war would save the Constitution precluded such action, for one thing. For another, both retained a respect for the document that was all the more vital because of its flexibility when the nation was endangered. They probably kept their constitutionalism without even thinking about it.

As with Lieber and Parker, the Kansas crisis directed Fisher's attention to the dangers and imminence of disunion. The passage

of the Kansas-Nebraska Act and the subsequent violence in the new
territory alarmed him, for he saw in Kansas a disease that might
spread. He thought the crisis portended a national breakdown in
order and respect for legal tradition. He was afraid that slavery
might well destroy or debase the nation's law.

The problem in Kansas, as Fisher understood it, was slavery and
the southern passion that human bondage should follow the American flag. He believed that the South had become so frightened of
the growing national and international hostility to slavery that it
was willing to repudiate the existing legal traditions and chart an
ominous course. It would accept the dangerous concept of popular
sovereignty.

The argument for popular sovereignty was a beguiling one. Its
roots and strength lay in the pervasive American admiration for self-
government, an admiration based on the fact that Americans did in
fact rule themselves in local units. Jefferson had endorsed the idea
of complete independent rule for the territories, and it had been
used, with modification, by Stephen Douglas in his bill to organize
the Kansas-Nebraska territory.[5]

The very attractiveness of the principle made Fisher fear it. However popular the idea that people should rule themselves, in the territories the law was that they did not. The Constitution, the
Northwest Ordinance, the Missouri Compromise, and the full pattern of congressional legislation on the territories, supported by
court decisions, had established in law the doctrine that popular
will was not the sovereign there. When the President and Congress
capitulated to southern threats and demands by supporting the
Kansas-Nebraska bill, they sacrificed the security of legal tradition
on the altar of popular passion. "We are at sea indeed," Fisher
wrote, "on the billows of change, and the law of the land ceases to
be any rule of conduct, but becomes merely the arbitrary decree of
any party that happens for a time to be uppermost."[6]

5. Bestor, "State Sovereignty and Slavery."
6. Sidney George Fisher (under pen name of "Cecil"), *Kanzas and the Con-*
stitution (Boston, 1856), 5–6; *Diary*, 258, July 9, 16, 1856. Both Fisher's neighbor
Horace Binney and political economist Henry Carey congratulated Fisher on this
pamphlet; 100,000 copies of it were circulated during the campaign of 1856. *Diary*,
259–261, Aug. 23, Sept. 25, 1856. Fisher heard that the expense of printing the

Territorial elections in Kansas confirmed his opinion. Along with other legal thinkers, Fisher read with growing sorrow and outrage of the corruption of self-government and law in Kansas. An ominous pattern appeared: a proslavery legislature elected with the help of intimidation from Missouri, a slave code which punished speaking or writing against slavery with penalties of up to two years in jail, laws which threatened death to those aiding or encouraging slave escapes, antislavery men excluded from juries which tried violations of the slave code. Popular sovereignty was rapidly being transformed into slave sovereignty.[7]

Fisher's dismay at events in Kansas was not based on antislavery feelings. Although he deplored the brutality of slavery, he recognized the vast complexity of the peculiar institution and believed that Negroes were better off in bondage in America than in Africa. He believed that slavery provided "without expense to the government, an efficient magistry to maintain order and subordination" in a much inferior race. He sympathized with Southerners who feared being absorbed or overwhelmed by the black race. Slavery was a force for order in the South, and as such it was protected by the Constitution. Fisher was disturbed by events in Kansas precisely because the South would not recognize that it was safe under existing law. Southern passion for slavery apparently overwhelmed understanding of, and respect for, law and the Constitution.[8]

As antagonistic to abolitionism as many Southerners, Fisher recognized that the South's best protection from northern opinion was the existing legal structure, not an attack on it. Although human

---

pamphlet had been paid by a man who had changed from favoring Buchanan to supporting Fremont after reading Fisher's words. *Diary*, 261, Sept. 20, 1856.

7. Fisher, *Kanzas and the Constitution*, 50–58; "Howard Report," 34th Cong., 1st sess., House Report 200, Serial Set No. 869, pp. 3–100. This report received wide circulation in the North as a pamphlet, *Subduing Freedom in Kansas* (New York, 1856). The laws of the legislature are also available in the memoirs of the freesoil leader of the state in the 1850s, Charles Robinson, *The Kansas Conflict* (New York, 1892), 157. Indictment of proslavery forces is found in Allan Nevins, *Ordeal of the Union*, II, 380, 384–387.

8. Fisher, *The Laws of Race as Connected with Slavery* (Philadelphia, 1860), 7–15, 27–29, 48–57; Fisher, *The Law of the Territories* (Philadelphia, 1859), 1–5; *Diary*, 317, Feb. 17, 1859. Arthur Bestor calls *The Law of the Territories* "One of the ablest statements of the conservative position [on the *Dred Scott* opinion]." "State Sovereignty and Slavery," 152n.

bondage was repugnant to many Northerners, they understood that the Constitution sanctioned it, and they were devoted enough to that Constitution to respect its sanctions. But once slave interests showed disrespect for the Philadelphia charter, they would place slavery in dark peril. White men did not care overmuch for black men, but they cared a great deal for the law enshrined by the Constitution. Southern actions in Kansas were demonstrating to the nation that slavery was hostile to law. "Not one in a thousand," Fisher observed, "cares much whether [Kansas] be a slave State or a free State; but millions do care, most deeply, whether the Constitution of their country is to be repealed for the sake of slavery; whether their government is to be used as an instrument to accomplish the schemes of sectional ambition in violation of the obligations of truth and justice."[9]

It appalled Fisher and others like him that disrespect for established law did not seem to be confined to the territories. In their view presidents Pierce and Buchanan had both yielded to southern threats and supported the proslavery government of Kansas, and so the corrosive malignancy of slavery was spreading to federal institutions. As indicated earlier, such an attitude ignored the complexity of the Kansas situation. In their responses to the territorial elections both presidents were trapped by the circumstances of popular sovereignty and their limited view of federal power. Once the proslavery government had been declared legally elected by the territorial officials, there was little they felt they could do. Pierce denied the President's power to interfere with local elections in states or territories. Buchanan's secretary of state, Lewis Cass, explained his Chief Executive's belief that all electoral matters were local questions. Determination of the legality of voters was a question for election judges appointed by county commissioners. If disputes arose over the validity of election returns for legislative offices, the legislature itself would have to decide whom to seat. Local judges were to make this determination if court offices were in question.[10]

9. Fisher, *Law of the Territories*, 108–110; *Diary*, 294, March 4, 1858; Larry Gara, "Slavery and the Slave Power: A Crucial Distinction," *Civil War History*, XV (March, 1969), 5–18.

10. Klein, *President James Buchanan*, 298; Franklin Pierce, *Message from the President of the United States . . . at the Commencement of the Third Session of the Thirty-fourth Congress* (Washington, 1856), 12, 14.

Had the Kansas question rested only on the matter of the territory's first elections, it is possible that Fisher, at least, would have come to soften his criticism of the federal administration. But Buchanan destroyed this possibility when, in the winter of 1857–58, he took up the cause of the Lecompton Convention. This convention was chosen after a census which omitted fifteen of Kansas's thirty-four counties. Because the freesoilers boycotted the election, less than a fourth of the eligible voters took part. Proslavery delegates controlled the convention, writing a constitution which endorsed and defended slavery. In addition, the delegates decided not to submit the constitution to a popular vote. Voters would only be permitted to express their opinions on a proposal which gave them a choice between "the constitution with slavery" or "the constitution without slavery." But even if they voted for the latter, the right to hold slave property in the territory would not be interfered with. The ensuing election was again boycotted by the freesoil element. Not surprisingly, "the constitution with slavery" won.[11]

Buchanan himself had promised that the constitution under which Kansas would be admitted to the Union would be submitted to the people. But now, faced with pressure from southern members of his cabinet and with threats of secession, he turned around and urged that Congress accept the Lecompton Constitution as the fundamental document for the new state. This was too much for Fisher, as for thousands of other Americans. It seemed that the presidency was now a hostage of proslavery forces.

Fisher was so bitter about this expanding evil that, even when Buchanan offered a minor concession to freesoil sentiment, he still attacked him. The President suggested that Congress should accept the slave constitution of Kansas; after that territory became a state, its people could change it into a freesoil document. Fisher did not see this as the ordinary workings of politics. Rather, to him it was another indication of disrespect for law, another surrender to the forces of disorder, not an act of political expediency.[12]

He pointed out that the Kansas constitution in question declared that it should not be changed for seven years. Yet there stood the President, sworn to uphold the law, urging that this constitutional

11. Allan Nevins, *The Emergence of Lincoln* (New York, 1950), I, 229–249.
12. *Ibid.*, Fisher, *Law of the Territories*, 104–106.

provision be ignored, overridden by the mere will of a congressional majority. Buchanan had simply adopted for his own ends the abolitionist insistence that a mere majority could overturn a constitutional provision. Abolitionists sought to end slavery; the President, to preserve it. But they agreed on a principle inimical to ordered liberty—whenever a majority vote could be mustered against established legal principles, those principles ceased to exist.[13]

Fisher had Buchanan coming and going. If the President supported slavery, he was damned; if he suggested that freesoil sentiment might dominate, he was damned again. But there was a basic consistency in this two-edged attack. Both views rested on the feeling that chaos opened before men when they ignored the law. Fisher's commitment to established legal institutions was so strong that, unlike Joel Parker, he could not even support the freesoil government of Topeka which had been formed to oppose the recognized Lecompton body. Although the provocation for Topeka's revolutionary act was almost unprecedented, still that government was outside the law; hence Fisher repudiated it.

This admirable legal consistency left no solution to the Kansas question. It simply damned both North and South for allowing extremism to replace respect for law. Fisher probably recognized the hopelessness of the situation. As early as 1850 he had predicted the dissolution of the Union; through the rest of the decade he showed the same pessimism. There was no national or moderate party in the country. All seemed mad and willing to destroy the nation. The fate of the United States seemed to be to copy the chaotic cycles of revolution that marked Latin America. Fisher only hoped that the Union would survive him, for he considered dissolution to be "synonymous with civil war, anarchy & misery & disaster of every kind."[14]

Events showed little sign of conforming themselves to his wishes. The sectional quarrel intensified alarmingly. The South seemed willing neither to abide by established legal guarantees nor to accept

13. Fisher, *Law of the Territories*, 104–106; Fisher, *Kanzas and the Constitution*, 7–9; *Diary*, 308, Oct. 13, 1858.

14. *Diary*, 233, 258, 294–295; March 4, 1850, July 16, 1856, March 4, 1858, March 29, 1858. Fisher, *Kanzas and the Constitution*, 10–11; Fisher, *Law of the Territories*, xx–xxiv.

as adequate existing constitutional protections. The attack on Sumner, the *Dred Scott* decision, and continued disunion threats all expressed southern militancy and a willingness to sacrifice to slave expansion what northern men believed were their rights. Fisher sensed a growing feeling that northern men would no longer be bullied into accepting southern demands. Their devotion to liberty, law, and civil rights was too strong to allow it. In the winter of 1859 he put the matter most clearly:

> The Union was made to secure these rights. Events are showing that they, the Union, and slavery are incompatible . . . Which shall we sacrifice? The Union, slavery, or civil rights? Every right thinking conservative man will answer, preserve all three if possible; if that be not possible sacrifice slavery first, if it must be, give up slavery and the Union rather than that freedom which the Union was intended to maintain.[15]

The statement was almost a resignation of the Union, evoked as it was by a continual outpouring of extremist speeches from both sections. But there was a prospect of steel behind this dejected theorizing. While Fisher was disturbed by radical northern orators, he was irate with the South. Already angered by some of the outrages which slavery permitted, he was enflamed at what seemed to be an aggressive slave power. The South had removed the ancient landmarks of law, had introduced dangerous new constitutional theories, had "at length abandoned all principle whatever" and declared "that it will either rule . . . or break the Union." Even in his fear of the destructive potential of John Brown's raid, there was a grudging respect. "This one man," he remarked, "has done more to reveal the true nature of the slavery question than all others who have acted on it."[16]

15. *Diary*, 341, Dec. 12, 1859. Abolitionist Lysander Spooner reported that Calhoun had once characterized northern opinion as "five percent . . . were for slavery, five percent abolitionists, twenty percent opportunists who would side with the stronger party, and the remaining seventy percent people who disliked slavery but were unwilling to defy the Constitution." Quoted in Kraditor, *Means and Ends in American Abolitionism*, 195.

16. Fisher, *Law of the Territories*, 40–41; *Diary*, 334, 339; Oct. 19, Dec. 3, 1859. Of *Uncle Tom's Cabin* he wrote, "It has the capital excellence of being true. It is a correct picture of the enormities of slavery, as I know from what I have myself wit-

As the crisis approached its climax in 1860, Fisher's outrage diminished. He again became troubled at the approach of a war in which a sense of outrage would be a cold luxury indeed. Conflicting imperatives of moderation and respect for law struggled with his desire somehow to restrain southern arrogance. Like most Northerners, Fisher was having reactions, not developing a philosophy. He thought in January that people in the North were becoming aroused and would no longer submit to rule by the South. He believed that the South would shy away from carrying out secession. It was a tactic "so desperate, so obviously destructive" that reason would surely prevail. Lincoln's nomination in May cooled his apprehensions; he saw the rejection of the more radical William H. Seward to be a sign of increasingly moderate sentiment. When southern states made Lincoln's election the signal for secession, he was again anxious. The Buchanan administration was unlikely to attempt coercion, and perhaps this was the best policy. Coercion would produce a bloody war which would scar the entire nation. He hoped that the seceders would soon see the folly of their actions and, having failed at blackmail, return peaceably to the Union.

Yet even as he entertained this hope that Buchanan's compromise effort would cajole disunionists back into the fold, Fisher was suggesting a means to resolve the dilemma by capitulating to the South. Hoping to preserve stability and to protect respect for law against the potentially anarchistic act of secession, he hoped to make secession legal. He proposed the passage of a law allowing any state to secede legally, providing it could obtain the support of two-thirds of its people. This idea may have been intended to create time for passions to cool. But as he thought more about it, Fisher became convinced that legalized secession was the only way in which the nation might preserve respect for law in such a disruptive environment. He watched Buchanan declare it his lawful duty to protect public property and then make no attempt to execute the law. He justly feared that the whole authority of government was becoming

---

nessed & heard from others thoroughly experienced & acquainted with the subject & whose prejudices were all in favor of the system. My full belief, indeed, is that not half the truth is told & that if the whole were told the description would be too horrible and revolting to be read." *Diary*, 243–244, Dec. 26, 1852.

the object of contempt. Secession was going to be successful in any case; if it were extralegal, the law would be dishonored and defied. Therefore, though despairing of the Union, Fisher thought that legalizing secession might at least preserve respect for law.[17]

The idea of legalized secession, poor though it was, appeared to be the best bargain for an appalling situation. Lack of a real alternative, the result of Buchanan's confused actions, led Fisher to suggest such a scheme. Then on March 5, 1861, he read Lincoln's first inaugural address, and some hope returned; the alternative of law enforcement by the federal government became real. The new President who had been unknown to Fisher before his nomination now became a hero, a man wise in the true philosophy of government. The speech showed Lincoln's firmness, strong convictions, and powerful sense of duty. Fisher retained some doubts about his "strength of personal will," but he felt that the new chief executive understood the crisis clearly. "He evidently appreciates his position, its duties and powers," the theorist wrote. "I shall be disappointed if he does not prove equal to either.... He who wrote [this address] is no common man."

Fisher especially admired Lincoln's view of governmental power. There was no rigid constitutional dogmatizing, none of that frightened legal rigidity which paralyzed the government while the Union fell apart. On the contrary, Lincoln said things which Fisher admired so much that he copied them into his diary: "No organic law can be framed with a provision specifically applicable to every case that may occur in its practical administrations." Here was a suggestion that action might replace paralysis, that there might be alternatives to secession other than passive acquiescence.[18]

On the last day of 1860 a despairing James Russell Lowell had asked, "Is it the effect of democracy to make all men cowards? An ounce of pluck just now were worth a king's ransom. There is one comfort, though a shabby one, in the feeling that matters will come to such a pass that courage will be forced on us." Lincoln's speech gave new energy to Northerners disillusioned with this nation's capacity to save itself. It provided the ounce of pluck that Lowell

17. *Diary*, 344, 353, 372, 377; Jan. 25, May 18, Dec. 4, 1860; Jan. 14, 1861. Fisher, "Legalized Secession," *Philadelphia North American*, Dec. 31, 1860.

18. *Diary*, 380–381, March 5, 1861; Stampp, *And the War Came*, pp. 201–203.

asked for, and it also suggested new options to the tragedy posed by a nation dividing.[19]

Four days after the President spoke, southern delegates appeared before Congress to ask recognition as members of a foreign government. Reacting to this situation with Lincoln in the White House, Fisher showed an enlarged understanding of the implications of legalized secession. Congress was faced with the necessity of accepting or rejecting the constitutional right of secession. Should legislators yield this right, Fisher now recognized, it would constitute "a virtual abdication of the powers of government." By April 1 he was criticizing a plan for constitutional secession that Secretary of the Treasury Chase had suggested. Now Fisher realized the practical dangers of carrying out such a plan: "It would require the calling of a convention, would open the question of one or more confederacies . . . nearly equivalent to authorizing anarchy."[20]

Two weeks later the question of peaceful secession became academic. When Confederate soldiers attacked the U.S. government, there was no longer any chance that the question of the future form of the Union would be decided in courtrooms, legislative halls, or libraries. The battlefield would now add the weight of its opinion to the debate; war necessity would be added to logical necessity as a major factor in any decision. Fisher was swept up in the passions of the post-Sumter days. He visited Philadelphia and savored the emotion with which men rushed to arms. The President had asked for 75,000 men. Fisher thought that ten times that number were ready to fight. The thought of his own service crossed his mind; despite his gout, he envisioned himself standing behind a tree pulling a trigger in the service of at least the home guard.[21]

He was willing to make many sacrifices to preserve law in America, to counter what he and others viewed as an outright southern attack on the rule of law. Whatever his feelings about the legality of secession in time of peace, he knew that secession extorted by force was intolerable. What was at stake, he would

19. James Russell Lowell to Charles Nordhoff, *Letters of James Russell Lowell,* ed. Charles Eliot Norton (New York, 1894), I, 308; Stampp, *And the War Came,* 201–203; Hyman, "Reconstruction and Political-Constitutional Institutions," 1–22.
20. *Diary,* 381–382, 384; March 9, April 1, 1861.
21. *Ibid.,* 385–386; April 15, 22, 1861.

write in 1862, was not so much the Union as the ability of the nation to retain a government of laws. "The primary object of the war," he insisted, "is to vindicate the outraged dignity and honor of the Government and to maintain the authority of its violated laws." Of course it would be tragic to lose the southern states— but far more tragic would be a government disgraced and mocked, a government unable to protect itself or its people. The act of violent secession was in effect a question: "Does the United States have a government?" Lincoln had replied

> that the Government of the United States still existed, and he announced the fact to them and to the world in resounding cannonade, whose meaning is plain enough. What they say is that the laws must be executed in Charleston and Savannah, and Richmond, and New Orleans, in order that they may have authority in Philadelphia and New York, in Chicago and San Francisco; that our flag must fly again at Fort Sumter, that it may be honored on the high seas and in foreign ports, and that when this Government discusses the right of secession it will not be with secret plotters of treason and armed rebels to its authority.[22]

Fisher's words mirrored Lincoln's vital interest in the legal aspects of the war. In his July 4, 1861, message the President, rather than simply asserting the right of the nation to respond to attack, had chosen also to argue on the legality of secession and on methods of conducting the war. He had devoted over a third of that message to constitutional argument. He differed from Fisher in denying the right of peaceful secession, but both men sensed the importance of legal elements of the conflict. Both knew the significance of demonstrating that the laws of the nation were adequate to the crisis.[23]

Such a demonstration would be a challenge. This was a war for which no adequate legal precedents existed. It provided continually unique legal situations which would have to be dealt with within

22. Fisher, *Trial of the Constitution*, 185–188. In a private interview Lincoln had expressed similar sentiment: "The Constitution will not be preserved and defended until it is enforced and obeyed in every part of every one of the United States. It must be so respected, obeyed, enforced and defended." Quoted in Stampp, *And the War Came*, 196.

23. Basler, ed., *Collected Works of Lincoln*, IV, 421–441.

the law. Each day of conflict made that fact clear to increasing numbers of jurists; Fisher was no exception. When the Merryman arrest occurred, he immediately saw the important constitutional issue at stake: that the conflict between civil and military authority might become a major question in the war. The law was going to have to settle that conflict. In early June sailors captured the Confederate ship *Savannah*. Fisher wondered about the legal status of the crew. If the Union was legally unbroken, then the men were pirates and would have to be hanged. But such a penalty would surely evoke reprisals. What legal remedy was there in this situation? Slaves were reported escaping in large numbers from border states. Would the fugitive slave law apply? Fisher thought not; but this question, like the others, was more than academic. They all were tests of the adaptability of the nation's law.[24]

The question of great importance was, of course, which form of the nation's law would provide the necessary legal justification? Operating in unique circumstances, how much of the nation's legal past would be useful? How much of the Constitution would be relevant to the war environment? These were complex questions with many possible answers. Significantly, almost no one answered that the Constitution should be completely ignored during the war. (Lieber's voice was virtually unique.) The nature of the conflict precluded such a response. The question really became, which Constitution would be most acceptable for wartime conditions? Would it be the Constitution which restrained power to protect liberty? Would it be Jefferson's Constitution, or the even less active Buchanan-Pierce document? Or would it be a constitution which marshaled power in the service of liberty, the Constitution of Hamilton, Webster, and Clay?

Supporters of the war for the Union emphatically endorsed the Hamiltonian view. Indeed, the reputation of Jefferson declined in the war era; Lincoln, having espoused the words and ideals of the third president throughout his prewar years, gradually ceased to mention him. Hamiltonian ideas were given new life by the necessities of the conflict, and Fisher was one who encouraged this revitali-

24. *Diary*, 387, 391, 394; April 27, May 29, June 16, 1861. Hyman, "Reconstruction and Political-Constitutional Institutions," 13–14.

zation. The Philadelphian repudiated the Jeffersonian Constitution as not merely incapable of saving the nation from disunion, but actually responsible for it.[25]

As he wrote his most important work, *The Trial of the Constitution*, Fisher was in the grip of those critical days which stretched from the troubles in Kansas to secession. He recalled years when the Constitution and laws had, one after another, been abused or ignored by Southerners while Pierce and Buchanan stood inactive, numbed by incantations of Jeffersonian ideology. His work was an attack on those years and that ideology. But it was an attack which revealed Fisher's own thralldom to the pre-Lincoln experience, for he often equated the Constitution itself with the hated Jeffersonian document and seemed almost to be attacking one in the name of the other. At other times, however, he was able to escape the hypnotic image that Jefferson's was the real Constitution and to invoke the true Constitution to exorcize the Jeffersonian heresy. Then he could write, "What is false in our Constitution, or in the interpretation of it should be got rid of; for only thus can it be preserved."[26]

Fisher believed that the major defect in the nation's charter lay in the fact that it was a written document, not adequately adaptable to change, and at times vague on important questions. The amendment provision, for example, had not allowed peaceful change when the nation faced the secession crisis. Fisher believed that law ought to restrain passion, not encourage it. But in order to function, the amendment article demanded that the people be aroused to demand change and that agitation be maintained during legislative discussion. There was little chance for calm deliberation of whatever constitutional change was demanded by crisis. Recognizing this fact, American leaders had avoided calling for necessary change. Instead of liberating the government for necessary adaptation to challenge, the amendment provision froze it.

Equally dangerous, in his opinion, was the respect that the nation had for written constitutions, a respect so powerful that it lifted the

25. Peterson, *The Jefferson Image in the American Mind*, 209–226. After December 3, 1861, Lincoln mentioned Jefferson once (July 7, 1863) when he responded to a serenade with a reference to the Declaration of Independence. Basler, ed., *Collected Works of Lincoln*, VI, 319–320.

26. Fisher, *Trial of the Constitution*, vi.

document out of the political arena and made it sacrosanct. The Constitution could be used to defy the very processes of government which it established. Those men who did not get their way in the usual operation of governmental institutions could always appeal to the Constitution. They could claim (and had done so repeatedly) that the will of the people, acting through those institutions, was unconstitutional. They could thus stifle the government and inhibit its ability to govern. More dangerously, they could claim that they were the true disciples of the nation's organic law and, calling upon the people's respect for the Constitution, rally them against the government. Such was the cause of disunion. The South had claimed that the popularly elected government was in fact violating the Constitution in following the popular will. Southern leaders had convinced their people that such an action was "a breach of the Constitution [which] not only justifies resistance because it is a wrong which admits of no other redress, but . . . it dissolves the Union and releases the citizen from the obligations of allegiance." The Constitution, the blueprint for union, could be used for union-breaking.[27]

Under the Constitution which Fisher attacked, the nation was falling apart; as it engaged in this malignant mitosis, the Buchanan government stood practically paralyzed. But Lincoln suggested that the Union might be saved, that the government might have a soul of steel and not of jelly. He had indicated that the law need not shackle but save. The problem was to find the legal power to perform the acts of salvation, to make or discover a constitution that empowered rather than debilitated, a constitution for the 1860s, not the 1780s. Fisher, among others, was in search of a constitution for the nineteenth, not the eighteenth century. "The Constitution," he insisted, "has failed to protect us from the calamity of a bloody and destructive civil war; but it does not follow that free government is to fail."[28]

To legitimize the government's efforts to survive, Fisher sought a

27. *Ibid.*, 20, 32–38, 56–57. For another criticism of the Constitution as a cause of the war, see the article by foreign-born E. L. Godkin, "The Constitution and Its Defects." Godkin's article parallels the logic in *Trial of the Constitution* to a marked degree, although he does not mention having read the book.

28. Fisher, *Trial of the Constitution*, 55.

new source of power, a view of the Constitution and a form of government which would be adaptable to the war crisis. He found it in the British system of parliamentary government. He believed that this system would reconcile the problems of change and stability, at the same time resolving the potential conflict between popular will and constitutional law. He hoped to make the American Congress accept the role of the British Parliament. It was an effort which defied the spirit of the American Revolution and ignored great parts of the last seventy-five years of American experience, but Fisher was so concerned to find power for the preservation of law that he could dispense with these possible objections. He was also freed from any obligation to accept responsibility for implementing his policy, and so was not obliged to consider the likely popular reaction. Uninvited into the seats of power, from his quiet study Fisher spun forth the first American constitutional argument which dispensed with the nation's hallowed belief in the separation of powers. It would be thirty years before a major American thinker, Woodrow Wilson, would suggest a similar theoretical proposition—and Wilson made the suggestion before he held political office.[29]

Observing the actions of the government in the prewar era, Fisher recalled an irresolute executive, snared by cowardice and misguided constitutional devotion. He recalled a Supreme Court which lost claim to popular respect by the nefarious *Dred Scott* decision. By rendering a decision so at odds with legal traditions and popular will, the Court had made itself a nullity, a condition fortified by Taney's *Merryman* opinion that a blatant traitor should go free. That left only Congress, the American Parliament, as a trustworthy instrument of government. To Fisher the war had served at least one beneficent purpose: it had demonstrated that Congress was the most vital and of necessity the dominant body in the government. In this crisis Congress would have to accept the role of the British Parliament, becoming supreme in all matters of policy, legislation, and constitution. If legislators accepted such a role, they would solve the two major weaknesses of the American constitutional system, rigidity and uncertain constitutionality. They would regu-

29. Riker, "Sidney George Fisher and the Separation of Powers during the Civil War," 397–400.

late change and constitutionalize any necessary piece of legislation.[30]

If Congress accepted such a role, it would become the sole judge of all laws it passed. There would be no possibility that some opponent would defy the law by raising the standard of the Constitution. The laws of Parliament became part of the British Constitution the moment they were passed. Such being the case, there would be no need to agitate the people by calling for constitutional amendment in the midst of an emergency. Congress would respond immediately to crisis; its response would be constitutional change. Law and power would be joined together in response to crisis.

Fisher was untroubled by the prospect of such radical alterations in the structure of government. He thought the times demanded change and that the alternatives to his suggestions had been proven dangerous to law and destructive of union. When President Lincoln asked Attorney General Edward Bates to provide legal sanction for presidential suspension of the privilege of the writ of habeas corpus, Bates's Jeffersonianism asserted itself. The three branches of the government were coordinate, he argued, and therefore the President had just as much responsibility for suppressing the rebellion or reacting to crisis as any of the other branches of government. Since he had this power, the President had to be the judge of the constitutionality of his actions in suspending the writ.[31]

This common argument was historically legitimate. Presidents Jefferson and Jackson had adopted it, as had Lincoln himself in debating Stephen Douglas. Even John Marshall had suggested his agreement with the principle that each branch of government was the proper judge of the constitutionality of its actions. The modern conception of judicial review, that the Supreme Court is the final arbiter of the meaning of the Constitution, arose in the post–Civil War period.[32]

Indicative of his fascination with the awesome consequences of

30. Fisher, *Trial of the Constitution*, 62–64, 39.

31. "Opinion of Attorney General Bates, July 5, 1861," *Official Record of the War of Rebellion*, Series II, II, 20–30; Randall, *Constitutional Problems under Lincoln*, 124; Cain, *Lincoln's Attorney General, Edward Bates of Missouri*, 147–152.

32. Alfred H. Kelly and Winfred Harbison, *The American Constitution*, 229–231, 392; Basler, ed., *Collected Works of Lincoln*, II, 400–403, 496, 516–517; III, 232; Kutler, *Judicial Power and Reconstruction Politics*, 114–142.

divided power, Fisher attacked Bates's argument as the product of a theory "flatly contradicting nature, truth and reason." The idea that the vital decision of constitutionality should rest in three hands was not only "unphilosophical"; it was "subversive of order." Without a single arbiter of constitutionality, each branch of government would either continually quarrel with the others or be stymied by them, remaining inert when action was demanded. If Bates's idea were true, Fisher insisted, then we simply did not have a government. We had the same sort of anarchy, chaos, and misrule that had caused the war. The concept of divided power had produced a divided nation.[33]

The obvious recourse on the question of constitutionality was the Supreme Court—obvious, at least, in the twentieth century. But when Fisher wrote, the question of the Court's ability to exercise review power was unsettled. The high bench had established its right to review state laws, but only twice in its history had it vetoed a federal law. The second time was the *Dred Scott* decision, and the resulting outcry did not suggest widespread public approval for such judicial imperialism. Indeed, Fisher blamed that decision for contributing to the onset of secession and war. Then Taney's *Merryman* opinion had suggested that a single judge might nullify the power of the President to save the Union. It was hardly the sort of environment which would encourage an elevated opinion of the Supreme Court. Fisher was happy to see that the people had rejected judicial sovereignty. When the Court had tried to assert its will against the nation's desire for survival, it had been "swept aside by the impetuous rush of events, of opinion, of passion. Its voice could scarcely be heard amid the tumult and din of elemental passion."[34]

This public reaction suggested to Fisher an important constitutional fact: the function of the Court needed to be reevaluated in

33. Fisher, *Trial of the Constitution*, 58–60. Bates's argument was so unsatisfactory that over forty pamphlets and articles appeared to debate the habeas corpus question. See Sydney G. Fisher, "The Suspension of Habeas Corpus during the War of the Rebellion," *Political Science Quarterly*, III (Sept., 1888), 454–488. The author was Sidney George Fisher's son.

34. Fisher, *Trial of the Constitution*, 75–79; Charles Warren, *The Supreme Court in United States History* (Boston, 1928), II, 369–373. While the *Dred Scott* decision did produce an outcry against the court, few people suggested that judicial institutions had failed generally. Kutler, *Judicial Power*, 7–29.

terms of natural law, not just constitutional law, and natural law demanded that a nation struggle to survive, whether judges understood how it was to survive or not. However American benchmen might feel about their duty to restrain the dangerous tendencies of democracy by acting as checkreins to legislatures, the fact remained that only the national legislature could save the union.

Would such a capitulation to democracy lead to anarchy and disorder? Privately Fisher had his doubts, but publicly he reasoned, with some force, that attempts to limit the people's desires for a vigorous government fighting for a viable union would have even more anarchical consequences. The indispensable requirement of the nation now was power; the power of the government had to be demonstrated as sufficient to save the nation. If not, then "every interest of society may perish in a raging sea of violence and anarchy." Laws had to be enforced in Charleston so that they could be respected in Philadelphia. Those who insisted that the Constitution restricted the capacity of the nation to preserve itself needed to understand a crucial fact: If they were successfully to shackle the government, then "the Constitution for which they profess so much respect will soon cease to exist, and the war they deprecate, will speedily be brought with added terrors to their own homes."[35]

He urged frightened judges to understand that "the Constitution belongs to the people . . . to the people of 1862, not to those of 1787. It must and will be modified to suit the wishes of the former, by their representatives in Congress, just as the English Constitution has been modifed by Parliament, or it will be destroyed." The Constitution was best preserved not by using it to resist change, but by making it an instrument for change. Fisher recognized judicial fears; he shared them to some extent. However, under the American form of government there was simply no alternative to popular rule. Between rule by the people and rule by judges, Fisher chose the first. "If the people cannot preserve the Constitution," he insisted, "it must perish, for it cannot be preserved by the judiciary. The only reliance in a popular government is the intelligence of the people."[36]

This was a strange paean to the people to come from such an

35. Fisher, *Trial of the Constitution*, 96; *Diary*, 496–497, April 27, May 5, 1864.
36. Fisher, *Trial of the Constitution*, 96–97.

elitist, but Fisher's understanding of parliamentary government diluted its force. One of the more attractive features of the British system was that members of Parliament were gentlemen, "the most intelligent, highly educated, critical, fastidious and thoroughly practical assembly of men on earth." In short, they were admirably like Sidney George Fisher. He admired popular rule as a theory supporting legislative sovereignty, not as a beneficent practice in itself.[37]

Armed with popular sovereignty and the British parliamentary model, Fisher had an impressive theoretical tool. It justified practically any increase in governmental vigor and did so within a recognizable legal tradition. "Unless the Government can be armed with sufficient power, *legal* as well as physical," he had argued, "neither the Constitution nor the nation can be preserved." Such power was now available.[38]

But Fisher was apparently not satisfied with these two liberators of government energies. He added to them the most potent justifier of all—a Lieberlike appeal to higher law. Expanding the range of legal options, he argued that "whatever the letter of the Constitution may be . . . whatever was the intention of the framers," natural law "invests every government with power to attain the ends of government, power to exercise its own necessary functions, power to satisfy the wants and demands of the people which can in no other way be satisfied." The embattled Union government was emphatically no exception.[39]

He seemed by such statements to free himself and the Union government from the shackles of an antiquated constitution. Yet, as though there were some unconscious commitment to the Constitution, Fisher was not content to reject it. He had somehow to show that not only natural law but even the Constitution itself justified the extra-constitutional actions he believed necessary for the survival of law and union. When he wrote *The Trial of the Constitution* in 1861–62, he presented both a view of a national charter proven inadequate for national survival and one which en-

37. *Ibid.*, 255–257.
38. *Ibid.*, 98, my italics.
39. Sidney G. Fisher, "A National Currency," *North American Review*, XCIX (July, 1864), 213.

compassed almost any innovative idea necessary to save the nation. His performance revealed the enormous hypnotic power of constitutionalism in American life. After arguing that the Constitution was inadequate to the existing crisis, that it was in major degree responsible for it, Fisher insisted that the Constitution justified the remedies necessary for national survival. After saying that the British Constitution was a better model for our government than was the American, he argued that the men who wrote our constitution were trying to copy the British.

He believed that the image of a union of states came from English society, where counties managed their own affairs and the king or Parliament handled national matters. Further development of the American system had come from the experience of colonial rule. The Constitution had created a nation essentially in the image of the British Empire. Our union was based on the same principles as those of the 1707 Act of Union between England and Scotland. Just as members of that union might not secede, so secession was impossible in this country. Fisher claimed that when Hamilton and Madison wrote the Federalist Papers in 1787–88, they were describing the same sort of government which Burke had described as existing in England in 1774. In short,

> our General Government is invested with the same power over the fact of Union, to preserve it or to dissolve it, that is possessed by an English Parliament. In its relation to the States, the General Government is placed in the same position that the British Government held to the Colonies, with this difference, that the people of the States are represented in the Federal Government whereas the Colonies were not represented in Parliament, the only grievance of which they complained.[40]

Fisher here expanded his argument outside fact and reason. The surest indication that the American idea of federalism was not that of the British was the fact that Americans had rejected the British idea in the revolution. If colonists had spoken of representation, they had also insisted (ultimately by revolting) on the right of nullification of repugnant imperial legislation. The Act of Union of 1707 did not represent conditions existing in America, a fact that

40. Fisher, *Trial of the Constitution*, 99–138.

Americans protested. The ultimate result of the British theory of
federalism had been a revolution. Now Fisher was trying to argue
that that theory was the one adopted by the Americans and that it
did not permit a revolution by the South.[41]

Fisher's historical analogy served his argument better than it
served the facts, but he was not writing a history of the Constitution. He was trying to convince Americans that their constitutional
traditions might serve them. He was seeking a useful, not an abso-
lutely honest, past. He recognized that his parliamentary solution to
national woes would not be acceptable as a substitute for the Constitution that men claimed to be defending. He therefore suggested
(convincing himself, if not others) that his solution conformed
perfectly to constitutional traditions.

Responding to an expected charge that he was proposing one
revolution to end another, Fisher insisted that the essential elements
of the existing constitutional system would not be endangered by his
proposed institutional change. Protection of the rights of states, for
example, would still exist even with the expansion in the Senate,
and the natural devotion of the people to their locality would preserve state functions and liberty. Even while insisting that states
should always yield to federal power, Fisher still described the
nation as "a union of States, sovereign within their appropriate
limits."[42]

He believed also that judiciary's role might properly be diminished within the Constitution. He called forth Madison and Story
to support his contention that the judiciary would have to bow to
majority will on political questions such as the conduct of a war,
taxation, regulation of commerce, and direction of foreign affairs.
He illustrated his idea of the Supreme Court's proper constitutional
role with the example of extreme legislation passed in a moment of
great crisis.

Suppose that, in response to overwhelming demand from the people, Congress should pass a law saying that the President should hold

41. Bernard Bailyn, *Ideological Origins of the American Revolution* (Cambridge, 1967), 198–229; Andrew C. McLaughlin, "The Background of American
Federalism," *Political Science Review*, XII (1918), 215; Bernard Knollenberg,
Origin of the American Revolution, 1759–66 (New York, 1960), 13, 157, 175.
42. Fisher, *Trial of the Constitution*, 65–66, 148–149.

office for life. Although this action would violate the words of the 1787 document, it should be accepted by the Court. The justices should declare that the primary responsibility for the safety of the nation rests with the legislature, and that it must have the power to provide that safety in any manner it believes necessary. Fisher believed that the proper role of the courts was simply "to carry out and apply to private rights the laws made by the Legislature, which is the creature of the ballot box."[43]

In Fisher's view there was simply no question that any action taken toward the end of saving the nation was constitutional. He insisted that the Court understand this fact and repudiate the constitutional nit-picking of its chief justice. "Shall all the laws but one go unenforced?" Lincoln had asked when Taney condemned his habeas corpus suspension. Fisher posed the question similarly: Shall the survival of the Constitution and the laws be threatened by judges who read the words but ignore the spirit of the nation's fundamental law? Not if Fisher could help it. "The Constitution itself, its declared purposes, its English models, its inherited principles, the opinion of its ablest founders and contemporary advocates and the eternal, immutable law of nature, on which all governments rest, say, that the Government of the Union itself has and must have unlimited power to preserve the Union and itself, through a future whose exigencies can neither be limited nor defined."[44]

Every act of Congress taken in the fight for the Union received Fisher's support. When legislators enacted the February, 1862, legal tender bill, opponents raised the plausible constitutional objections that the measure violated the obligation of contracts and transgressed the limits of congressional power. Fisher's reply rested on the necessity of the action to pay for the war and on his personal relief that the nation was apparently returning to the Hamiltonian principles which Andrew Jackson had defied in the service of states' rights principles.

In December, 1862, West Virginia applied for statehood. In a series of dubious proceedings the forty-eight western counties of

43. *Ibid.*, 69, 81–85.
44. *Ibid.*, 145; Fisher, "National Currency," 206, 228–229; Basler, ed., *Collected Works of Lincoln*, IV, 430. Lincoln's exact words were, "Are all the laws, but one, to go unexecuted, and the government itself go to pieces, lest that one be violated?"

Virginia had repudiated the state's secession ordinance and created
a new state government which agreed to the formation of a state
within its borders, i.e., "Virginia" agreed to part with the forty-
eight counties so that they could become West Virginia. It was a
situation similar to the Confederate government's claiming to be the
real government of the United States and then agreeing that the
eleven southern states might become a new nation. As mentioned
above, the formation of this new state was justifiable in terms of
strict constitutional logic, but it actually had little reality to recom-
mend it. Thaddeus Stevens admitted: "We may admit West Virginia . . . under our absolute power which the laws of war give us. . . .
I shall vote for this bill upon that theory, and upon that alone; for
I will not stultify myself by supposing that we have any warrant
in the Constitution for this proceeding." Fisher concurred, "The
Constitution in this case [is] obliged to yield to necessity."[45]

Even when he agreed with Roger Taney, he managed to justify
the exercise of national power in the Union-saving effort. When
Lincoln suspended the privilege of the writ of habeas corpus in
Maryland, the Chief Justice argued that suspension was a congressional prerogative and that Lincoln's action portended tyranny.
Defenders of the President accepted this ground for argument and
insisted on executive, not legislative, power over suspension. But
Fisher agreed with Taney as to the locus of this power. The remedy
for Lincoln's act was simple, however: Congress might constitu-
tionlize the unconstitutional by passing a bill ratifying presidential
suspension, indemnifying those persons responsible for arrests, and
declaring the suspension of the privilege of the writ for the duration
of the war. It was an eminently practical solution to a problem
which had agitated the legal profession for almost three years. It
accorded with Lincoln's expressed wishes and was echoed by historian George Bancroft a year later, on February 20, 1863. On
March 3, 1863, Congress took almost precisely this course.[46]

Faced with a situation in which power was the prerequisite for

45. *Congressional Globe*, 37th Cong., 3rd sess., pp. 50–51; Fisher, "National Currency," 204–245; *Diary*, 443–444, 460–461; Dec. 12, 1862; Sept. 16, 1863.

46. Fisher, *Trial of the Constitution*, 230–248; Randall, *Constitutional Problems
under Lincoln*, 186–214; Basler, ed., *Collected Works of Lincoln*, IV, 429; Williams,
"Northern Intellectual Reaction to Military Rule during the Civil War," 339.

national survival, Fisher created a remarkable argument which increased national power to almost unlimited dimensions. Although he argued for its constitutionality, his theory defied traditional constitutional scruples. But he was untroubled by this fact, for to him the idea that an instrument creating a nation might be used to destroy it defied reason and nature. Power was necessary to save the Union and the Constitution; therefore the power that was available might be exercised constitutionally. War could be lawfully waged so that the laws would be obeyed both north and south of the Mason-Dixon Line, so that order would be preserved in New York as well as in Richmond, in Philadelphia as well as in Charleston.

Sidney George Fisher II:
Racism and National Power

In the British model Fisher had discovered constitutional justification for federal efforts to save the Union. He had found a power vast in scope and all the more potent because it was lawful, not simply naked, power. However, his eagerness to concede, create, and justify federal power had one exception. It did not extend to the question of emancipation. This question was too complex; it touched too many of Fisher's prejudices to allow his usual sweeping assertions of federal power. It involved his profound belief in the basic inferiority of the Negro and his great fear of the black race's power to weaken and destroy white society.

Even while recognizing the fact that the war would profoundly affect slavery and might end it, he could not erase from his mind the image of "this conquering negro race . . . so formidable because of its weakness, its unteachable ignorance, its tame docility." The black man had "the power to blight morals, to unnerve industry, to wither the intellect, and to blast, like the sirocco of its native deserts, the fair promises of culture and civilization." Contact with Negroes was the cause of the South's degradation, both because of the evil effects of race-mixing and because this "inferior race must in some way be held in subjection [by] irresponsible power, with all its baneful moral effects." Enslaved by the need to be tyrants, Southerners created a society marked by "a rank growth of cruelty . . . arrogance, pride, sensuality, and sloth."[1]

This image of the South once led him to contemplate the possibility of ousting that region from the Union after the rule of law had been guaranteed by putting down secession. After all, he reasoned, the South was behind the North in industry, intellect, and

1. Fisher, *Trial of the Constitution*, 361–362, 274–275.

morals. Would it not benefit the nation to be free from this incubus which could only drain strength from the North and might, ominously, draw blacks northward? However, Fisher dropped this idea as the war progressed.

But the slavery question would not die. The war inexorably imposed the question of what should be done with the institution. Despite his racism, Fisher recognized that slavery had caused the war. The South had seceded to protect a society founded on bondage, and the North had become angered to the point of violence by southern attacks on northern liberties. He believed, however, that the peculiar form of American slavery was the cause of the disunion crisis. The inequality of the two races made slavery per se a natural solution to the dangers of interracial encounters—but the great fault of the South was that it failed to recognize that slavery was a relationship between men, not between men and property. Had the South only ameliorated the conditions of slavery, it would not have provoked the humanitarian outcry against it. Southerners would not have provided fuel for abolitionist fire, nor would they have felt the need to infringe on northern rights in order to protect their own.

Yet even the beginning of the war did not end the possibility of southern repentance, in Fisher's opinion. As he wrote *Trial of the Constitution* in 1861 and 1862, he suggested that, if the South reformed its attitudes toward slavery while still preserving the institution, the war would stop and a new nation would be born. It was an unrealistic suggestion, of course. The South naturally refused, as it had before the war, to make slavery its own local problem. Having made a rebellion to protect its form of slavery, it was hardly likely that the Confederacy would seek reconciliation on the terms he proposed. It therefore remained necessary for the North to try to solve a problem which Southerners would not and could not solve for themselves.

Fisher found Lincoln's compensated emancipation proposal to be the best northern solution offered in the early war years. The President urged that slave states free their bondsmen and that federal and state government join in compensating slaveowners for their loses. States might delay granting freedom until 1900; if freedmen would go willingly, they were even to be colonized abroad. Displaying amazing constitutional scruples for a man arguing that Congress ought to act like Parliament, Fisher felt that this proposal went as far as the Constitution allowed. It respected the states' rights to control their domestic institutions, and he believed that it would recognize the states' right to control the new freedmen. They would be allowed to pass laws necessary to keep Negroes at work, making sure that they did not become "lazy lazzaroni, a mass of ignorance, pauperism and crime."[2]

Yet Congress rejected Lincoln's plan, as Fisher had feared. The rejection provoked him to greater consideration of the war and human bondage. Feeling that the nation could not and should not use war powers to emancipate, he was still haunted by a vision: a black army standing behind rebel forces in the field. Docile workers were manufacturing the provisions which allowed Confederate soldiers to kill Union soldiers so that slavery might be preserved. He began to doubt that union and slavery were compatible. Maybe abolitionists were right—maybe slavery would have to be destroyed so that union might survive. The section of *Trial* dealing with slavery is practically a debate between his views on the compatibility of slavery and union. As such, it mirrors changes in northern thought being wrought by the war.

Fisher ultimately reached the conclusion of the northern majority: slavery, being the cause of the war and the main prop of the Confederacy, would have to die in the struggle. Yet he did not foresee a sudden death. He proposed that existing property in slaves be protected, but that all children of slaves born after a certain date be considered free. Those persons still enslaved would be given certain rights as men, though still remaining under state control. He suggested that a constitutional amendment to this effect be passed and that, as a condition of returning to the Union, southern states would have to accept the amendment.[3]

That was before September 22, 1862, when Lincoln issued the preliminary emancipation proclamation. Fisher responded happily to this measure. The vision of that black army haunted him again, and he could see no reason why the Union government might not weaken the South in any way possible. He had concluded that the

2. *Ibid.*, 342–344, 297–309.
3. *Ibid.*, 307–309, 314–315.

laws of war might justify emancipation as a measure to save the Union. If the South truly cared for slavery, then the measure might end the war without further bloodshed.

But Fisher's support for Lincoln's proposal had little relevance to the question of the black man's condition. He supported the proclamation not because it would help Negroes gain their freedom, but because it would help whites preserve their union. What intrigued him was the question of national power to emancipate, not the humanitarian results of emancipation. Like Joel Parker and Lincoln, Fisher insisted that "the Proclamation . . . is strictly a military measure, applicable only to public enemies in time of war, and does not touch the question of slavery under the Constitution in any State subject to its authority and entitled to its protection."[4]

What would happen to slavery after the conditions of war no longer applied? He may have hoped that the earlier proposal of emancipation and amelioration of chattel slavery would be applied. He did not say in 1862. But over a year after the preliminary proclamation was issued, Fisher wrote "The Bible and Slavery" for the *North American Review*. Here he trotted out the same argument he had previously made—that even though blacks were obviously inferior, they ought to be treated like men, even while they were slaves. Relying heavily on the arguments of the British writer Goldwin Smith, Fisher insisted that the only form of servitude sanctioned by the Bible was that which recognized that slaves were not simply chattel.

The Philadelphian's article was a strange performance. Published in January, 1864, it never mentioned the Emancipation Proclamation, which was a year old at the time. Fisher rambled on about the history of slavery and laws of nature. He wearied his readers with the views of Moses, Jesus, St. Paul, Egyptians, Hindus, Persians, Greeks, and Romans. He even spoke of a war that was changing the face of American thought and society, of "the collision of free thought, stimulated by great events and the jeopardy of great interests, hoary prejudices, and forms whose use has past, [which] may be destroyed, as decayed trees of the forest are prostrated by a tempest to make room for new growth." Yet Fisher's commitment to the inferiority of Negroes was so strong that he could not write

4. *Ibid.*, 361–373; Basler, ed., *Collected Works of Lincoln*, VI, 29, 428.

this article on any other foundation than the thought that slavery was going to endure; the South needed to treat slaves with the same humanity that the Bible demonstrated, not to free them.[5]

Fisher hoped (indeed, insisted) that the war would stimulate new thought and encourage more advanced views of governmental powers. He engaged himself in part of this mind-expanding process. In its view of separation of powers *Trial of the Constitution* was at least thirty years ahead of its time. Fisher's assertion of national power was among the most extreme of the war years. Yet in matters involving race, his thought moved much more slowly.

It was not that he was unaware that minds were changing on the slavery question. One fall evening in 1863 the noted abolitionist Miller McKim visited the Fishers and spent the evening discussing his favorite subject. Though impressed by McKim, Fisher was much more struck by the fact that any antislavery extremist should even have visited:

> The time was when a visit from him would have been very unwelcome to us, but the war has changed our notions in regard to slavery and like most others, if we are not abolitionists, in the old sense, we are emancipationists and wish to see slavery destroyed since it has attempted to destroy the nation. . . . The term "abolitionist" has ceased to be one of reproach.

Five days later he began his article on "The Bible and Slavery."[6]

Although Fisher might privately entertain the possibility of continuing slavery, by the spring of 1864 the institution's survival had become a practical impossibility. In April the Senate had adopted what would become the Thirteenth Amendment. The House failed to provide the required two-thirds majority for passage, but that clearly would come with the next election. The Republican party had renominated Lincoln, and in his acceptance the Chief Executive had paid special attention to the platform's call for an abolition amendment. Clearly this idea's time had come.[7]

5. Sidney George Fisher, "The Bible and Slavery," *North American Review*, XCVIII (Jan., 1864), 48–74; Goldwin Smith, *Does the Bible Sanction American Slavery?* (Cambridge, 1863); *Diary*, 462, 465; Nov. 1, 1863; Jan. 2, 1864.

6. *Diary*, 462, Oct. 27, Nov. 1, 1863.

7. McPherson, *The Struggle for Equality*, 126–127; Basler, ed., *Collected Works of Lincoln*, VII, 380.

Aiding its arrival were public constitutional discussions which convinced the doubtful that this humanitarian goal had legal legitimacy. Fisher's public writings show a growing conviction on the subject, which probably helped convince others. Arguing for national power to save the Union, defending the legality of the Emancipation Proclamation as a war measure, he had learned by early summer of 1864 that slavery could not just be the concern of southern states and that states' rights would have to yield to federal power. In 1862 he argued that southern states were the sole legal guardians of a slave's future. By 1864 he was urging the possibility that the founding fathers had seen some things as local which had become national. These subjects were "thus withdrawn from State power into the province of national power." This was eminently the case with slavery: "Regarded at first as local in its nature, it afterwards grew to be a gigantic interest and influence, affecting all other interests, claiming to rule the nation, and failing that, attempting to destroy it. Rightfully, therefore, does the central power consider slavery now within its proper sphere, and take possession of it and govern it."[8]

However, even while accepting the idea that federal power would have to be exerted to deal with slavery, Fisher had not changed his belief in Negro inferiority. The extent to which that power would be exercised was still in question, and Fisher showed no disposition to agree with abolitionists who insisted that the power to free the slave implied the necessity to guarantee him equality. Although he had supported Lincoln, he was afraid that the President's victory in 1864 might encourage the extremists in the Republican party. When he heard that such radical, pro-abolition sentiment was taking over the Union League, he reversed his earlier decision to join. When James Russell Lowell suggested in April, 1865, that blacks be given the vote, Fisher's elitist racism flashed. He commented in his diary, "The absurd plan gains many supporters. The abolitionists cannot bear to lose so fruitful a theme of excitement as the position of the Negro race, so that now, having emancipated him, they propose going a step farther by granting him political power." Most thinking men already believed that universal suffrage, marked by "the ignorance and recklessness of the mob," was "the chief source of

8. Fisher, "National Currency," 230–231.

danger to our government." And yet "these fanatics wish to add the mass of abject and degraded Negro population to make, what was already bad enough, a great deal worse."[9]

Such prejudice did not diminish his belief that federal power might be used constitutionally in slave-related questions. Whether black men were inferior or not, they were still the subject of federal, not local power. Thus though Fisher's racial views were those of many hardened southern slaveowners, his belief in federal power placed him in a much more radical camp—alongside the very radicals whose excessive egalitarian zeal deeply disturbed him.

This was a position shared by many Northerners. They were discomforted by abolitionists' egalitarian demands, for they believed that Negroes were biologically inferior. But the question of power to act on behalf of their interests seemed largely resolved by the war. The major question concerned the extent to which this power might be limited by those traditional constitutional restraints unchanged by war; and that would have to be resolved when disunion was crushed and emancipation realized. If they listened to Fisher, they would conclude that federal power had few restraints—that, since the war made the use of power imperative, the Constitution made it legal.[10]

Although apparently agreeing in sentiment with Fisher's view, the wartime Congress did not adopt the parliamentary model which he urged. Indeed, there was little need to do so. The President was not Buchanan, shackled to a frightened and threatening South, seeking to reconcile the irreconcilable. The President was Lincoln, marshaling the North in support of an enormously popular cause, leading an essentially unified section whose disputes were resolvable within existing political and constitutional institutions. Congress and President usually worked together; neither usurped power.[11]

9. *Diary*, 456, 487–488, 491; July 8, 1863; Nov. 9, 1864; April 11, 1865. James Russell Lowell, "Reconstruction," *North American Review*, C (April, 1865), 540–559.

10. Fisher, *Trial of the Constitution*, 60–63. On northern beliefs about Negro inferiority, see Leon Litwack, *North of Slavery: The Negro in the Free States, 1790–1860* (Chicago, 1961); Stanton, *The Leopard's Spots*; C. Vann Woodward, "Seeds of Failure in Radical Race Policy," *New Frontiers of American Reconstruction*, ed. Hyman, 123–147.

11. Trefousse, *The Radical Republicans*; Belz, *Reconstructing the Union*; David

If anything, contrary to Fisher's philosophical inclinations, it was the President who showed the most initiative while congressmen debated alternatives or even refused to legislate on sensitive issues. This was especially the case at first, when Lincoln called the nation to war even before Congress had assembled. The legislative branch was hardly Parliament, while the executive was attacked in some quarters as a potential tyrant.[12]

At variance with Fisher's philosophy, Lincoln's efforts nevertheless conformed to the theorist's desire for quick action to save the Union. He reconciled the two in his own mind by the hopeful suggestion that Lincoln might prove to be an American Cromwell. He might rescue his nation from turmoil and while doing so suggest that a future powerful executive might be less trustworthy. Perhaps Congress would be encouraged to do what Parliament had done: take the power which logically and constitutionally was theirs.[13] Both Lincoln and Congress did very well without following this suggestion.

Similarly, the Supreme Court failed to conform to the fears Fisher expressed in writing *Trial of the Constitution*. The book was the product of the author's dismay at a constitutional system apparently incapable of preserving the nation. He struck out at those institutions which had contributed to the disaster, especially a Supreme Court tarred with the brush of *Dred Scott* and *Merryman*. He concluded that the Court could not be trusted to play any but an obstructionist role to the needs of the nation. This conclusion proved wrong. The Court, after *Merryman*, supported the fight for the Union. It did the very thing that Fisher was trying to do: it constitutionalized acts of war necessity. The decision in the *Prize* cases

Donald, "Devils Facing Zionwards," *Grant, Lee, Lincoln and the Radicals*, ed. Grady McWhiney (Evanston, 1964), 72–91; David Donald, "The Radicals and Lincoln," *Lincoln Reconsidered* (New York, 1947), 103–127. These essays are in reply to T. Harry Williams, *Lincoln and the Radicals* (Madison, 1941). Williams has moderated his view of the bitterness between radicals and Lincoln in an essay in the volume edited by McWhiney, "Lincoln and the Radicals," 92–117.

12. See chapters on Joel Parker; also the Democratic party press of the North during the Civil War, especially the *New York World*, *New York Sun*, and midwestern Copperhead papers such as the *Columbus Crisis*. See also *Ex parte Merryman*, 17 *Federal Cases* 144.

13. Fisher, *Trial of the Constitution*, 235, 240–242; *Diary*, 415, Jan. 13, 1862; Riker, "Sidney George Fisher and the Separation of Powers," 409.

gave legitimacy to the acts required at the war's beginning, and then offered a usefully ambiguous view of the constitutional nature of the war. Faced with the opportunity to disrupt the policy of arbitrary arrests, the Court sensitively decided that it could not accept jurisdiction of such cases as that of Copperhead leader Clement Vallandigham. Only after Appomattox did the judges challenge the policy of military arrest and trial.[14]

This disparity between Fisher's theories and the logic of events suggests that his unique call for an end to the tradition of separation of powers gained little notice. What attracted reviewers was the book's insistence that national survival and prosperity depended on more than a passive reverence for a rigid constitution. "Why could we not have had such books as this while they might have been of avail in averting our present calamities?" wrote the *North American Review*. The work would have dispelled the blind confidence in the Constitution which had led to war. But even during the conflict, the reviewer continued, there was much to be learned from Fisher. The most important message was that "war develops hitherto hidden power in our national structure [and that the nation] cannot survive its existing perils without being, through their instrumentality, strengthened and purified for a long and glorious future." The *American Law Register* agreed. The book was filled with "thoughtful and liberal patriotism . . . that demands the most attentive consideration."[15]

Whatever attention the book attracted was not reflected in sales. Two years after publication, Fisher still had 450 copies of the original 1,000. The book was certainly not a light evening's entertainment, and it does not appear that the publisher, Lippincott, pushed it aggressively. Fisher was naturally disappointed in the

---

14. Fisher, *Trial of the Constitution*, 87–90; *Prize* cases, 2 Black 635; *Ex parte Vallandigham*, 1 *Wallace* 243. After the war in the *Milligan* case (4 *Wallace* 2) the court took up the same question that it had refused to settle in the *Vallandigham* case and invalidated the conviction of Lambert Milligan. Here was an obvious demonstration of political sensitivity by the high bench. Writing in 1861–62, Fisher was unaware of the two cases.

15. *North American Review*, XCVI (April, 1863), 576–577; *American Law Register*, XII (1863–64), 767–768. Timothy Farrar, "Trial of the Constitution," *North American Review*, XCVII (Oct., 1863), 338–372, does not discuss Fisher's book at all, despite the title.

sales. Aside from the usual author's egotistical interest, he had hoped to make some money on the volume to offset losses on his farm. But *Trial* was hardly the sort of work that would inspire a public buying spree. A long essay in political theory, it attacked a philosophy of government that lay in the past and supported with scholarly prose an ideology which necessity had made almost commonplace.

However, Fisher's wartime ideas are not important because of his precocious rejection of the tradition of the separation of powers or because the North listened to or ignored him. They warrant study because they clarify the implicit paradox in the encounter of three facts. Power was discovered in the Constitution to save the Union. The northern majority recognized that emancipation was crucial to that salvation. These same people had an unshakable belief in the irredeemable inferiority of the Negro race. Our focus should rest on the reflective, not the directive nature of Fisher's thought.

In clarifying this encounter, the theorist's ideas reveal the ease with which Americans, facing a crisis in which the Constitution had apparently failed, were able to revivify that Constitution to legitimize the salvation of the Union. Fisher's work shows how far a man could go to find constitutional power to preserve the nation. He went far indeed—he was able to assert that a constitution written by Americans not four years free of Britain was intended to incorporate the British Constitution! Only when the question of emancipation arose did he hesitate. The hesitation was ominous in its forecasting of the future, but it was only temporary.

The particular solution that Fisher suggested, complete legislative sovereignty, is less noteworthy than the flexibility he discovered in a constitution apparently moribund. The unity shown by the three branches of government, driven together by the crisis, made his suggestion only interesting. Fisher himself was untroubled by the federal government's failure to conform to his model. He was delighted that the conditions of the secession winter which had spawned his 1862 argument no longer existed.[16]

16. Fisher's diary makes only one mention of the relationship between the actions of Congress and his desire that the body take up a parliamentary role. See *Diary*, 461, Sept. 16, 1863. He thought in that instance that Congress had done what he suggested in regard to passing a law which legalized Lincoln's suspension

But after April 15, 1865, conditions changed. Echoes of the pre-war crisis sounded. The fundamental harmony between branches of government vanished, and popular will was again stifled by an executive espousing southern ideology. Made president by the act of an assassin, Andrew Johnson soon began to act and speak like the people's chosen tribune. He initiated a reconstruction policy which imposed minimum conditions for the return of the defeated South. Under Johnson's plan former Confederate leaders would have been seated in Congress less than a year after the bloodshed of civil war had ended. His policy would have left southern Negroes free of their chains but devoid of the protection which their loyalty to the Union demanded. Not surprisingly, Johnson's ideas infuriated even the more moderate members of a Republican Congress which believed that its mandate from the people was as clear as the President's was dubious.[17]

The Reconstruction years resounded to the clash between the executive and the legislature. The struggle was won by Congress, largely because it discovered the constitutional power to exert its will despite presidential objections. *Trial of the Constitution*, written in 1862, describing conditions in 1860, actually is most illuminating in its description of the theory which Congress adopted by 1867. As proof of this assertion we have the direct testimony of a participant in the postwar quarrel.

In March, 1866, the struggle between Johnson and Congress was beginning to heat up. The Chief Executive had vetoed the Freedmen's Bureau bill in mid-February; three days later he celebrated Washington's birthday with an hour-and-a-half harangue in which he attacked congressmen by name, compared himself to Jesus, and suggested that radical legislators sought his assassination. The veto message had strongly intimated Johnson's belief that the President alone had responsibility for reconstructing the South and that Congress's sole duty was to seat delegates when he declared them en-

---

of the writ. Other than that, he remained mute about how well Congress was conforming to his theorizing. He continued to be pleased, however, with the way in which the war was proving to be a nationalizing experience. See *Diary*, 490, April 5, 1865.

17. McKitrick, *Andrew Johnson and Reconstruction*; Brock, *American Crisis*; Lawanda Cox and John Cox, *Politics, Principle and Prejudice, 1865-66*.

titled to representation. He had also raised the question of whether a president elected by all the people might be a better executor of the public will than a congress chosen from local districts. It was a surprising assertion for a president who had not been elected to that office, but it provoked Congress to consider the source of its power.[18]

Shortly after the veto message Pennsylvania congressman William D. Kelley visited the Philadelphia area and met Fisher. They exchanged political conversation for a while; Kelley mentioned that he was a great admirer of the author's work. As Fisher reported it, the congressman said that "he regarded *The Trial of the Constitution* as next to DeTocqueville's the best work on American institutions ever written." Fisher was delighted. He told Kelley that he had a few copies on hand; would the congressman like a dozen? Yes, Kelley replied, he would. He thought he could place them where they would be appreciated.

A year later, Kelley returned to Philadelphia to lecture on the efforts of the Thirty-ninth Congress. In 1862, he said, a Philadelphia citizen had published "a most remarkable book entitled *The Trial of the Constitution*, and he who will read that work will find incorporated in it the philosophy that pervaded the 39th Congress. In that work is embodied in elegant style all the theories that enabled Congress to grapple all the subjects and bring the country through safe."[19]

The implications of Kelley's statement are, of course, tantalizing. On one hand he seems to suggest that *Trial* was a guidebook for legislators. On the other it is possible that he meant simply that the work mirrored the effort of Congress and provided a theory by which outsiders might understand what Congress had wrought. Although I am naturally tempted to claim for Fisher some determining role, the evidence for such a possibility has just been presented—Kelley's statement.

It is possible that some congressmen read copies of the book which the Pennsylvania congressman seems to have provided. But I have not discovered any legislator who suggested that Fisher had provided a theory which would justify what they wanted to do.

18. McKitrick, *Andrew Johnson and Reconstruction*, 288–292.
19. *Diary*, 511, 526–527; March 15, 1866; March 25, 27, 1867.

Kelley himself did not mention the author in any Reconstruction speech in the year between their meetings.

It is probable that no one needed to read a book to see what the circumstances required. The President had adopted a policy which became increasingly unpopular throughout the North. Blatant and bloody evidence showed that Johnson's reconstruction methods did not increase loyalty in Dixie. They did not even provide simple security for those who had supported the Union cause. Individual and mob violence occurred frequently. At a time when men believed they had gained peace, there was no peace. Legislators therefore had the not too difficult choice of seeking harmony between Congress and the President, or listening to the people who had elected them.[20]

In the process of choosing the obvious alternative, they came very close to establishing legislative supremacy on the British model. They gave to a joint congressional committee power to determine Reconstruction policy—a broad mandate, considering the times. By ousting a pro-Johnson senator, Congress secured for itself the two-thirds majority necessary to override presidential vetoes. The Tenure of Office bill was passed to make officeholders more subject to legislative than to executive will. Congress wrestled with Johnson for control of the Reconstruction army. Ultimately, of course, they impeached and almost convicted him. As the British historian W. R. Brock suggests, "The adoption of something akin to the British parliamentary system was not so remote or impossible as has usually been imagined; the instruments were at hand. . . ."

But, as Brock adds, "The principle was rejected." As it had during the war, Congress refused to be Parliament. Legislators still respected the constitutional system secured by war. During debate on the Tenure of Office bill, Senator Timothy Howe was ignored when he suggested that Congress follow clearly the British cabinet model. His colleagues continued the discussion, citing only American constitutional precedents. Legislators continued to respect judicial institutions, despite their occasional outbursts against the Supreme Court. Congress was generally aware of the weaknesses of the

20. McKitrick, *Andrew Johnson and Reconstruction*, 422–427; John A. Carpenter, "Atrocities in the Reconstruction Period," *Journal of Negro History*, XLVII (Oct., 1962), 234–247.

British system, even while emulating some of its facets. It was well understood that what one legislative majority might do another could repeal. Amendments to the Constitution supplemented ordinary legislation to secure Congress's Reconstruction goals.[21]

In the battle between Johnson and Congress some legislators might have gained insight into the process that engaged them by reading Fisher's book. But it is more likely that even here the author's importance rests on the fact that he sensed a theoretical necessity to which experience would give life. His work clarifies the nature of the postwar encounter, even though it seems not to have influenced it.

As for Fisher himself, he was troubled by the postwar era. Declining income and worsening health deepened his anxiety about the world around him. Most troubling was an apparent decay in the fabric of society. The vulgar values of the common man seemed to be replacing a serious concern for the quality of state and society. There is a Henry Adams feeling about Fisher in the years from 1865 to his death in 1871. One senses a growing dismay that the best men were losing influence; their ability to affect society was passing away, and society itself seemed out of control.

Crime and disorder seemed to be increasing. For a long time there seemed to be two burglaries a night in his area; once Fisher's own house was broken into. The local government would not increase the size of the police force, and law-abiding citizens remained helpless. He was sure that the police were working with the criminals. Given the national example, he was not surprised. Bribed legislatures and venal politicians abounded. The temper of the times was best revealed, he thought, by the fact that a New York journal, *The Imperialist*, frankly advocated revolution and the establishment of an hereditary monarchy. That was a little extreme for Fisher, but he was alarmed by a world which no one worthy of respect seemed able to control.[22]

The burgeoning influence and irresponsibility of industrial corporations seemed to be part of this process. The responsible citizen

21. *Congressional Globe*, 39th Cong., 2nd sess., p. 383; Brock, *American Crisis*, 259.

22. *Diary*, 520, 533, 550, 557; May 16, 1869; Nov. 5, 1866; March 4, 1870; Oct. 9, 1867.

(indeed, everyone) was victimized by their conscienceless negligence. Fisher was especially appalled by the increasing number of railroad accidents; they seemed unpreventable because no one could call the railroads to account. These industrial giants were wealthy enough to bribe state legislatures into inaction, and the national extent of the rail network militated against effective piecemeal regulation.

National regulation of the railroads stood twenty-two years in the future, but already Fisher held two views which would later provoke the creation of the Interstate Commerce Commission. He was outraged at the power of these "soulless corporations," and, more important, he had resolved any doubts about the constitutionality of federal action in any sphere where he thought it necessary.[23]

He insisted that Congress should pass a law requiring railroads to provide a fixed sum of money to compensate accident victims. The money would be paid without any trial or investigative procedure to determine who was at fault. In effect, the railroad's funds were to be consigned by Congress to any person who could prove injury from an encounter with a train. However, just in the abstract, this suggestion came dangerously close to a deprivation of property without even procedural due process. It was remarkably like that ultimate assertion of legislative power which even the most tolerant supporters of state police powers declared they would oppose: a law which gave A's propery to B.[24]

Fisher was a firm believer in property rights, but his belief was the product of a society that was passing away. He seems to have envisioned a world in which the individual owner served the society whose laws protected his wealth. Such a man knew that his own

23. *Ibid.*, 521–522, Dec. 10, 1866; Sidney George Fisher, "Duties on Exports," *North American Review*, CI (July, 1865), 157–162; Sidney George Fisher, "The National Highways," *Nation*, I (Oct. 5, Nov. 16, 1865) 424–425, 616–617; II (Jan. 4, 1866), 8–9.

24. "National Highways," *Nation*, II, 8–9; *Wilkinson* v. *Leland*, 2 *Peters* 627 (1829); *Loan Association* v. *Topeka*, 20 *Wallace* 655 (1875); Alfred H. Kelly and Winfred Harbison, *The American Constitution*, 496–520, discusses the growth of constitutional law away from the attitude that Fisher displayed here, toward increased protection of corporate property. Of course, Fisher may have been simply insisting on applying strict tort liability to all railroad-pedestrian accidents.

actions influenced events, and he was checked from irresponsible action by his personal code of honor. He believed and lived the words of Francis Lieber: "No right without its responsibilities, no responsibility without its rights." But the corporation had no conscience. Because of its form, it could feel no responsibility. It simply claimed a right—the right to do what it wished. It might rampage unchecked across the whole society, leaving in its wake angry opponents who felt equally free from any responsibility save to themselves. The resulting clash between the two seemed ominous for a stable nation.

Society was not simply veering out of control at its upper level; its lower reaches seemed equally threatening. Fisher's doubts about democracy were furthered by increasing labor militance, as well as by a rising crime wave. The eight-hour-day movement seemed especially foreboding. The folly of its leadership was shown, he felt, by its startling ignorance of natural economic laws of wages and supply and demand. No man could safely interfere with the economic process by limiting hours of work. The only result of such action would be a reduction in the amount of goods available for sale, a consequent reduction in capital, and a lowering of wages. Fisher's great fear was that such uninformed men might come to dictate economic policy. Once such a calamity occurred, "the time [was] not far distant when all things will be in common, and grass grow in Broadway."[25]

This economic heresy was only one manifestation of the fearful growth of the power of the all too common people. Quality political leadership seemed awash in an ocean of corruption and incompetence. He placed most of the responsibility for this in the hands of venal politicians who controlled the nominating process and thus sent into office a gang of "gamblers and pugilists, drunkards and criminals."

Fisher suggested an alternative, a means to bring the control of politics back into the hands of men whose birth, wealth, and intellect prepared them for honest leadership. Admitting that the majority occasionally managed to secure worthy leaders, he wanted to make sure that such quality was not the exception. His solution was the

25. Sidney George Fisher, "The Eight-Hour Movement," *Nation*, I (Oct. 26, 1865), 517–518.

passage of a law establishing elected boards of nominators who would select candidates to run for office. Membership qualifications for these boards insured patrician dominance: "a native born American citizen of the white race, not less than forty years of age, educated according to a standard fixed by law, and possessive of an amount of income or property sufficient to elevate him above the class working for wages." Predicting the sentiments which would help spawn the 1872 Liberal Republican movement, Fisher hoped that such electoral reform would stabilize an excessively democratic society. He mirrored exactly the later words of Carl Schurz: "We want a government which the best people of this country will be proud of."[26]

This central core of Fisher's thought—a passion for stability and order—naturally controlled his response to the immensely complicated and ultimately tragic dilemma of Reconstruction. In responding as he did, he revealed the source of the North's, and the Negro's, inevitably hollow victory. Simply stated, the dilemma was this: safe and secure reconstruction apparently required an unprecedented peacetime outreach of national power to protect an apparently inferior race recently freed from two hundred years of spirit-crushing bondage.

When the Civil War ended, most Northerners would have welcomed a mild and early reconstruction. Some radicals demanded vengeance and severe measures, but the predominant sentiment was for leniency. The South simply had to demonstrate its loyalty to the sort of union for which victorious Northerners had fought. The victors had learned in the war to connect the condition of the Union with the condition of southern blacks. Slavery had caused the war, and the death of slavery had helped end the war. The way in which the South treated the former slaves would signal the extent of southern loyalty. Given the strong desire for "normalcy," it is most likely that the South could have satisfied northern opinion by ratifying the Thirteenth Amendment, repudiating secession, and acquiescing in the exercise by blacks of civil, but not political, rights.[27]

26. Sidney George Fisher, "Nominating Conventions," *North American Review*, CVI (Jan., 1868), 233–246; *Diary*, 503, Oct. 8, 1865; Schurz quoted in Eric F. Goldman, *Rendezvous with Destiny* (New York, 1956), 20.

27. McKitrick, *Andrew Johnson and Reconstruction*, 15–41, 153–213.

It did the first reluctantly, the second with infuriating equivoca-
tion, and the third not at all. Many of the southern "black codes"
seemed a reimposition of slavery, and the brutality practiced against
the freedmen served to amplify this impression. All these things
served to convince the North that there was practically no white
loyalty in Dixie. The obvious recourse was to counterbalance white
disloyalty with the loyalty which the freedmen would offer. Successful reconstruction would depend on how the North would be
willing to act to protect and secure that loyalty.[28]

A proper conjunction of attitudes would have guaranteed success.
If one could believe that the war had expanded the constitutional
power of the federal government beyond significant limitation, there
would exist the means of producing any desired result. If, in addition, it were possible to view the Negro as the white man's equal,
there would be an unshakable determination to employ those means.
Federal power would insure equality; loyal blacks would exercise
their liberties to produce a loyal South and thus a secure Union.[29]

Few Americans held either opinion securely. A rare statesman like
Charles Sumner might do so, but for most it had taken the pressures
of war to engender attitudes which provided the opportunity for
action facing them in 1866. And the manner by which they had
arrived there portended an ultimately tragic result. Focusing on
Fisher's experience, we can understand why this was so.

During the war Fisher had discovered an immensely permissive
constitution, one which even allowed emancipation. But the slaves
had gained their freedom only when it became evident that the
death of slavery was required to preserve the Union and the ordered
society which union guaranteed. Then for a season Fisher and those
like him overcame their racism in the service of their fear of anarchy.
After Appomattox it was evident again that the black man's freedom
was still the necessary instrument of a secure Union. As long as the

28. *Ibid.*, 153–213; *Documentary History of Reconstruction*, ed. Walter Fleming (New York, 1966), I, 273–314.

29. On the other hand, if successful Reconstruction is defined as the quickest
possible return of the South to its position in the Union, then another set of attitudes would have merit. A belief that Negroes were congenitally inferior, linked
to the idea that the war had not changed the relations between nation and state,
would provide the best foundation for immediate restoration. For Andrew Johnson the problem was as simple as it was for Charles Sumner.

cause of the Negro could be linked to preserving that security and the order it represented, blacks might hope for national protection. To this extent the "bloody shirt" was the Negroes' most sturdy shield.

But racism lurked always in the wings—an incurable belief that blacks were irresponsible, basically lazy, predominantly ignorant, and much less trustworthy than whites (with the possible exception of the Irish). Given this attitude, it was possible that belief in expanded constitutional power to protect freedmen might be overcome by the very commitment to order which had called it forth.

There were many ominous elements of disorder in the Reconstruction struggle. The quarrel between Congress and the President occasionally became so heated that many feared revolution in Washington. Southern riots and individual acts of violence demonstrated the bitter tenacity with which Southerners would fight to protect their caste system. Fisher became more and more worried as the South demonstrated the cost to the North of promoting its vision of loyalty. He feared that Reconstruction might produce the ironic picture of northern unionists forcefully subduing the very section whose return to the Union they sought. This would involve more than the simple passage of a federal law; he believed it would require "an exertion of the power of the general government as would be inconsistent with its plan and theory." [30]

But the most disturbing aspect of this reconstruction effort was the fact that the major tool at hand was the former slave. The only large loyal force in the South, the only means to insure a nation united and stable, was the freedman. As it became clear that only suffrage would sufficiently arm the blacks to fill their role, Fisher's anxiety grew. He had deep-rooted doubts about unlimited white suffrage. "A villainous Mumbo Jumbo" he called it, an invitation to "the refuse pauper population of Europe to come over and govern." But for the South to be subject to the voting influence of blacks was to be in the power of "a viler mob than that of the North." [31]

Yet on the other hand he knew that something had to be done to keep the South from practicing brutality against freedmen as though they were slaves. This fact was made quite clear to him in early

30. *Diary*, 499, June 8, 1865.
31. *Ibid.*, 508, 525; Jan. 20, 1866, March 21, 1867.

March, 1866, when a young relative and four-year veteran of Confederate service came for a visit. As they talked, Fisher offered his
ideas about the treatment of the freedmen. He hoped to see black
men in the South as a peasant class, working for wages, having all
civil rights but denied suffrage. He asked if the South would permit
this. Erroneously, the young man said yes. He then asked what
Fisher meant by civil rights. The author replied that he meant "the
right to acquire property, to make contracts, to sue and be sued, to
give testimony in court, to work for whomever he pleased, and the
right of self-defense." He asked what white Southerners would do if
they saw a black man strike a white man in self-defense. "Most
men," the visitor said, "would kill him."

"And public opinion would justify the act?"

"Certainly . . . more than justify, almost require it."[32]

The young man's reply showed how much effort would be needed
to produce a loyal South, but that of course did not produce a solution. Fisher was troubled; he did not see how what had to be done
could be done. Even before the visit he had been concerned. "What
to do with the South and the Negro," he mused to his diary, "seems
as difficult a problem now as before the war. . . . Shall we let them
back as states & thus give them power over us, or shall we hold them
indefinitely as conquered provinces and, in order to do so, invest our
government with despotic power & keep their enmity alive forever?
Either plan seems equally dangerous."

Some action was required, but what? He didn't know. His philosophy failed him; he was reduced again to simply having reactions.
He hated Negro suffrage yet called it "poetical justice" for the South
to have to suffer under it. "I cannot help a feeling of satisfaction at
beholding [the southern plight] which does not overcome my
sympathy with those who are subjected to so terrible a curse," he
wrote.[33]

He believed that the South would have to be changed to insure
permanent national stability, but he feared the amount of power
required to produce that change. Most of all, he was frightened by
the Negro, the only instrument to secure a loyal Dixie. On the eve of
Reconstruction he had declared, "I can see no way out of these diffi-

32. *Ibid.*, 510, March 4, 1866. See also *Diary*, 509, 511; Feb. 16, March 15, 1866.
33. *Ibid.*, 509, 525–526; Feb. 16, 1866, March 21, 1867.

culties consistent with the preservation of the Union and free government." The passage of years did not change his mind. He had come face to face with the riddle of Reconstruction, a legal problem in the largest sense—one which involved the continued endurance of a properly ordered society. He did not know how it would be possible to secure the results of a war for union and order with an instrument that was incapable of the intelligent participation required in a stable polity.[34]

Having no answer, Fisher took refuge from the problem. By late September, 1867, he observed, "Of public affairs much might be said, but nothing cheering or satisfactory. I am tired of thinking about the subject of politics." He had not gone quite so far as an associate whose disgust led him to give up reading, but he admitted that "I do not care to write about it."[35]

Being only a theorist, Fisher could afford to escape this complex dilemma. In addition, age, illness, and severe economic straits served to draw his attention elsewhere until his death on July 25, 1871. Congress, however, did not have the opportunity to escape the problem; it had to seek a resolution which would balance goals and fears in an acceptable way. Legislators had committed themselves politically and personally to a reconstruction in which blacks might be protected and through which unionism in the South might be upheld. But, like Fisher, they were sensitive to the complexities with which they dealt. They thought very little of the instrument of unionism they were forced to use. Generally less committed to federal power than he was, they shared his fear of the excesses of democracy. (Many would later join the elitist Liberal Republican movement in 1872.) Their commitment to the black man could not then be whole-hearted, even though their devotion to a restored nation was. The legislation they wrote reflects this fact. They gave the black man equality, but couched in constitutional terminology ambiguous enough to permit the Constitution to later become, once again, a covenant with death—the death of the black man's equal liberty.

34. *Ibid.*, 499, June 8, 1865.
35. *Ibid.*, p. 531; Sept. 30, 1867.

John Norton Pomeroy:
States' Rights Nationalist

The experience lay forty years in the past, but the memory was green. In 1906 Elihu Root, secretary of state, still recalled clearly his years as a student of John Norton Pomeroy. "I look back at those years," he wrote, "as being full of intellectual delight and inspiration. It was not merely that Professor Pomeroy had broad and accurate learning and a powerful and discriminating mind, capable of the most accurate analysis, and a strong sense of proportion; he had all these; but he had also an innate and overwhelming impulse, which drove him at legal questions as if they were tribal enemies; he lived and moved and had his being with them; he rioted and rejoiced among them."[1]

Root's experience was not unique. Pomeroy was an impressive and innovative classroom teacher both at New York University, where the future statesman met him, and later at the Hastings School of Law in San Francisco. He introduced the case method of legal study almost a decade before Christopher Langdell made it famous at Harvard. He associated with his students continually, in the classroom, in the library, and at his home. His influence extended after graduation as his former pupils would submit to him briefs they had prepared for argument in the courtroom.

But Pomeroy was not only a classroom teacher. His writings brought him national attention and the admiration of Francis Lieber, Justice Oliver Wendell Holmes, Horace Binney (patriarch of the American bar), Justice Stephen J. Field, political analyst Lord James Bryce, and attorney David Dudley Field, among others. One

1. Elihu Root to John Norton Pomeroy, Jr., January 15, 1906, quoted in John Norton Pomeroy, Jr., "John Norton Pomeroy," *Great American Lawyers*, ed. William D. Lewis (Philadelphia, 1909), VIII, 101–102.

source, admittedly biased, suggested that Pomeroy was "perhaps the most important text book writer of the last third of the nineteenth century." The honor probably should go to Thomas Cooley, but Pomeroy's claim is strong, and the distinction is of some importance.

Law is not made solely by legislators and judges but by what Bentham called "Judge and Company." In interpreting statutes, jurists rely heavily on the briefs and arguments of counsel; both are dependent on legal textbooks. The authors of such works thus help to shape the law of their age. If Pomeroy was not the most important of these authors (considering, for example, the number of times he is cited in court decisions), his influence was still great and was added to by the sheer amount of his work. In eighteen years of writing he produced eight volumes of clearly written and exhaustively researched legal study, in addition to a stream of articles on the events of his times.[2]

His life was essentially a life of the mind. He enjoyed writing and wrote lucidly, convincingly, and constantly. His powers of concentration were such that he allegedly wrote his first book while presiding over a classroom at a boys' academy. He is also supposed to have written detailed and analytical legal lectures while listening to and commenting on moot court proceedings. He found more satisfaction in writing than in active participation in politics or even in the courtroom. However, when he did appear as counsel, he performed with marked influence—even though his nervousness led him to read his arguments instead of speaking them informally. Pomeroy's abilities brought him compliments from the bench and (more rewarding) the adoption of his reasoning as the law. He played an important role, for example, in shaping the Fourteenth Amendment into a tool to protect corporations when he argued the San Mateo rate case in California.[3]

But his greatest contribution was as author, not participant. Born in 1828 in Rochester, New York, Pomeroy studied law in the Cin-

2. *Ibid.*, 104–105, 108–109, 112, 123; Roscoe Pound, *The Formative Era of American Law* (Boston, 1938), 138–139; Charles Edward Larsen, "Commentaries on the Constitution, 1865–1900" (Ph.D. dissertation, Columbia University, 1952), Appendix.

3. *Dictionary of American Biography*, XV, 52; Howard J. Graham, *Everyman's Constitution: Historical Essays on the Fourteenth Amendment, The 'Conspiracy Theory,' and American Constitutionalism* (Madison, 1968), 400–403.

cinnati law office of Whig senator Thomas Corwin and in Rochester, where he was admitted to the bar in 1851. He was not successful in Rochester, so in 1861 he moved to New York and found a job teaching in a boys' academy. There he wrote his first book, *An Introduction to Municipal Law*. Four years later it was followed by *An Introduction to Constitutional Law* (1868), the first book on constitutional law published after the Civil War. In 1870 illness forced him to resign from his position at NYU and return to Rochester, where he published an edition of Theodore Sedgwick's *Treatise on Statutory and Constitutional Law*. In 1876, reacting to the need for a work which would clarify changes in practice resulting from the codification of law in many states, Pomeroy wrote *Remedies and Remedial Rights*. Under the title *Civil Remedies* the book was in use as late as the 1930s.

In 1878 the University of California opened the Hastings School of Law in San Francisco. Pomeroy's reputation was strong enough that he was asked to teach there, and to administer the school as well. These new duties did not take all his time. With a capacity for work which struck all who knew him, he combined teaching, administration, and writing to produce in 1879 *A Treatise on the Specific Performance of Contracts*. For the next four years he concentrated his efforts on what his close friend Justice Field called his greatest work, *Equity Jurisprudence*—a three-volume study which appeared from 1881 to 1883 and exercised considerable influence on the form of equity law in America. The most recent edition of this work appeared in 1947. Two years after the last volume appeared, Pomeroy died. He was fifty-six.[4]

He had not taken a significant part in the events of his age, but he did deal with the vital constitutional questions that arose during the Civil War and Reconstruction. Although he had some understanding of the strains and pressures of politics, he understood these questions basically as legal ones, as problems whose equitable solutions depended upon existing institutions. His basic question was not simply, "What is to be done?" It was, "How do we make sure that whatever we do is affected through the institutions which our nation requires for the preservation of its liberty and security?" Although he often conceded the beneficial intent of legislation, he wor-

4. Pomeroy, Jr., "Pomeroy," 124-133.

ried profoundly about the dangerous consequences of harmful legal precedents. He did not understand that "What is right?" and "What is the right way given present conditions?" might be two different questions.[5]

This myopia has its obvious usefulness in clarifying the constitutional issues of the Civil War era. It gives us the opportunity to see more clearly the constitutional points and issues, to abstract from the political rhetoric the legal ideas and assumptions which were ultimately so deadly to hopes for equality.

Pomeroy first revealed that constitutionalism which formed the foundation of his thought in his first book, *Introduction to Municipal Law* (1864). Primarily a survey of the origins and practices of the American legal system, the work contained one of the clearest justifications of a vigorous fight for national integrity in the Civil War crisis. It placed the constitutional issue foremost; passion for national survival did not lead the author to sell his respect for the law to pay the price of union. Unlike Lieber, who had suggested ignoring the Constitution, or abolitionist theorists, who claimed that the document sanctioned their boldest egalitarian dreams, Pomeroy insisted that the law itself was the prize of war. He believed that men who argued that the necessities of survival required rejection of the nation's legal traditions were advancing an ominous thesis. To pay for the Union by sacrificing the Constitution was to sell the very thing being defended. "We cannot," he insisted

> in search of a practical basis on which to rest any assumption of authority, raise the nation itself above the organic law. The notion that we may resort to the instinct of self-preservation, or to the pleas of necessity for the source of power to do acts unwarranted by the Constitution, is in the highest degree pernicious, leading to anarchy, and therefore to tyranny. We must stand by the charter which we have adopted for ourselves, or else we become disintegrated, and our national interest destroyed.[6]

5. John Norton Pomeroy, "Amnesty Measures," *Nation*, XII (Jan. 26, 1871), 52–54; "Political Precedents," *Nation*, XII (May 4, 1871), 300–301; "The Proposed Legislation for Louisiana," *Nation*, XX (Jan. 21, 1875), 37–38.

6. John Norton Pomeroy, *An Introduction to Municipal Law* (San Francisco, 1883), 2nd ed., 402–403. The book was first published in 1864.

To be sure, similar statements were common throughout the war. Again and again anti-administration orators lashed Lincoln with the constitutional whip. Coming from Copperheads like Clement Vallandigham, Fernando Wood, and Samuel Medary, or even such moderate Democrats as Samuel Tilden and New York governor Horatio Seymour, the statements can be seen as much as political rhetoric as meaningful constitutional concern. But when pro-war, pro-administration figures like Pomeroy showed similar respect for the nation's charter, there was a significant portent for the future. Pomeroy's commitment to law even in the midst of a struggle for national survival suggested that he would support legislation on the basis of its constitutionality, not just its desirability. If his hopes for a more libertarian future, for example, should ever collide with his respect for traditional restraints, there was little doubt as to which would have to yield. The hand of the past would restrain, and might cripple, movement toward that future.

During the war, however, Pomeroy's constitutionalism revealed no serious paralyzing bent. His Constitution was viable and capable of justifying the fight for the Union. His document demanded nationhood and sanctioned measures taken to assure it. More conservative men might cry "dictatorship" at Lincoln's expansion of presidential power. Pomeroy was proud of such actions and vigorous in supporting them. More frightened men might see the tentacles of tyranny behind the outreach of martial law, but Pomeroy declared that martial law "may co-exist with the ordinary operation of civil liberties and in rare cases may supplant them." To be sure, the Constitution was written primarily for a time of peace; but "the framers knew that the progress of hostilities brings with it, amid other evils, a revolution in the social order; that for a time, all other interests are secondary to the absorbing purpose of repelling force with force." *Inter armes silent leges* was a principle recognized by the nation's fundamental law.[7]

7. *Ibid.*, 404; Pomeroy to Francis Lieber, July 28, 1863, Lieber Papers. In 1868 Pomeroy wrote, "There is something exquisitely absurd in the supposition that a civil, any more than a public, war can be waged under the protection of the Bill of Rights." *An Introduction to the Constitutional Law of the United States*, 9th ed. (Boston, 1886), 379.

Still, there were signs that Pomeroy's justification of wartime efforts retained important elements of constitutional conservatism. His discussion of the extent and operation of martial law relied heavily on the article that Joel Parker had written for the *North American Review*. He accepted Parker's definition of martial law as "the most complete and accurate definition which I have met." He agreed with the Harvard professor that this law did not allow complete, unrestrained military rule of all aspects of life. It was limited to a particular place and circumstance and controlled only those actions directly related to military operations. Like Parker, Pomeroy cited the "binding authority" of Taney's opinion in *Luther* v. *Borden*. He agreed with the Chief Justice that civil courts should remain open even in areas under martial law, and that military officers who too zealously exercised their powers might be punished by those courts.[8]

Municipal Law brought Pomeroy widespread applause. In addition to being the first American study of the historical roots of existing practice, its sections on war powers attracted reviewers. At Harvard both Theophilus Parsons and Theodore Dwight welcomed the book. Yale's president Theodore Wolsey complimented the author, as did Lieber at Columbia. The faculties of Princeton, Harvard, and Yale either adopted it as a text or gave it serious consideration. The message that Pomeroy treasured most of all, however, came from aged Horace Binney, widely revered apologist for Lincoln's habeas corpus suspension. "I have read it with as much pleasure, and with as little fatigue," he wrote, "as some old men read a novel, myself among the number."[9]

Those modern scholars who have noticed Pomeroy see in him an example of the nationalist school of thought which arose out of the disunion crisis. In part, this reputation is well deserved, for he did argue eloquently for perpetual union. He insisted regularly

8. Pomeroy, *Municipal Law*, 405.

9. Binney's comment quoted in Pomeroy, Jr., "Pomeroy," 96–98, along with other letters of praise. Isaac Redfield, Vermont's chief justice and an editor of the *American Law Register*, wrote, "We have never read two consecutive pages without finding just cause for admiration . . . in manner and style almost without fault. . . . There is not a cultivated man in the country who could afford to dispense with it in his private library." *American Law Register*, XII (May, 1864), 446–448.

and forcefully that the doctrine of state sovereignty was both fool-ish and dangerous. Second only to a man's duty to God, he wrote in 1868, was his duty to his nation. "How wonderfully has this truth, forgotten perhaps for a while been recognized, accepted, and acted upon with the last six years." Now men recognized that sovereignty could not be divided. Now they knew that the government was strong enough to preserve itself. Now they understood that states had to be submissive to legitimate national power. The United States was not many nations but one nation. State sovereignty, which had raised up the sword, had died by it.[10]

Taking such statements from Pomeroy and from philosophers of organic nationalism such as John W. Draper, Orestes Brownson, and Elisha Mulford, many historians have called states' rights a casualty of war. This conclusion is wrong. State sovereignty died in combat; states' rights remains a debatable issue one hundred years and more after the end of the Civil War. A distinction must be made between states' rights and state sovereignty, or the possibility of understanding the history of civil rights in America vanishes. Despite the fact that politicians have always confused the two and despite the fact that modern dictionaries perpetuate the con-fusion, insight into the failure of the struggle for equality depends on clear differentiation.[11]

Sovereign means "above or superior to all others . . . supreme in power, rank, or authority." In statecraft it applies to the status of a nation—to its ability in international law to make its will the supreme law of its people. When a state of the Union is sovereign, it may not only determine what shall be law in matters of only local concern; it may also decide whether or not federal law shall apply to it. State sovereignty may thus be exercised to nullify a single federal law or

10. Pomeroy, *Constitutional Law*, 23-25, 30-31, 51-56.
11. Gettell, *History of American Political Thought*, 363, 400; William B. Hes-seltine, *Lincoln and the War Governors* (New York, 1948), 392; Nichols, *American Leviathan*, 273; William Weeden, *War Government: Federal and State in Massa-chusetts, New York, Pennsylvania and Indiana, 1861-65* (Boston, 1906); *Webster's New World Dictionary* (Cleveland, 1959), 1395. McLaughlin, *A Constitutional History of the United States*, 340, and Dunning, *Essays on the Civil War and Reconstruction*, 63, avoid this error. Burgess, *Reconstruction and the Constitution*, 1, says, "The key to the solution of the question of Reconstruction is the proper conception of what a 'State' is in a system of federal government." See especially Walter Bennett, *American Theories of Federalism* (University, 1964).

to reject all connection with any federal laws, i.e., to secede. The crucial test of sovereignty then rests upon the right to decide to what extent a federal law or the Constitution may affect a state, if at all. The Civil War settled this question in favor of the federal government.[12]

But that does not mean that the war destroyed state influence or responsibility. The Union's victory did not create a unitary nation; it did not end federalism. Remaining in state hands were a large number of important functions which states would control and with which the federal government might not interfere. The control over and exercise of these functions constituted the rights of the states. What distinguished these rights from state sovereignty was the fact that the President, courts, and Congress would have the final say in cases where there was a question over whether the subject in question was properly a state or a federal one.

After the war there remained crucial decisions to be made about the balance between national and state authority. All that was really settled was that, in case of a disagreement between them, the federal government's will would be done. But no one doubted that that will would prevail within a system in which states exercised some important functions and the federal government others. No one questioned the idea that a federal law, however apparently beneficial, might still be denied operation within a state by the decision of a federal court, or that it might even fail of enactment should congressmen believe that it encroached excessively on state responsibility. The nation that emerged from the war was one nation, but still a nation of states. As the legal rhetoric of the conflict had demonstrated the viability of the Constitution, so it had also thereby protected the federal system which the Constitution enshrined.[13]

In evolving and defending the concept of a viable wartime national charter, Pomeroy came to share the respect for it demonstrated in the Reconstruction Congress. Although he believed, with senators like Fessenden and Grimes, that the postwar period required a more restrictive constitutional view, like them he came to support congressional programs. He believed in the kind of legis-

---

12. *Webster's New World Dictionary*, 1395.
13. Kelly, "Comment," 40–58; Howe, "Federalism and Civil Rights," *Massachusetts Historical Society Proceedings*, LXXVII (1965), 15–27.

lative protection for freedmen which the Congress passed. Like the majority, he was unwilling to abandon completely the constitutional past in the service of an egalitarian future; unlike them, however, he could look directly at the effect of the post-Appomattox conflict upon the nation's constitutional institutions.[14]

The conflict that developed between the Supreme Court and Congress was the most clear-cut example of an encounter between legislative hopes and existing institutions. After individual members of the court had initially shown a disposition to favor Reconstruction measures, the full court by late 1866 showed signs of hostility. In the *Garland* case the jurists struck down a congressional loyalty oath which disallowed former rebels from practicing law before federal courts. In *Cummings* v. *Missouri* they invalidated an oath required of teachers, ministers, and lawyers which was intended to keep rebel sympathizers from these professions. And in the *Milligan* case the court seemed to imperil military Reconstruction by ruling that civil courts must try civilians for their crimes whenever such courts were open. Military tribunals might not do so.[15]

The response from Congress was an understandable sense of anger. Legislators denied that the court's respect for the Constitution was unique or should be controlling. They had their own oaths to respect and defend the document, but they were equally sensitive to the popular demand that the freedmen be protected and the Union be safely reconstructed. They did not believe that their duties and those oaths conflicted. Memories of *Dred Scott* and *Merryman* revived, and conservative Republicans joined their more radical colleagues in speaking ominously of ending judicial review. In the winter of 1867–68 the House passed a measure to require a two-thirds vote of the court to invalidate acts of Congress. Though

14. Brock, *An American Crisis*, 250–273; Kelly, "Comment," 55–58; McKitrick, *Andrew Johnson and Reconstruction*, 93–119.

15. Initial favorable response came from Justice Swayne in *U.S.* v. *Rhodes, Federal Cases*, 16,151 (1866); and Justice Chase in *In re Turner, Federal Cases*, 14,247 (1866). *Milligan* is 4 *Wallace* 2; *Garland*, 4 *Wallace* 333; *Cummings*, 4 *Wallace* 277. The three best studies of the Supreme Court in Reconstruction are Kutler, *Judicial Power and Reconstruction Politics*; David Hughes, "Salmon P. Chase: Chief Justice," *Vanderbilt Law Review*, XVII (March, 1965), 569–614; and the monumental Charles Fairman, *Reconstruction and Reunion, 1864–88* (New York, 1971).

tabled in the Senate, the proposal did indicate that tempers ran high when judges impeded the will of legislators. Outside congressional halls there was similar anxiety about the judicial decisions. The *Washington Chronicle* called the oath cases "the fortification behind which impertinent rebels may renew or continue their war against the government." Lieber's earlier respect for the judiciary weakened as he asked a friend if the power of judicial review "might be diminished at least." [16]

Pomeroy was worried about the prospect of diminished judicial influence. He was frightened at the prospect of popular government unchecked by the bench: "A pure democracy must be the most terrible of tyrannies, because there is no . . . limit upon the exercise of authority." The prospect of legislative dominance was similarly worrisome. He did not equate popular rule with free government; he believed that the legislature, being the most powerful branch of government, was therefore potentially the most dangerous. What troubled him most was a growing tendency to exalt the position of Congress to equal status with the judiciary as the proper interpreter of the Constitution, thus supplementing its law-making power with the ability to act as judge of its own cause. He saw this as a sure step toward consolidation and tyranny: "I am strongly of the opinion that the people of the United States are not so much in danger from an undue stretch of authority by President or by judges, as from unlawful assumptions by Congress." Judicial review was an imperative shield of liberty. [17]

But Pomeroy was aware that the instrument of diminishing influence might prove to be the court itself. The questions posed by the war and Reconstruction were vital ones which evoked hot feelings and strong rhetoric. In such an environment the court might forget that its strength lay in establishing an image of judicial objectivity, in avoiding sweeping political pronouncements, in appearing to

16. Kutler, *Judicial Power*, 64–88, places the congressional response in its proper perspective, although he does not deny the initial anger of legislators. Harold M. Hyman, *The Era of the Oath* (Philadelphia, 1954), 113–114, discusses response to the test oath cases. Lieber to A. D. White, Feb. 24, 1867, Lieber Papers.

17. Pomeroy, *Introduction to Constitutional Law*, 61, 91–92, 121–122; Pomeroy, "Criminal Procedure," *North American Review*, XCII (April, 1861), 297–318, reflects his distrust of democracy by an attack on grand juries and trial by jury.

serve no master but the law and the Constitution. He saw disturbing signs that the judiciary was heedless of these facts.

In the *Milligan* case, for example, five judges' zeal for civil liberty carried them far beyond the language necessary to decide the case and helped to ignite congressional wrath. Milligan and some associates had been arrested in Indiana in 1864 for conspiring to release rebel prisoners and march to the aid of southern armies. A military court convicted him and sentenced him to death. He appealed the conviction; in 1866, with the war ended, the case reached the Supreme Court. By a vote of 9-0 the court sustained his appeal and released him, but it divided over the reason. A minority of four argued that the trial procedures had simply violated a congressional law which provided that civil courts try such cases. But the majority, with Justice David Davis as spokesman, took the occasion to come forth with a declaration of libertarian principles which has attracted the admiration of modern civil libertarians but which put the Reconstruction court in a difficult position.[18]

Pomeroy was bothered because the same decision might have been reached without endangering the court. Davis's argument was weak anyway, he believed, confusing total military rule with a limited and infrequent exercise of martial law. But more important, it was an unnecessary declaration of potential hostility to congressional Reconstruction efforts; as such, it might bring retribution.[19]

For the same reason he was concerned about the court's decisions in the oath cases. He agreed with the results of both cases: neither congressional nor state oaths were constitutional. They were both ex post facto laws which deprived men of rights they had exercised before the war, doing so by creating crimes and punishments where none had existed before. He was troubled because the court had not been satisfied simply to settle the cases in the most limited and re-

18. 4 *Wallace* 2; Randall, *Constitutional Problems under Lincoln*, 180–183.

19. Pomeroy, *Introduction to Constitutional Law*, 596–597. Justice Davis, displaying surprising naivete, was taken aback by the congressional outcry. He claimed that the opinion did not apply to military Reconstruction, since the question at issue in the *Milligan* case was the legality of military trials in the North. But the opinion itself did not reflect a similar sensitivity to fine distinctions; it provoked much public discussion about the effect it would have on Reconstruction. Kutler, *Judicial Power*, 67, reports Davis's opinion but does not question it.

strained way possible. Instead of restricting themselves to precise legal issues, certain judges seemed to find it necessary to announce expansive policy doctrines which were direct challenges to the most powerful branch of government. In both the *Cummings* and *Garland* cases the court struck down oaths as bills of attainder, as well as ex post facto laws, and Justice Stephen Field (later Pomeroy's close friend) especially had put a chip on the court's shoulder. He announced not only that were men who had practiced the teaching, legal, and ministerial professions before the war free of penalties from wartime oath restrictions, but also that oaths might not be valid for those licensed after the laws in question had been passed. Pomeroy was appalled by Field's assertion; he attempted to exorcize it. "A mere dictum," he insisted. Field's opinion had "no binding efficacy as a precedent, no quality of an express adjudication upon an actual state of facts in a legal controversy."[20]

To a man so vitally interested in preserving constitutional institutions, such injudicial conduct must have been exasperating. Faced with a Congress where rhetoric often seemed to outrun institutional stability, it was at least to be hoped that judges would not respond with counterbombast. Pomeroy did what he could to restrain the judiciary, but he did not content himself with appeals to it for more restraint. He tried arguments to the people and their representatives as well.

He seems to have sensed that one reason for the bitterness of the Reconstruction quarrels between Congress, the President, and the court was the persistence of the Jefferson-Jackson concept of judicial review. Both presidents faced courts which asserted a monopoly over determining whether or not a law was constitutional. In answer, the executives had insisted that each branch of government had sworn to uphold the Constitution, and therefore each

20. Pomeroy, *Introduction to Constitutional Law*, 417–418, 435–436, 579. Hyman, *Era of the Oath*, 113–114, does not note that opposition to the decision came from supporters of Congress like Pomeroy. He limits the opposition to "Democrats and almost all southerners." Such a view obscures understanding of the seeds of failure within congressional policy itself. The most recent work on Pomeroy, other than my own, calls the discussion of the oath cases the best part of the volume. John C. Leary, "John Norton Pomeroy, 1828–85," *Law Library Journal*, XLVII (May, 1954), 140.

might decide such questions for itself. This view persisted into the Civil War, when Attorney General Bates used similar arguments to justify Lincoln's right to suspend the privilege of the writ.

But there was an obvious danger in so dividing this crucial power, a danger noted by Fisher in discussing secession and by Pomeroy in discussing this very question. Given the profound respect of Americans for the Constitution, the absence of a single arbiter of constitutionality produced bitter, and sometimes irreconcilable, conflicts. Whether these conflicts were intersectional or between federal departments, they threatened stability and thus required resolution. The Supreme Court, Pomeroy insisted, had to assume its proper role as arbiter of all constitutional questions. It would thereby reduce tensions and preserve order.[21]

But to insure this position for the court would require more than a request from Pomeroy that both President and Congress listen to the judges. Andrew Johnson was unlikely to listen to anyone, and legislators had reason to doubt that the Court was as devoted to secure nationhood as they were. After all, four of the judges had Democratic party loyalties, and recent efforts of the bench hardly fostered trust.

Pomeroy recognized the need to direct attention not to specific decisions, but to the overall role of the court as a protector of nationhood. He was aware of the power of the argument that national integrity was the highest good, and that northern blood had already been spilled to defeat the ideas that the court seemed to be supporting in defending men like Garland, Cummings, and Milligan. Therefore he argued that to attack the bench in the name of the nation would be seriously to harm both. It would be "an act of suicide," he said, "for those who uphold the principles of government which emerged victorious from the agony of the late war [to] weaken the authority of the court." The nation's history demonstrated that the Supreme Court had consistently been the strongest bulwark of nationhood. Presidents had wavered, Congress had often been weak, but the Court persisted in the belief that Americans were "a sovereign people, one and indivisible." "Without [the

21. Pomeroy, *Introduction to Constitutional Law*, 91–93; Fisher, *Trial of the Constitution*, 58–60; Randall, *Constitutional Problems under Lincoln*, 124.

Court] there would have been no national party," he said, "simply because there would have been no nation." The continued national opinions of the federal bench had become the settled convictions of the people, educating them to the true nature of the Union. Without such tutelage there would have been no war against the rebellion.[22]

He did note that there had been three instances in the past few years in which the court had decided against federal laws, but he denied that *Dred Scott, Milligan,* and the oath cases seriously endangered the federal government. He called for a longer view of the results of diminishing the court's power than its detractors did. Action weakening or ignoring the federal court would harm not just the bench, but national authority and the supremacy of federal law as well. A decline in the influence of federal courts would increase the power of state courts. "The laws of the General Government," he explained, "must operate within the states, and the officers of the general government must act within the jurisdiction of state tribunals. Remove the supervisory function of the national judiciary, and these laws will become the sport of local partisanship, upheld in one commonwealth, they will be overthrown in another and all compulsive character will be lost."[23]

Pomeroy overstated the case. Congressional antipathy was momentary and directed only at the Supreme Court, not at all federal courts. As a matter of fact, the most lasting outthrust of federal power produced by the Reconstruction period was the expansion of the judicial function. Military courts were established to try violations of freedmen's rights. The Civil Rights bill of 1866 incorporated under federal jurisdiction the protection of those rights secured by the bill to equal protection of the laws. And, as the most recent student of the courts in the postwar era reports, "The reorganization schemes of 1862, 1863, and 1866, the creation of intermediate courts of appeal, and the expansion of federal jurisdiction . . . all indicated a positive thrust, a desire and a willingness to incorporate the judiciary into the Republicans' vision of national development." Whatever the talk about a Reconstructon revolution, its perpetrators used

22. Pomeroy, "The Use of the Supreme Court," *Nation,* VI (Feb. 20, 1868), 146–147.
23. *Ibid.*

most traditional channels—indeed, the most conservative ones available—to work their will.[24]

In addition, in this period the Supreme Court itself, despite the occasional excesses that Pomeroy deplored, secured the foundations of its late-nineteenth-century ascendancy. The wide-ranging arguments of justices like Field would appear again and again to strike down state legislatures' efforts to regulate corporations. Indeed, Pomeroy himself would encourage this enterprise in the 1880s.[25]

But in the post-Appomattox era this remained in the future. Focusing only on an immediate crisis, Pomeroy believed that the court was besieged; he was concerned that respect for legal institutions might be threatened in such turbulent times. If Congress could intimidate the judiciary, or should excessive judicial zeal provoke reprisals, then there might be implanted in the public mind a disrespect for judicial institutions everywhere. People might come to view the courts as hindrances to liberty instead of liberty's imperative guardians.

Pomeroy's fear was proven groundless. Despite the turmoil of the period, legislators, judges, and apparently the population in general retained a tenacious legal commitment, perhaps partly due to the efforts of constitutional theorists and publicists like Pomeroy. Despite the expansive rhetoric, apparently ground-breaking legislation, and three major constitutional amendments in five years, Reconstruction has properly been termed an "ultraconservative revolution." For all the apparent change, things remained much the same.[26]

I believe this tragic fact is best explained by the phenomena so far presented: in a fight to secure order, the only possible result of victory would be a retention of the existing legal structure, purged only of its disruptive elements. It is illustrated most precisely by studying the reaction of a dedicated constitutional nationalist such as Pomeroy to the apparently revolutionary Fourteenth Amendment.

24. Kutler, *Judicial Power*, 167–168; Morgan, *Congress and the Constitution*, 125–133.

25. Kutler, *Judicial Power*, Ch. 7.

26. Eric McKitrick, "Reconstruction: Ultraconservative Revolution," *The Comparative Approach to American History*, ed. C. Vann Woodward (New York, 1968), 140–159. This article notes the constitutional conservatism shown by Congress but does not offer an explanation for it.

The basic purpose of the amendment was to secure constitutional protection against state action which denied equal protection of the laws or due process of law to any citizen. It was an attempt to overthrow the 1857 *Dred Scott* decision that blacks were not national citizens and hence could not enjoy the privileges and immunities of national citizenship. This amendment also sought to provide federal protection for a number of not very clearly defined rights—possibly including those in the Bill of Rights—which had previously been subject to state control.[27]

This lack of clarity reflected the fact that the measure was a compromise between two major groups. Radical egalitarians hoped to secure full political and social as well as civil equality between the races. Moderate congressmen recognized that the freedmen needed protection from their former masters but hoped to limit that protection to a guarantee of civil equality. Agreement between the two was reached by an amendment with its most crucial terms undefined. The all-important first section says, "All persons born or naturalized in the United States, and subject to the jurisdiction thereof, are citizens of the United States and of the state wherein they reside. No State shall make or enforce any law which shall abridge the privileges or immunities of citizens of the United States; nor shall any State deprive any person of life, liberty, or property, without due process of law; nor deny to any person within its jurisdiction the equal protection of the laws."[28]

It was a splendid announcement, but what did it mean? Exactly what were the privileges and immunities of citizens of the nation? Of the states? Did they differ in each jurisdiction? What constituted due process of law? What was the equal protection of the laws? When was a denial of liberty within a state the action of the state

27. For a survey of the extensive literature on the question of the extent to which the framers of the Fourteenth Amendment sought to incorporate the Bill of Rights, see Henry J. Abraham, *Freedom and the Court: Civil Rights and Civil Liberties in the United States* (New York, 1967), 26–46. Abraham concludes that full incorporation was intended, as does the author of the most complete book on the amendment, Joseph B. James (*The Framing of the Fourteenth Amendment*, 99, 180, 186, 197). See also Graham, *Everyman's Constitution*, 320–321n.

28. Randall and Donald, *Civil War and Reconstruction*, 581–584; Alexander M. Bickel, "The Original Understanding and the Segregation Decision," *Harvard Law Review*, LXIX (Nov., 1955), 1–64.

itself? The rights which Negroes might actually claim depended to a considerable degree, not on this rhetoric, but on precise, legal definitions of the rights in question.

Pomeroy's definition apparently promised much. He welcomed the all-important first section of the amendment. He announced his belief that civil rights should be protected from state as well as federal interference. With the single exception of the emancipation amendment, he thought that the Fourteenth was "far more important than any which has been adopted since the organization of the government." Under the amendment states would be prevented from making laws abridging the equal right of citizens to pass through a state, to acquire, hold, and sell property, to make contracts, to sue and be sued, to hold any lawful occupation. His position on what had been done by the amendment mirrored the congressional view of the rights protected under the Civil Rights bill: though no political rights were secured, all civil rights were now under the protection of federal law. The amendment, in Pomeroy's opinion, gave the nation "complete power to protect its citizens against local injustice and oppression." He believed that both *Dred Scott* and *Barron* v. *Baltimore* had been remedied by the Fourteenth Amendment.[29]

Although falling short of radical goals of complete equality, Pomeroy's view of the amendment was as advanced as most proponents of the measure could wish. It coincided with the intentions of the amendment's sponsors in Congress. Both Congressman John Bingham and Senator Jacob Howard explained their intentions in terms equivalent to his, and Congress accepted these views in passing it. Pomeroy's concurrence with congressional wishes was clearly

29. Pomeroy, *Introduction to Constitutional Law*, 154–160, 180; *Statutes at Large*, XIV, 27; *Congressional Globe*, 39th Cong., 1st sess., pp. 474–476. The first section of the amendment was the only section he approved of. He believed that section two (which provides penalties for failure to permit Negroes to vote) violated state control over suffrage. He thought that section three (which denied federal office to former rebels) was an ex post facto law. He wanted the amendment to give federal control only over federal elections. He suggested the following as a proper measure: "The House of Representatives shall be composed of members chosen every second year by the people of the several states, and the electors shall have the qualifications which Congress may from time to time prescribe, which shall be uniform throughout the states." Pomeroy, *Introduction to Constitutional Law*, 138–141; "Amnesty Measures," 52–54.

shown in 1873 when the Supreme Court, while deciding the Slaughterhouse cases, completely ignored the intentions of the framers of the amendment.[30]

In determining whether or not the Fourteenth Amendment protected competing New Orleans butchers against a state-established slaughtering monopoly, the court for the first time announced its view of what rights now fell under federal, not state, custody. Justice Samuel Miller announced the decision of a five-to-four court that the amendment had produced no new federally protected rights. "The Court," Senator George F. Edmunds responded, has "radically differed in respect both to the intention of the framers and the construction of the language used by them." Edmunds had taken part in framing the amendment.[31]

Pomeroy agreed with the senator and with the four-judge minority that Miller's opinion was wrong. "Properly viewed," he insisted, "This beneficent amendment throws the protection of the nation, of its Congress and its courts, around the lives, liberty, and property of all its citizens, and enables the supreme tribunal to annul all oppressive laws which the partisanship of local courts might perhaps sustain."[32]

These words and ideas seem to contain a bright promise of equality for the freedmen, and many historians have been beguiled by them. Pervading the historiography of the Slaughterhouse cases and their meaning for the Negro is the assumption that, had the minority of the court prevailed, the black man's future would have been different and better. Casting the judicial argument as one between national protection and states' rights opposition, historians have made the plausible argument that had the nationalism of Field, Bradley, Chase, and Swayne prevailed over the majority's states' rights commitment, the egalitarian promises of Reconstruction would have been kept.[33]

30. See note 27.

31. :6 *Wallace* 36; Charles Warren, *The Supreme Court in United States History* (Boston, 1928), II, 541.

32. Pomeroy, *Introduction to Constitutional Law*, 177–178; Theodore Sedgwick, *A Treatise on the Rules which Govern the Interpretation and Construction of Statutory Law*, ed. John N. Pomeroy (New York, 1874), 563–564.

33. Warren, *Supreme Court in United States History*, II, 547, claims that, "had the case been decided otherwise, the States would have largely lost their autonomy and become, as political entities, only of historical interest." Kutler, *Judicial Power*,

Such an opinion is wrong—it would be true only if nineteenth-century jurists were devotees of twentieth-century nationalism. They were not. They were Jacksonian nationalists who respected the duties and rights of the states even as they asserted the sovereignty of the nation. For example, Justice Miller's record is heavily laced with decisions upholding national power against state interference. The same is true, in fact, of the full Reconstruction court. Post-Appomattox nationalism was sufficiently states' rights–respecting to produce the example of strong supporters of the war for national supremacy applauding the Slaughterhouse decision. The *Nation*, the *Chicago Tribune*, the *New York Times*, and the *New York Tribune* all hailed the court for its action. The Chicago paper declared, "The Supreme Court has not spoken a moment too soon or any too boldly on this subject."[34]

Even those who deplored the decision retained a sufficient commitment to the federal nature of the Union to deprive the freedman of his apparent victory. Pomeroy was one with such a commitment. His belief in increased national responsibility under the Fourteenth Amendment was not profound enough to provide actual protection for the rights which he insisted might legally be claimed. This fact became clear when the South responded to northern Reconstruction measures.[35]

166, asserts that "the Court's decision had devastating effects for the freedmen." Miller, *The Petitioners*, p. 109, says of Justice Miller's dual citizenship distinction: "That duality boded ill for the Negro, just as it had in Dred Scott's day and for the same reason." See also Blaustein and Ferguson, *Desegregation and the Law*, 90; Graham, *Everyman's Constitution*, 297.

34. Newspaper reaction quoted in Warren, *Supreme Court in United States History*, II, 543–545. For Miller's nationalism, see Fairman, *Mr. Justice Miller and the Supreme Court*, 124, 137–138. The nationalism of the court is discussed in Kutler, *Judicial Power*, 141–142.

35. Harold Hyman calls Pomeroy a "front runner" in his views of the egalitarian nature of the Fifth and Fourteenth Amendments. He says that both Pomeroy and Charles Sumner believed that the two amendments merged the Declaration of Independence and the Bill of Rights into the Constitution "as negative limitations on the nation and the states in the old sense of a bill of wrongs, and as positive goals which all American governments must protect" ("Reconstruction and Political-Constitutional Institutions," 37). Although Pomeroy's rhetoric may have paralleled Sumner's, his commitment to federalism led him far away from the senator's truly revolutionary position that whatever had to be done to protect the freedmen was allowable by the Constitution. For Sumner's view, see *Congressional Globe*, 38th Cong., 2nd sess., p. 791; 42nd Cong., 2nd sess., p. 727.

Reconstruction brought the vanquished South face to face with an experience for which it was completely unprepared: the challenge to absorb into free society approximately 4.5 million blacks previously excluded by force. The survival and maintenance of slavery had demanded beliefs, practically instincts, about the Negro which made any self-generated absorption impossible. These same beliefs suggested that any externally imposed assimilation could not be faint hearted if it were to be successful.

Having convinced themselves that the slave was congenitally ignorant, lazy, dishonest, and potentially savage, white Southerners were hardly prepared to believe that freedom changed the leopard's spots. A vast free black population raised the spectre of an end to civilized order. In the midst of the already insecure atmosphere of defeat, groups organized to make sure that, whatever his legal status, the freedman would remain at the only level of society where he could not endanger it—the bottom. Spontaneous riots and clashes between blacks and whites expressed the southern determination to keep him there. Organized groups, especially the Ku Klux Klan, acted as instruments of that determination.

Organized in 1865 as a secret social society, the Klan quickly became a large midnight militia whose goal was to terrorize freedmen who took advantage of their freedom and whites who sought to help them. Between 1865 and 1871 about a thousand of these "uppity niggers" and "niggerloving carpetbaggers" were killed. Klan violence became so extreme that in 1869 Nathan B. Forrest, head of the far-flung organization, called for its dissolution.[36]

But the violence, which members insisted was necessary to preserve social order, continued. In Meridian, Mississippi, in 1871 the Klan placed on trial a group of Negroes who had made "inflammatory speeches." A crowd of freedmen gathered to show support for their leaders, a shot was fired, and shortly a number of blacks lay dead. One white man had been injured. Most of the freedmen ran away, and the aforementioned speechmakers were dragged from jail and hanged. The incident was typical of others throughout the South. They seem to have reached a peak in 1870–71.[37]

36. Chalmers, *Hooded Americanism*, 8–21.
37. *Ibid.*

In response, Congress passed three bills known as the Force Acts. These measures attempted to secure civil and political rights for the freedmen. They contained extremely specific provisions which attempted to curb every conceivable evasion by describing that evasion as unlawful and by punishing officeholders for failure to enforce the law. To further insure protection, they provided that federal courts should have exclusive jurisdiction of violations. The Force Acts were a stark commentary on the extent to which the promises of the war amendments were being repudiated in the South.[38]

The act which received Pomeroy's attention was the third, the so-called Ku Klux Act. This act made it a federal crime to interfere with "the privileges and immunities" of any citizen, state laws to the contrary notwithstanding. Interfering with the execution of federal laws was punishable by fines from $500 to $5,000 and jail terms from six months to six years. In cases where domestic violence inhibited the enforcement of state or federal laws, the state would be liable if it did not take action against such violence. If the disturbance impeded the course of justice under federal law, the President was authorized to use whatever force he believed necessary to suppress it. In service of this responsibility, the President could suspend the privilege of the habeas corpus writ. When prosecutions began under this act, jurors were to swear that they had never assisted any of the acts in question. If they lied, they were subject to federal prosecutions for perjury. Failure to report violations of the act or to stop them if possible might subject the quiescent individual to suit by the injured party.[39]

The Force Acts were efforts to give meaning to the implicit promises of the Fourteenth and Fifteenth Amendments. They arose from the fact that, despite such sweeping announcements of equality, black men and their white friends could not exercise their rights without fear of violence. Here was the opportunity to test the extent of Pomeroy's nationalist commitment. Was his expansive view of the Fourteenth Amendment broad enough to turn promises

38. *Documentary History of Reconstruction*, ed. Walter Fleming (Cleveland, 1907), II, 102–128.
39. *Ibid.*, 123–128.

into reality? Would soldiers protect the new citizens when they moved to collect Reconstruction's promissory notes? Pomeroy's answer was no.[40]

"Never in the political history of the country," he charged, "has so direct a blow been aimed, under color of legal authority, at the supremacy of the Constitution, or a precedent been established so dangerous to free institutions." Pomeroy asserted that the measure allowed the President to act like an unrestrained despot, defining domestic violence to suit himself and then marching troops to the destruction of liberty. Congress shared the despotic inclination; it attempted to define what constituted a rebellion in order to suppress conditions it disliked. But the definition of a rebellion was clearly established in law, and legislators could not simply create a rebellion where none existed. The habeas corpus privilege, according to the Constitution, could be suspended only during rebellion or invasion. The action of Congress in trying to define a rebellion into existence so that the privilege might be suspended, he insisted, was clearly unconstitutional.

Although Pomeroy was a defender of judicial prerogatives, he even objected to the way in which the bill augmented judicial power. He saw the central idea of the whole measure as a plan "by which the United States courts may exercise full criminal and civil jurisdiction over any and all acts of violence to the persons and property of private citizens; by which, in short, Congress and the national tribunals may assume and wield a complete police power throughout the states."[41]

He was too much of a nationalist not to concede that the federal government might indeed act to protect its citizens. But (and this conjunction is crucial) it could do so only in national spheres. Al-

40. Everette Swinney, "Enforcing the Fifteenth Amendment, 1870–1877," *Journal of Southern History*, XXVIII (May, 1962), 202–218.

41. Pomeroy, "The Force Bill," *Nation*, XII (April 20, 1871), 268–270. Similar fears for the federal system were felt by E. L. Godkin, influential editor of the *Nation*, and by Oliver Wendell Holmes, Jr., though Holmes did support the Force Bill. *Nation*, XII (April 20, 27, 1871), 265, 282; Mark De Wolfe Howe, *Justice Oliver Wendell Holmes: The Proving Years* (Cambridge, 1963), 35–36. Howard J. Graham incorrectly implies that Pomeroy favored this bill; he is misled, I believe, by the fact that Pomeroy believed that the Fourteenth Amendment incorporated the Bill of Rights. See *Everyman's Constitution*, 324n.

though national power had been increased by the war amendments, state police power, the power to legislate to secure the health and safety of its citizens, had not been surrendered at Appomattox, nor had it been rescinded by the Fourteenth Amendment. This amendment had only made it illegal for a state to use its laws to discriminate against one group of its citizens. It secured to all an equal right to enter or leave the state, to acquire and transfer property, to sue and be sued, to make contracts and to hold a lawful occupation. Pomeroy's catalogue was more than the Supreme Court would concede in the Slaughterhouse cases, but considerably less than the freedmen required for protection, as soon became clear.

When might the federal government move to protect its citizens? Why, Pomeroy said, that is perfectly clear: the amendment says, "No *state* shall." Until a state, as a state, legislated in violation of the rights mentioned above, no federal action might take place. Private citizens acting on their own initiative to deprive other citizens of their rights were not in violation of the amendment. "The only way possible for the [Fourteenth] Amendment to be violated by anyone," he insisted, "is by the passage of a law in conflict with its mandates."[42]

There remained only the question of enforcing the amendment's provisions, and that was easily settled. Since federally protected rights could only be violated by state action, the remedy for violations had to be judicial, not legislative. No congressional legislation was even necessary to enforce the amendment, because any state laws conflicting with it were null and void and would be declared so in a courtroom.

But suppose that states had equality legislation on the books but failed to enforce it, or that private actions took place which made the legislation a farce. What recourse did the citizen have then? Federal enforcement laws were directed precisely at such conditions. To Pomeroy this legislation, however well intentioned, imperiled the federal system. After all, what sort of federalism gave a state exclusive jurisdiction over something and then allowed the

42. Pomeroy, "The Force Bill," 270. Five years later the Supreme Court would use the same argument to invalidate the Force Acts, and in 1883 it would do the same to the 1875 Civil Rights bill. *United States v. Cruikshank*, 92 *United States Reports* 542; *Civil Rights Cases*, 109 *U.S. Reports* 3.

federal government to invalidate the state effort when it believed
that the state had not done its job properly? Such a view of federal-
state relations simply made the federal government a perpetual po-
liceman of all state activities.

No citizen, he insisted, might properly secure a federal guarantee
that a state would always operate at the optimum level of efficiency
and honesty. "When the laws of a State are proper, the citizen has
no jural right, as against the State, that prosecuting and police officers shall be vigilant in acts of prevention, of inquisition, and of
apprehension, that grand juries shall be ready to find indictments
and petit juries to convict, that judges shall be quick and stern to
punish. All this is beyond the reach of United States constitutional
sanctions and, we may add, of State constitutional sanctions." The
offended citizens should seek redress at the ballot box, not in the
courts, if the existing government denied them the proper execution
of its laws.[43]

Reality made such theorizing sheer sophistry. The Force Acts had
been passed because freedmen could not resort to the ballot box
for any purpose whatsoever. They could not vote to change an
unfair government; they could not vote to change or retain anything in most places in the South. Their very presence at the ballot
box was anathema to most Southerners. Despite claims that Klans-
men and others rode to preserve the peace, what they in fact objected to was, in David Chalmers's words, "the Negro as a citizen,
rather than a lawbreaker."[44]

Pomeroy's sophistry would later become hypocrisy. He had ad-
monished freedmen to seek redress at the polls and not in the courts.
Six years later the Supreme Court spoke practically the same words
to the corporations of the nation. *Munn* v. *Illinois* raised the question
of whether a state might regulate a large warehousing business by
fixing rates for grain storage. Operators raised the due process clause
of the Fourteenth Amendment and argued that such regulation
constituted unlawful deprivation of property. The court denied the
claim and told the operators that "for protection against abuses by
Legislatures the people must resort to the polls, not the courts."[45]

43. Pomeroy, "The Rights of Citizens," *Nation*, XII (May 18, 1871), 335–336.
44. Chalmers, *Hooded Americanism*, 13.
45. 94 *U.S.* 113 (1877).

Although the court might have been echoing his earlier ideas, Pomeroy was outraged at its decision. "No other decision . . . in the course of our judicial history," he announced, portended "such disastrous consequences to the future welfare and prosperity of the country." Apparently the nation's welfare depended more on the liberty of the corporation than on the liberty of the freedman.[46]

Certainly the nation came easily and quickly to that decision. Unchallenged by public outcries, the court in the years 1875–1898 transformed the Fourteenth Amendment from an instrument to secure equal rights for the freedmen into a protector of corporate freedom. While the amendment's power to inhibit state regulation of business grew, its influence in shielding the Negro dwindled. By 1898 the Supreme Court had ruled that state regulations which separated the races (and thus denied true equality to the blacks) were constitutional, while state laws which regulated the rates charged by corporations were not.[47]

Pomeroy reflected this double standard. Strict consistency and pure devotion to liberty would have required that he insist on equal treatment for both businessmen and black men. In fact, a precise reading of the evidence of congressional intention would have demonstrated that under the amendment black men had much the better claim. But he increasingly neglected the Negro; his attitude toward equality measures became even mocking.

In 1877, the same year as the *Munn* case, the Supreme Court decided the case of *Hall* v. *DeCuir*. A Negro woman had attempted to get first-class accommodations on a riverboat operating between New Orleans and another town in Louisiana. She was refused and was sold a second-class ticket. However, the lady was not easily convinced that she could legally be treated in this way. The state's Reconstruction legislature had passed a law requiring equality in public accommodations, and she thought it was time to enforce this law. When she got on the boat, therefore, she took possession of a whites only, first-class cabin. She was forcibly ejected and sued the company for damages. Two state courts upheld her claim, but the Supreme Court of the United States did not.

46. Pomeroy, "The Supreme Court and State Repudiation," *American Law Review*, XVII (Sept.–Oct., 1888), 712.
47. Kelly and Harbison, *The American Constitution*, 492–493, 496–518.

Adopting an expansive interpretation of federal jurisdiction over interstate commerce, Chief Justice Morrison Waite announced that the Louisiana law must fall. The state regulation was an unwarranted interference with the power of Congress to regulate interstate river traffic, even though the law in question applied only to Louisiana waters. "If the public good requires such legislation," Waite said, "it must come from Congress and not from the states."[48]

"This case," Pomeroy observed derisively, "is a striking example of 'the engineer hoist by his own petard.'" Political and social reformers had zealously sought "to force blacks into a social equality with the whites." These men were not satisfied with civil or even political equality; they had even advocated "a social intermingling of the two races." The foundation for this reforming enterprise had been the legal argument that the Congress might exercise national power in the freedmen's behalf. "It is therefore rather amusing," he sneered, "that the scheme of social equality should be overthrown by the very national power which had always been invoked as its sure and sufficient foundation." Less than four years later Pomeroy would argue eloquently that the Fourteenth Amendment gave the protection of the national constitution to the nation's corporations.[49]

Yet, however hypocritical this contrast between his treatment of corporate and black persons, his firmly rooted constitutional conservatism gave some consistency to his views. The crucial determinant of Pomeroy's attitude toward the amendment (indeed, toward any law or constitutional provision) was the extent of legal change that it portended. Clearly, an interpretation of the amendment which made it a shield for corporations was much less revolutionary than an interpretation that made it the protector of freedmen. Although the legal legerdemain which offered corporations shelter while the Negro languished involved a change from what the framers had intended, to do successfully what they intended would have required considerably more than courtroom magic.

48. 95 *U.S.* 485. In 1888, when Mississippi passed a law requiring segregated accommodations for railroads passing through the state, the Supreme Court upheld the law despite the objections of Justices Harlan and Bradley that there was no difference between the regulation of interstate commerce in the two cases. *Louisiana, New Orleans and Texas Railroad* v. *Mississippi*, 133 *U.S.* 587.

49. Pomeroy, "The Power of Congress to Regulate Interstate Commerce," *Southern Law Review*, IV (1878), 371n; Graham, *Everyman's Constitution*, 400–403.

The protection required by corporations was minimal. Their major need was the exercise of a judicial veto against some state legislatures' regulative efforts. They had sufficient wealth and power to influence elections, hire the nation's most skilled attorneys, and corrupt lawmakers. In addition, these corporations were often engaged in enterprise solicited and supported by state and federal governments. They could therefore count on support within the legislature. Also, there was enough popular belief in the mythology of laissez faire to insure popular backing for court decisions. Perhaps of greatest import in securing judicial backing, corporate lawyers could call upon a legal tradition in favor of vested property rights which, since at least John Marshall's time, had protected property against state governments.[50]

In contrast, what claims could the freedman make upon society to secure protection? Only that of justice. He could not guarantee increased national wealth, bribe legislators, or win elections. More than this—while he could offer nothing, he had to demand a great deal. His liberty required more than the judicial declaration that a state law was void. It required what no government in the United States had ever continually provided in normal times: the active use of power on behalf of individual liberty, a positive relationship between liberty and government, not liberty against government, but liberty protected by government whatever the obstacle, whatever the cost in constitutional tradition. It required particularly a revolution in federalism.

Pomeroy could never allow this revolution. Notwithstanding his fervent nationalism and sweeping libertarian rhetoric, he insisted that the states were still vital parts of the federal union. This belief allowed him to advance a view of the Fourteenth Amendment which promised much but delivered practically nothing. His view of the nature of the Union was all the more ominous because it was

50. This is not to say that most precedents were against state regulation; that is not the case. It required what one historian calls a "revolution" in constitutional interpretation to make the Fourteenth Amendment into the breastplate of corporations. However, there was a significant tradition in the nation's law which protected property rights with great vigor by insisting that such rights might be vested rights basic to human liberty. The revolution referred to was simply that of turning the amendment's due process clause into a protective device for those vested rights. See Kelly and Harbison, *The American Constitution*, 496–518.

not uniquely his. The majority of the Supreme Court shared Pomeroy's view of the condition of the post–Fourteenth Amendment
Union.

Pomeroy believed that, while the concept of state sovereignty
was "illogical, absurd, opposed to the truth of history," states did
retain rights "as perfect within their sphere as those of the general
government." He believed that the Constitution gave "to the agents
appointed to manage the national affairs, power enough to meet
any emergency." He believed also that the nation's charter had
"clothed the separate states with capacities to limit and restrain any
unlawful exercise of that power, and to preserve our liberties to
all time."[51]

The undercurrent of all his apparent liberalism, therefore, had
been an unfailing commitment to states' rights. His beliefs made him
delighted with the Supreme Court's *Texas* v. *White* decision. Here
the court was called upon to decide two major questions. First, had
the southern states legally seceded—in other words, what was the
nature of the Union? Second, which branch of government had the
authority to reconstruct the South? It upheld the right of Congress
over Reconstruction, thereby suggesting that federal power might
be used broadly in the former Confederacy. But when the judges
described the nature of the Union, they robbed this power of
significant meaning. They provided Pomeroy's definition of the
nation's legal nature.[52]

On August 9, 1869, Chief Justice Chase wrote to the New York
jurist, "You have doubtless seen some traces of your own thinking
in the late judgment of the Supreme Court." Modestly, Pomeroy
added the letter to a footnote in *Constitutional Law*. For there were
more than traces of his thought in the court's action. The decision
coincided so well with his views that he lost all restraint describing
it. It was "remarkable for its clearness and for the cogency of its

51. Pomeroy, *Introduction to Constitutional Law*, 103–104.

52. Most authors share the view expressed by Kelly and Harbison (*The Ameri-
can Constitution*, 481) that *Texas* v. *White* was "a major victory for the Radicals."
See McKitrick, *Andrew Johnson and Reconstruction*, 117; Rembert Patrick, *The
Reconstruction of the Nation* (New York, 1967), 116–117; William A. Dun-
ning, *Reconstruction, Political and Economic 1865–1877* (New York, 1907), 258.
But see the informative William Whatley Pierson, *Texas versus White: A Study in
Legal History* (Durham, 1916), 49.

reasoning." The decision "struck the solid ground of historical fact" and, most significant, it provided "the greatest security for the nation [and] also the greatest security for the several states."[53]

In *Texas* v. *White*, Chase had described a view of the nation which the full court continually affirmed throughout the Reconstruction era. "The Constitution in all its provisions," he declared, "looks to an indestructible Union composed of indestructible states." Pomeroy strongly agreed. He was equally pleased to hear from Justice Nelson in *Collector* v. *Day* that there were "sovereign powers vested in the states by their constitutions which [remain] unaltered and unimpaired, and in respect to which the state is as independent of the general government as that government is independent of the states." The professor thought he heard the sound of truth also from Chase in *Lane County* v. *Oregon*. "[I]n many of the articles of the Constitution, the necessary existence of the states, within their proper spheres, the independent authority of the states are distinctly recognized. To them nearly the whole charge of interior regulation is committed."[54]

Pomeroy believed that the Civil War had guaranteed a perpetual union. But that union was still composed of active, viable states. If the federal government were permitted to move troops into these states at its will, or if federal courts were allowed to assume unlimited jurisdiction, then that union under the Constitution, for which so high a price had been paid, would no longer exist. Even as he extolled nationalism, therefore, he deplored what he saw as a dangerously increasing consolidation of federal power in the Reconstruction period. He welcomed the 1874 republication of Lieber's *Civil Liberty* as "especially needed in our . . . country to counteract those tendencies of the day toward a complete centralization."[55]

As he believed in union, Pomeroy believed in equality under law for all men. He was delighted with the promises of such equality implicit in Reconstruction legislation. But he could not conceive of

53. Pomeroy, *Introduction to Constitutional Law*, 78–82, 103–104. Chase's letter cited by Pomeroy in a footnote to p. 81.

54. Pomeroy, "The Supreme Court and Its Theory of Nationality," *Nation*, XII (June 29, 1871), 445–446; *Texas* v. *White*, 7 *Wallace* 724–725; *Lane County* v. *Oregon*, 7 *Wallace* 76; *Collector* v. *Day*, 11 *Wallace* 113.

55. *Nation*, XVIII (June 18, 1874), 397.

equal justice outside the law, and he could not envision an American law that did not rest on an "indestructible union of indestructible states." He supported the principles of the Fourteenth Amendment, but only as they operated within the existing federal structure; he believed in that structure more than he believed in equal justice, for he could not visualize one without the other. He was ultimately more devoted to states' rights than to human rights, more to the structure of law than to its uses on behalf of liberty. He thought the Civil War had preserved that structure—and, tragically for the Negro, it had.

Thomas M. Cooley:
Liberty against Equality

In 1868, as the Fourteenth Amendment was being ratified, Thomas McIntyre Cooley published *Constitutional Limitations*. It was a propitious conjunction of circumstances. The amendment was an attempt to limit the ability of states to infringe on the liberties of their citizens. Cooley's book was a lucid and learned discussion of constitutionally imposed restrictions on the legislative powers of the states. Men who sought to determine how the amendment affected the exercise of state power in the post–Civil War world soon came to regard *Constitutional Limitations* as authoritative and indispensable. As the importance of the amendment expanded, so did Cooley's reputation. It became America's second constitution. Cooley became the most influential legal author of the late nineteenth and early twentieth centuries.[1]

Pervading the hundreds of cases, principles, and illustrations of *Constitutional Limitations* was a fundamental Jacksonian faith in equality. "Equality of rights, privileges, and capacities," he wrote, "unquestionably should be the aim of the law." Further, he emphasized that the word "liberty" had broad meaning; it was not confined to acting as a code word to defend intrusions upon property rights. The word "embraces all our liberties, personal, civil, and political." Freedom of worship, of speech, "the right of self defense

---

1. Fine, *Laissez Faire and the General Welfare State*, 128–129; Larsen, "Commentaries on the Constitution," 146; Alan Jones, "Thomas M. Cooley and 'Laissez-Faire Constitutionalism': A Reconsideration," *Journal of American History*, LIII (March, 1967), 759; Edward S. Corwin, *Liberty against Government* (Baton Rouge, 1948), 116–118. A former student of Cooley's, George Sutherland, sat as a justice of the Supreme Court from 1922 to 1938 and promulgated his mentor's ideas. See Joel Francis Paschal, *Mr. Justice Sutherland* (Princeton, 1951), 16–20, 170–172.

against unlawful violence," the right to attend the public schools, the equal right to buy and sell—all were included. Looking back in 1873 at the Civil War amendments, Cooley saw a culmination of Jacksonian ambitions. "Freedom is no longer sectional or partial," he exulted. "There are no privileged classes." Apparently persons who needed protection for their liberties would now receive it.[2]

Corporate persons did. Black persons did not. With amazing swiftness lawyers and judges made the Fourteenth Amendment, intended to protect Negro freedmen, into corporate property; they used Cooley's writings as their instrument. Again and again counsel turned to *Constitutional Limitations* to argue that their clients might not be deprived of liberty or property without due process of law. With equal frequency the bench cited the same book to agree with them and to strike down state regulative laws. The power of corporations increased as the century passed, and national constitutional guarantees secured the environment of their growth.[3]

Meanwhile, the position of the freedmen declined. The nationwide announcement of their access to equal liberty ceased to resound. Soon they became the prisoners of state laws, local custom, and private violence. Penned in by federalism, they could only watch the progress of the corporate giants who had stolen their amendment from them. Although he intended neither industrial growth nor the Negroes' decline, Cooley's writings were an important vehicle in the accomplishment of both. His role in the first has been described. His importance in the second requires attention.[4]

He was born in Attica, New York, in 1824 into a farming family. Despite this, his interests were intellectual. His mother encouraged him to read and study all that he could, but his father wanted Thomas to help with the farm work and to follow a plow, not carry

2. Thomas M. Cooley, *Constitutional Limitations* (Boston, 1890), 393; Joseph Story, *Commentaries on the Constitution*, ed. Thomas Cooley (Boston, 1873), II, 689.

3. Jones, "Cooley," 751n; Fine, *Laissez Faire*, 128–129.

4. Jones, "Cooley," 751–771; Clyde E. Jacobs, *Law Writers and the Courts* (Berkeley, 1954); Benjamin Twiss, *Lawyers and the Constitution* (Princeton, 1942). The most complete and thoughtful study of Cooley is Alan Jones, "The Constitutional Conservatism of Thomas McIntyre Cooley" (Ph.D. dissertation, University of Michigan, 1960). I am much indebted to this study, although Jones slights the relationship between Cooley's thought and equal rights.

a book. Perhaps because of this tension in his life, Cooley left New York in 1843 and headed for Chicago. However, his money ran out by the time he got to Adrian, Michigan, and he decided to stay there and continue the legal studies he had been able to begin at home. He entered a local law firm and was admitted to the state bar in 1846.[5]

He began his political life as a Jacksonian Democrat but joined the Republican party soon after its formation. When the Republicans carried Michigan in 1856, this new affiliation paid off. Cooley was appointed to compile the state statutes. He performed this task with his characteristic thoroughness and with sufficient skill that the judges of the state supreme court asked him, in 1858, to become the reporter of the court's decisions. Another appointment followed quickly. The next year the board of regents of the University of Michigan chose Cooley to be one of three professors for the newly formed department of law. His affiliation with the university would last until his death in 1898.

His connection with the supreme court and his growing reputation at the university gave Cooley increased stature within the legal profession of the state. It was natural, therefore, when a position on the court opened, that he would be considered and ultimately given the appointment. He joined the court in 1865 and served on it for twenty years, maintaining his position at the university at the same time.[6]

Although well known in Michigan, Cooley had no national reputation until the 1868 publication of *Constitutional Limitations*. Then his fame as a judge as well as a legal commentator grew outside the state borders. His writings on torts (1879) and on taxation (1876) further expanded his reputation, as did an 1871 edition of Blackstone and an 1873 edition of Joseph Story's *Commentaries on the Constitution*. In 1880 he wrote a small volume, *General Principles of Constitutional Law*, which was widely used as a text, and five years later he published a short history of Michigan which revealed his interest in history as well as law.

5. Harry Burns Hutchins, "Thomas McIntyre Cooley," *Great American Lawyers*, ed. William Draper Lewis (Philadelphia, 1909), VII, 429–492.

6. Alan Jones, "Thomas M. Cooley and the Michigan Supreme Court: 1865–85," *American Journal of Legal History*, X (April, 1966), 97–121.

After 1885 Cooley's time was taken up with railroad affairs. In 1886 a federal court appointed him receiver of the Wabash Railroad lines east of the Mississippi. Under his guidance the road prospered; his knowledge of the law was shown to have a practical side. He demonstrated his understanding of operating procedures and methods so well that in the spring of 1887 President Cleveland made Cooley the first chairman of the Interstate Commerce Commission. During that commission's first years Cooley was its mainspring, writing many of its reports himself and directing its operations with great skill. When he died in 1898, the legal world and the nation lost a man whose ideas had profoundly influenced law in America. His observations on the problems of the Civil War era are thus eminently worth study.[7]

I have been emphasizing the Jacksonian origins of Civil War thought. Up to now, however, only the Whig opposition has spoken. Lieber, Parker, and Pomeroy would have agreed with Fisher that Andrew Jackson was "a concentrated mob."[8] All deplored the ominous democratic rumblings that echoed when the words "Jacksonian democracy" were spoken. Their Whig backgrounds gave their thought a Hamiltonian cast.

Thomas Cooley spoke for the other side, the majority. He supported the Jeffersonian-Jacksonian ideology. He read and listened eagerly to the apotheosis of this ideology, William Leggett. This was Leggett's theme:

> We hope to see the day ... when the maxim of "Let us Alone" will be acknowledged to be better, infinitely better, than all this political quackery of ignorant legislators, instigated by the grasping, monopolizing spirit of rapacious capitalists. The country, we trust, is destined to prove to mankind the truth of the saying that "The world is governed too much," and to prove it by her own successful experiment in throwing off the clogs and fetters with which craft and cunning have ever combined to bind the mass of men.[9]

7. Hutchins, "Cooley," 486–492; Alan Jones, "Thomas M. Cooley and the Interstate Commerce Commission," *Political Science Quarterly*, LXXXI (Dec., 1966), 602–627.

8. Fisher, "National Currency," 217.

9. *The Political Writings of William Leggett*, selected by Theodore Sedgwick (New York, 1940), I, 104. Richard Hofstadter calls Leggett "The Spokesman of Jacksonian Democracy," *Political Science Quarterly*, LVIII (Dec., 1943), 581–594.

It was an argument in support of greater freedom of foreign and domestic trade, favorable to equality in rights, liberties, and opportunities. Resting on an image of a strong, independent yeoman, it was an assertion of belief in the sort of government that Jefferson *talked* about—one whose duty was simply to keep men from injuring one another and otherwise, in Jefferson's words, to "leave them free to regulate their own pursuits of industry and improvements."[10]

Cooley shared this bias and would maintain it in one form or another throughout his life. His father had a reputation as a strong Democrat and, despite the fact that the area around Attica was to spawn the Whig party in New York, young Cooley supported the Democratic cause. When he moved to Michigan, he took this cause with him. A catalogue of his heroes and intellectual mentors in the 1840s would be practically a hagiography of economic laissez faire: Richard Cobden, Ebenezer Elliott, Leggett, John Greenleaf Whittier, James Russell Lowell, and William Cullen Bryant.[11]

But the laissez faire of Jacksonian America did not exist in pure form. Citizens of all classes recognized that pure laissez faire was simply anarchy. They understood and acted on their understanding that law, properly used, was the fundamental precondition of the sort of economy and life they envisioned. Thus they used law in the way described by James Willard Hurst to support, encourage, and secure the greatest possible release of individual energy. They provided the legal instruments which made men willing to risk their fortunes and lives in search of greater wealth and hence, in their opinion, greater happiness, not only for themselves but for the nation.[12]

Cooley was in general agreement with this use of law, but he did not carry his agreement into every sphere. It was common throughout the century for state governments to support the activities of private business by using taxation and the power of eminent domain in its behalf. Cooley opposed this conjuction of state power and private enterprise whenever it seemed to offer a special privilege

10. Quoted in Marvin Meyers, *The Jacksonian Persuasion* (New York, 1957), 29.
11. Jones, "Constitutional Conservatism of Cooley," 88–95; Jones, "Laissez Faire Constitutionalism," 753.
12. Hurst, *Law and the Conditions of Freedom in the Nineteenth-Century United States*, Ch. 1.

which benefited only a few. A poem he wrote in 1852 reveals this sentiment most clearly:

> There is not room if one may
> Own the land that others toil on,
> If gold be dug or grain be sown
> For drones to gorge and spoil on.
> But, if to each the equal chance
> To plow and dig be guarded,
> To competence may all advance
> Through honest toil rewarded.
> There's room, and more than room, here
> And gold beyond the mountains.
> Then let the land, and chance for gold
> Be free as nature's fountains.[13]

Cooley's Jacksonian roots are easily documented. He shared the vision of the independent individual, astride his environment, reins securely in his hands. But it was a vision to be realized only if some distressing weaknesses in society might be remedied.

Jackson had focused his attack on the Bank of the United States as the symbol of the major evils of his age. It was the perfect image of private power supported by government power, taking advantage of men striving to make it on their own. But more than that, the bank was something which worked its evil on society in obscure, unfathomable ways; it destroyed hopes so subtly, so deviously that one might doubt that the fault lay really with the bank itself. Jackson was sure, violently sure, and so were millions of his followers. They were so sure that it is easy to doubt that they understood what the trouble really was; it seems likely that the bank was simply the most obvious scapegoat for failures throughout the society itself. The vision of a society of independent yeomen was predicated on the optimistic view that a society of such men might exist and preserve itself. But such a society had existed in the past (at least, so Jacksonian oratory insisted), and it had been corrupted. What guarantee was there that, even if restored, it would not fail again?[14]

Pervading the vision of a glorious future of equality, wealth, and

13. Quoted in Jones, "Constitutional Conservatism of Cooley," 81.
14. Meyers, *The Jacksonian Persuasion*, 10–14.

freedom was an undercurrent of doubt and anxiety. Intellectuals were sensitive to it. Hawthorne, Melville, and Poe, to name the most obvious, somberly suggested the possibilities on the American scene. Emerson's early hopeful essays were followed by darker musings that perhaps the ordinary man was too ordinary to build from a liberal society the exalted transcendental soul.[15]

Jackson himself reflected the ambivalence of his age. His farewell address mixed hopes and fears in a bittersweet potion. "The progress of the United States under free and happy institutions has surpassed the most sanguine hopes of the republic . . . never have thirteen millions of people associated together in one political body . . . enjoyed so much freedom and happiness." The optimistic hope was there. But one sentence later the latent fear of the easy corruptibility of the people asserted itself. External dangers need not be feared, the President asserted, but "it is from within, among yourselves, from cupidity, from corruption, from disappointed ambitions, and inordinate thirst for power, that factions will be formed and liberty endangered." In the final words of this address, where some ringing avowal of hope might have been expected, Jackson did not assure the nation that it would succeed. He could only hope that God might help the people to defend the charge given into their keeping. If Jackson was "the symbol for an age," then that age must be recognized for its fears as well as its hopes, and the intertwining of both fear and hope.[16]

There was manifest reason for fear in the economic realm. Burgeoning liberal capitalism and increasing democracy fed on each other. Increasing wealth increased the influence of wealth in politics; desire for democratizing economic opportunity encouraged the loosening of economic restrictions. In the law the goal was to release individual creative energies, but the result was naturally enough to allow the most able and/or least scrupulous to prevail, and to permit cycles of boom and bust to work their will. "For the sake of present

15. R. W. B. Lewis, *The American Adam*; Stephen Whicher, *Freedom and Fate: An Inner Life of Ralph Waldo Emerson* (Philadelphia, 1953).

16. Joseph Blau, ed., *Social Theories of Jacksonian Democracy* (New York, 1947), 20; John William Ward, *Andrew Jackson, Symbol for an Age* (New York, 1955); Fred Somkin, *Unquiet Eagle: Memory and Desire in the Idea of American Freedom 1815–60* (Ithaca, 1967).

boom," James Willard Hurst remarks, "we recurrently subjected ourselves to future breakdown."[17]

The hopes of the day could become the nightmare of the future. The periodic panics of the pre–Civil War years show that the nightmare was frequent and troubling. There was an economic basis for the era's underlying doubts, and in a society as economically oriented as America's, economic insecurity suggested potential weakness in the whole societal fabric.

Responding to this insecurity and anxiety, the nation engaged in an outburst of reform activity. Reflecting the non-specific nature of the apprehension, reformers of all types set off to reform practically everything about the United States. Religious revivals endeavored to purify the American soul; educational changes were sought to broadcast more widely the virtues of the nation; moral uplifters urged changes in the drinking habits of democrats; dedicated humanitarians insisted that American prisons and asylums abandon brutality. Those who despaired of saving the nation sought to save themselves by founding utopian communities and new religions, or preparing for Armageddon.[18]

Most threatening of all to the realization of national ideals was the fact of slavery. It was a clear repudiation of the belief in equal liberty for all men which formed the crux of Jacksonian thought. But for a time human bondage was only a theoretical contradiction, maintained by widespread belief that Negroes deserved slavery and that the Constitution protected it. Generally, northern Jacksonians kept slavery in the back of their thoughts and sought their ambitions and hopes in the future of the country.

But then slavery protruded itself into their thoughts and seemed to endanger their hopes. Victory in the Mexican War raised the spectre that territory which had been part of the white man's future would not be occupied by Jeffersonian yeomen, but by a rigid slave society. To foreclose such a possibility, Pennsylvania Congressman David Wilmot offered his famous proviso that slavery might not exist in

17. Hurst, *Law and Conditions of Freedom*, 67.

18. Tyler, *Freedom's Ferment*; Clifford S. Griffin, *Their Brother's Keepers: Moral Stewardship in the United States, 1800–1865* (New Brunswick, 1960). For a thoughtful and handy bibliographical study of pre-Civil War reform, see Clifford S. Griffin, *The Ferment of Reform, 1830–60* (New York, 1967).

any territory acquired by the United States as a result of the war.

Wilmot struck a Jacksonian note in advocating his measure. He told his colleagues that his goal was "to preserve for free white labor in a fair country, a rich inheritance, where the sons of toil, of my own race and color, can live without the disgrace which association with negro slavery brings upon free labor." Walt Whitman took up the cry. The free soil question issue involved the "question between *the grand body of white workingmen, the millions of mechanics, farmers, and operatives of our country*; with their interests on one side and the interest of the few thousand rich, 'polished' and aristocratic owners of slaves at the South on the other side."[19]

Cooley shared this sentiment. He was among the leaders and founders of the Free Soil party in southeastern Michigan. The program of this group reflected its Jacksonian origins. It was antislavery but also against what one of its leaders called "anti-democratic social conditions." The movement reflected the general sentiment that freedom from all unrestrained power was the goal of true democrats.[20]

But this creation of new parties also suggested that something was wrong with the nation. It reflected a feeling that existing institutions had failed, and that men would have to discover other paths to the realization of their dreams. Cooley's move from party regularity thus suggested more than a personal feeling that slavery was incompatible with his ideals. It revealed a general feeling that society itself was sick, that his youthful optimism was unfounded, that there was more to liberty than unexamined egalitarian oratory. He showed a growing awareness of the possibilities for evil and failure in man and society. By the 1850s his favorite authors were no longer Emerson and Leggett, but Hawthorne and Dickens.[21]

As the prewar crisis intensified and sectional quarreling threatened to tear the nation apart, his apprehension grew. Events in Kansas and the *Dred Scott* decision troubled him; when the national

19. Wilmot and Whitman both quoted in Arthur Schlesinger Jr., *The Age of Jackson* (Boston, 1945), 450–452.

20. Jones, "Laissez Faire Constitutionalism," 753–754; Salmon P. Chase to Samuel Beaman quoted in Jones, "Constitutional Conservatism of Cooley," 54; William O. Lynch, "Anti-Slavery Tendencies of the Democratic Party in the Northwest, 1848–50," *Mississippi Valley Historical Review*, XI (Dec., 1924), 319–331.

21. Jones, "Constitutional Conservatism of Cooley," 109.

administration endorsed proslavery actions in Kansas, Cooley joined the ranks of anti-Nebraska Democrats who would soon supply the new Republican party with such men as Salmon Chase, Lyman Trumbull, Benjamin Butler, Gideon Welles, Hannibal Hamlin, and Walt Whitman. In 1856 he officially joined the Republicans. This party seemed to him to be least equivocal in its devotion to equal liberty.

More important than his political affiliations, however, was the effect of the prewar societal crisis on his legal thought. Although his papers are scanty for this period, there is evidence of a growing interest in Blackstone and the common law. He came to revere James Mackintosh, a noted apostle of conservative Edmund Burke. Reflecting a feeling later described by T. S. Eliot, Cooley became more and more interested in history and studied the relationship between common law and American liberty. "This is the use of memory," Eliot would write, "for liberation—not less of love, but expanding of love beyond desire, and so liberation from the future as well as the past." The Michigan jurist focused on the history of England, which told him that principles of liberty were given by God to Anglo-Saxon nations who embodied them in their customs and traditions. Common law was the structure of tradition and custom which preserved and promoted individual liberty; it was the perfection of natural reason and artificial reason. He accepted Matthew Hale's reverence for the common law "not as the product of some one man or society of men in any one age; but of the wisdom, council, experience, and observation of many ages of wise and knowing men." Even as the nation apparently fell apart, Cooley came more and more to believe that an institutional framework, such as that provided by the common law, was imperative for liberty. With the nation secured in 1868, he would extoll the common law, in spite of its faults, as "on the whole the . . . best foundation on which to erect an enduring structure of civil liberty which the world has ever known."[22]

This respect for the common law did not, however, place Cooley with legal experts like Kent, Story, Webster, Joel Parker, Francis Lieber, or Sidney George Fisher. Cooley modified his Jacksonian-

22. *Ibid.*, 102–108; Cooley, *Constitutional Limitations*, iii, 23.

ism; he did not repudiate it. He was sensitive to the need for law and a respect for history in a democratic society, but he was equally sensitive to the need for liberty. He was much more concerned than those men with maintaining an open society—one which, though restrained by respect for law and history, offered every man an equal chance to exercise his talents and abilities. In contrast to more conservative legalists, Cooley disliked the Dartmouth College decision. He deplored the support given by the Supreme Court to an ancient contract over the popular desire to permit the legislature to change established institutions for the people's benefit. "It is under the protection of [that] decision," he said, "that the most enormous and threatening powers in our country have been created."[23]

The common law which Cooley admired protected liberty first, then order, though it protected both most tenaciously. It was a common law that was suspicious of legislation, insistent about the equality of law, and always opposed to arbitrary power. Cooley's common law respected Jacksonian goals when it emphasized the idea that constitutional government was limited government, and that under just law all men's rights were equal. The law which Cooley admired was one which opened opportunity and formed a structure which protected liberty and property already won, but which also guaranteed the continued search and reward for enterprise. It was a law for liberal capitalism which opposed privilege. Its spirit: no one shall receive from the law special privileges; all shall have equal opportunities; no one shall be allowed to concentrate power to such an extent that liberty is impossible.[24]

This fusing of liberty and institutional structure was common to all the figures of this study. It is seen in Lieber's nationalism, in Parker's strict constructionist constitutionalism, in Fisher's commitment to established societal and class relationships, and in Pomeroy's federalism. Cooley's thought might be classified as common law Jacksonianism. In his case, as in the others, the fusion process was a natural result of a troubled Jacksonian world. The result of their efforts was generally to restrain power by the use of institutions

23. Cooley, *Constitutional Limitations*, 335; Jones, "Laissez Faire Constitutionalism," 755.
24. Jones, "Laissez Faire Constitutionalism," 757–758.

(certainly a completely tenable position), but, more specifically, it was to equate the preservation of existing institutions with the survival of liberty (a considerably more suspect claim).

Cooley engaged in this more dubious process by insisting that the Jacksonian goal of equal liberty under law might only be achieved safely if men recognized liberty's deep historical and institutional foundations. Supporting his contention, he hit upon the common law roots of American liberty. In doing this he joined a widespread effort of the legal profession in the prewar years, and he revealed the basic weakness in the era's legal thought: its fear of the exercise of governmental power in innovative ways.

Although American law was heavily dependent upon the English common law, reliance upon its restraining influence was unnecessarily conservative in this instance. In England the restraining power of common law is kept from being too effective by the unitary form of parliamentary government. Parliament not only makes the laws; it is also responsible for their execution and is the ultimate arbiter of their constitutionality. Although the principles of common law can restrain, they cannot inhibit Parliament from exercising the nation's power to any extent necessary to respond to challenge. "Parliament," Blackstone insisted, "may do anything but make a man into a woman, or a woman into a man."

In the United States, born of a rebellion against that assertion, the federal government is restrained considerably short of parliamentary power. Our constitutional troika already restrains the exercise of national power, and federalism further diminishes the power that remains. The insistence on the restraining power of the common law was in fact redundant; it revealed just how fearful of unrestrained power many jurists were. It mirrored a devotion to institutional restraints which made most of them equate liberty with the negation of power.

Such an attitude was an effective antislavery instrument. Slavery involved the ultimate assertion of both state and national power against individuals. It also seemed to threaten the institutional sinews of the nation by the way in which it turned representative bodies into armed encampments, courts into political forums for dubious constitutional rhetoric, and presidents into advocates of territorial tyranny. It was easy for Jacksonians like Cooley to believe that the death of slavery would mean an end to arbitrary power and to en-vision a future in which free men boldly and successfully exercised their now unshackled talents.[25]

The fallacy of such a view was its failure to recognize that the age of the free omnicompetent individual was in the past, not in the future. Even when applied to the white man it was an illusion. So-ciety grew more complex every day, and concentrations of eco-nomic power grew, fostered by freedom from the exercise of adequate governmental regulative power. Freedom there was and would be, but not freedom equally enjoyed. The myth of a society of equality conflicted with the fact of a society of unequal indi-viduals. Equal freedom would ultimately require not the negation but the exercise of governmental power. That power would not be provided in ample portion to protect even white men until the first half of the twentieth century. Blacks would wait an additional half-century before they could claim its benefits. When such power was available and combined with a willingness to use force to secure freedom, men not free might hope; without such willingness, the hope was chimerical.

Cooley would never clearly understand the contradiction be-tween equality and individualism; neither would he recognize the extent to which an exercise of power might help resolve the con-flict. He was too occupied with securing existing institutional ar-rangements to consider the possibility that they might be inadequate to the nation's future needs. In any event, the Civil War effectively ended any possibility that he might seek new options. As an attack on the old order, it made the salvation of that order the measure of victory. Coming as the culmination of a decade of doubt and dis-order, it committed him all the more to the maintenance of the institutions he had come to equate with the survival of ordered liberty.

He was most anxious about the potential turmoil of wartime. He did not agree with abolitionists who insisted that the conflict offered

25. On use of common law by American jurists to restrain democratic natural law impulses, see Miller, *Life of the Mind in America*, 99ff. On slavery as a threat to northern liberties, see Russell Nye, *Fettered Freedom: Civil Liberties and the Slav-ery Controversy, 1830–1860* (East Lansing, 1963). On slavery as a threat to institu-tions of government in the North, see chapters on Lieber, Parker, and Fisher, above.

an opportunity for revolution against all the institutions that protected slavery. He did not agree with men like Fisher and Lieber that the great benefit of this conflict was that it opened minds for new ideas. Although certainly a greater believer in democracy than either of those men, Cooley's democratic faith was woven with doubt. He did not share their joy at the outpouring of popular support for any new measure which might save the country.[26]

Given a chance to talk at length about the meaning of the war, the Michigan lawyer spoke of the need for order in the midst of potential revolution. Addressing a crowd assembled to dedicate the new law building in Ann Arbor in the fall of 1863, he focused on the stable elements, the old institutions, for which the nation was fighting. He reminded his listeners of the Anglo-Saxon roots of American law. He emphasized the long national experience with local self-government. At a time when many were concerned with increasing nationalism, Cooley, like Parker, insisted on the traditional benefits of local self-government in the way that it "fitted men to larger responsibilities [and] made them conscious of the public purposes which government was to serve." No law that he ever taught, he insisted, would ever have "any tendency to strengthen the State at the expense of the nation, or to exalt the nation on the ruin of the state."

Recognizing that in wartime men might resort to what he termed "desperate remedies," Cooley still sought to limit the occasions and justifications for their use. Echoing John Norton Pomeroy, he insisted that in times of disorder it was "the part of wisdom to keep an eye to the old landmarks, and so to shape action that when the commotion is quelled there shall be apparent, not mere heaps of materials from which to build something new, but the same good old ship of state, with some progress toward justice and freedom." Great danger to those landmarks could result from yielding to "those temporary excitements which sometimes sweep over the people and from which no body of men can at all times be free." Only respect for established legal tradition would protect Americans from the dangers of such momentary passions.[27]

26. Fisher, *Trial of the Constitution*, v–vi; Lieber, *Miscellaneous Writings*, ed. Gilman, II, 147.
27. Quoted in Jones, "Constitutional Conservatism of Cooley," 112–119.

To further secure the stability of the nation and society, Cooley emphasized the crucial role that the legal profession was to play in guiding the nation through the war and in securing the results of the fighting. Echoing the urgings of lawyers and congressmen throughout the nation, he insisted that the legal profession was uniquely qualified for such an important task. Untrained persons "would cut and hew blindly in their ignorance until the beautiful fabric which has required ages to build may be utterly defaced by vandal hands." But lawyers could promote change without loosing anarchy. "The lawyer is and should be conservative," he insisted. "However radical the change he may desire to make, the lessons of our judicial history admonish him that they can only be safely brought about in the slow processes of time."[28]

A Jeffersonian who read Hawthorne, a Jacksonian who respected Blackstone and the common law, a devotee of individual freedom who feared the masses, Thomas Cooley encountered Reconstruction with ideas and assumptions which would severely limit uncompromising devotion to its legislation. Obstacles stood in the way of an unconditional commitment to human freedom. Innovations, he believed, required historical basis, and American history was singularly lacking in precedents for national power used in behalf of individual freedom. Distrusting power and revering liberty as he did, the Michigan lawyer was sure to feel discomfort where force was exercised to protect liberty. To Cooley, constitutional government was, by definition, government restrained. He was sure to suspect government action to guarantee liberty. When the Civil War ended, he was inclined to feel that the question of liberty and freedom for all men had been settled; he was not prepared to understand that it had only begun to be argued. He looked back at what had been preserved, too relieved to envision what had possibly been won.

Writing additional chapters on the Civil War amendments for his 1873 edition of Joseph Story's *Commentaries on the Constitution*, Cooley reviewed the impact of the war. He rejoiced that the "dangerous excrescence of slavery" had been removed from the nation. Human bondage had not only been a moral wrong; it had also threatened the permanence of the nation by a controversy made all the more bitter by the fact that each side had insisted that it alone

28. *Ibid.*, 117.

defended the sacred Constitution. This violent and fearful antipathy had been the cause of war.

The war had killed slavery by releasing the force of pro-union sentiment against the institution. Prior to Sumter, concern for the integrity of the Union had restricted anti-slavery sentiment to a small group of radicals. But when the South dissolved the bonds of union, fears for union no longer restrained criticism or action. Emancipation ceased to be solely the dream of the revolutionary and became the necessity of the patriot. The Thirteenth Amendment, born of necessity, had removed slavery as "a disturbance and danger to the body politic."[29]

Cooley recognized the post-Appomattox fear of Congress that the conflict might somehow resume should leaders of the rebellion regain control of their states. He saw that Andrew Johnson's Reconstruction measures "did not sufficiently protect the government against the danger of States passing under disloyal control." Neither did executive action provide sufficient protection for freedmen or loyal Southerners. Southern states had passed the so-called Black Codes, which practically reduced the freedmen to peonage. He understood the fears behind these codes but deplored them. They would only "perpetuate the degradation of this [recently enslaved] people." He was pleased that Congress had responded to these measures with the Civil Rights Act of 1866, which made the freedmen citizens. He was even more pleased when Congress ended all doubt about the constitutionality of this act by initiating the Fourteenth Amendment. The subsequent ratification of this measure settled the vexing question of the status of the Negro in the United States.[30]

This was Cooley's history of the meaning of the war era. It conformed to his Jacksonian hopes and fears. As Huck Finn said of Mark Twain, "He told the truth, mostly." But Cooley left out the crucial part: the spawning in the war era of new constitutional possibilities which would make Jacksonian goals realities for the freedmen. Hiding in the Michigan lawyer's apparent support for equalitarian legislation were attitudes poorly designed to bring these measures to life.

29. Story, *Commentaries*; Cooley's additions, II, 633–646.
30. *Ibid.*, 649–654, 661–662.

To have impact, the measures would have to be seen as the beginning of a new constitutional era, a promise by the federal government that it would do what it had never done before: act in behalf of a citizen's personal liberty. Abolitionists and radicals, and even more advanced moderates, argued plausibly that the federal government's power to free the slave implied a promise that such power would exist to secure that freedom should it be endangered. But to Cooley the Fourteenth Amendment, the legitimizer of future federal action, was a promise kept, not a promise made. It was the end of a crusade, not its beginning.[31]

Cooley supported the amendment as a means to end doubts about the legal condition of the black man in America. The whole war crisis had been generated over this fundamental question. The time had come, he insisted, to cool this passion. The people wished to forget the war and to resolve its bloodstained uncertainties. They were turning their thoughts in new directions, but before they finally did so, they wished to tie together the loose ends of civil war. "The number was few indeed," he said, "who would have been disposed to deny citizenship to this portion of the people, or to object to a settlement of the question by express declaration of the Constitution."[32]

He spoke here for millions of war-weary Americans, but the ideas he expressed did not suggest to him an abandonment of equality as he understood it. He did not seek to achieve normalcy by knowingly sacrificing equal justice under law. He believed that the war, by purging the constitutional system of slavery, had secured it. With the Fourteenth Amendment securing to Negroes their citizenship rights, and the Fifteenth Amendment proscribing race or previous slavery as a condition of voting, he insisted that no "particular or invidious distinction" could infringe on the legal equality of Americans.[33]

Cooley did more than write about equality; he showed his belief in it as a member of the Michigan Supreme Court. For example, an 1869 case raised the issue of educational discrimination against a

31. Brock, *An American Crisis*, 250–254; McKitrick, *Andrew Johnson and Reconstruction*, 93–120.

32. Story, *Commentaries*, 654.

33. *Ibid.*, 656.

Negro boy. In 1867 Michigan had amended her general school law to say that any resident of a school district might attend any school in the district as long as such attendance did not interfere with the system of grading schools according to the intellectual level of the students. But the Detroit schools had special legislation which allowed students to be racially segregated. When the youngster attempted to enroll in an all-white school, he was denied entrance. His parents insisted on his right to enroll; the case reached Cooley's bench. The judge ordered the school board of Detroit to admit the student, ruling that the state law overturned the city's special legislation and meant that Negroes might not be excluded from white schools because of their race. In addition, Cooley observed that the young man had been deprived of advanced education, since the Negro schools in Detroit were only elementary schools. Although the judge was only enforcing a law, he intimated that even without the law the court would have taken the same position under the due process clause of the state constitution.[34]

This action and others like it on the bench showed that he meant it when he insisted in 1873 that the Fourteenth Amendment made it a "settled rule of constitutional law that color or race is no badge of inferiority and no test of capacity to participate in government." In addition, he doubted "if any distinction whatever, either in right or privilege, which has color or race for its sole basis, can either be established in the law or enforced where it had previously been established." That question had been settled.[35]

But the only settlement that had in fact been made was a legal settlement, one to be defined in terms of existing legal limitations and structures. The amendment declared, "No State shall make or enforce any law which shall abridge the privileges or immunities of citizens of the United States; nor shall any State deprive any person of life, liberty, or property, without due process of law; nor deny to any person within its jurisdiction the equal protection of the laws." These were principles with which Cooley agreed. But the vital question was how these principles would secure *de facto* the equal

34. *People v. Board of Education of Detroit*, 18 *Michigan* 400 (1869). *People v. Dean*, 14 *Michigan* 406 (1866); Jones, "Cooley and the Michigan Supreme Court," 119; Cooley, *Constitutional Limitations*, 494.

35. Story, *Commentaries*, 676.

justice promised *de jure*. How would they operate in relation to the federal system? Would they change or preserve it?

As he described the actual working of the amendment, it became clear that, despite sincere words of acceptance of its egalitarian principles, Cooley would not allow them to be experienced as facts in the lives of the freedmen. Defying the intentions of Congress, ignoring expressed statements of law, rejecting the possibility that the war had altered the federal system, he offered an explanation which made the amendment simply rhetorical. Most important, his description was not *sui generis*; it rested securely on widely recognized and respected constitutional principles. Although Cooley falsified the intentions of the framers of postwar changes, his argument was plausible enough to gain the acceptance of the many war-weary people who sought an explanation that demanded little of them.

The amendment, he said, had been passed to strengthen the guarantee of citizenship provided under the 1866 Civil Rights Act. It was to overturn the *Dred Scott* decision that blacks were not citizens. According to the bill and the amendment, he noted, "The freedmen were to have the same right in every State and territory of the United States to make and enforce contracts; to sue, be parties and give evidence; to inherit, purchase, lease, sell, hold, and convey real and personal property; and to full and equal benefit of all laws and proceedings for the security of persons and property as is enjoyed by white citizens, and to be subject to the like punishments, pains and penalties and to none other, any statute, ordinance, regulation, or custom to the contrary notwithstanding." (This was a direct quotation from the bill.) Then came an immensely crucial qualifier. These rights which the national legislature was establishing for the freedmen became, in his words, "the privileges and immunities of citizens of the States."[36]

These last words are so important because Cooley believed that the phrase "No state shall make or enforce any law which shall abridge the privileges or immunities of citizens of the United States" did not refer to the rights of state citizens but only to those of national citizenship. "The difference," he stated, "is in high degree important . . . the privileges which pertain to citizenship under the general government are as different in their nature from those which

36. *Ibid.*, 653–656.

belong to citizenship in a State as the functions of the one government are different from those of the other." The vital question then
became, what were the privileges and immunities which each government protected? On this definition would hang the extent of
protection that could be claimed by the freedmen—in short, their
access to equal justice rested on it.

Cooley's catalogue of federally protected rights was minuscule.
He suggested that the 1823 description of those rights provided by a
federal circuit court in *Corfield* v. *Coryell* was the only proper one.
The following were exclusively federal rights: protection against
wrongful action by foreign governments, use of passports, use of
all navigable waters of the nation, use of post office facilities. "Such
rights and privileges," Cooley magnanimously asserted, "the general
government must allow and insure, and the several States must not
abridge or obstruct; but the duty of protection to a citizen of a State
in his privileges and immunities as such is not by this clause [of the
Fourteenth Amendment] devolved upon the general government
but remains with the State itself, where it naturally and properly
belongs."[37]

37. *Ibid.*, 558–560, 657–659. The consensus of twentieth-century scholarship holds
that the dictum of Justice Washington in the *Corfield* case supports an expanded
view of nationally protected privileges and immunities. See Arnold J. Lein, *Concurring Opinion: The Privileges and Immunities Clause of the Fourteenth Amendment*
(St. Louis, 1957), 27–28, 55–56; Roger Howell, *The Privileges and Immunities of
State Citizenship* (Baltimore, 1918), 19–20; W. J. Myers, "Privileges and Immunities
of Citizens in the Several States," *Michigan Law Review*, I (1902), 291–292; Graham, *Everyman's Constitution*, 48, 180, 307–311, 331–332. The evidence against this
view seems much more convincing, however. First, the issue in the case is not that
of expanding nationally protected privileges and immunities; it is whether or not
one state, New Jersey, may deny to a citizen of another state, Pennsylvania, a right
which it grants to its own citizens. Second, the lawyers for the plaintiff who rejected New Jersey's restrictions did not demand an expanded view of national privileges and immunities. They simply argued that New Jersey had to treat Pennsylvania
citizens the same way it treated its own citizens. Third, the court rejected this argument and upheld the restrictions which New Jersey had applied. Fourth, Justice
Bushrod Washington, in discussing the source of the privileges and immunities
clause, points to its origin in the Articles of Confederation, hardly the sort of heritage for an allegedly nationalizing clause. Fifth, although Washington's language
is not the model of precision, he does seem to insist on the rights of the states to
control the privileges and immunities of their citizens; nowhere does he suggest that
there are new privileges and immunities of national citizens which require either
legislative protection or judicial definition. It would be surprising to find the former, but when even the latter is absent, I find it difficult to accept the predominant

Had this view been isolated, it would deserve only passing mention. But it was the opinion adopted by the U.S. Supreme Court in April, 1873, the same year that Cooley offered his views. In the Slaughterhouse cases Justice Samuel Miller spoke for a 5–4 court in accepting Cooley's division of state and national privileges and immunities. He cited and quoted *Corfield* vs. *Coryell* as precedent. It would be 1935 before the Court would expand upon this list of federally protected privileges and immunities. Neither Cooley nor Miller provided reasons why the amendment should be so emasculated. Both were so firmly gripped by a commitment to the old federal Union that they seemed to think that their assumptions required no argument. Both simply made fact out of personal belief. Miller declared that it was not possible to believe that the framers had intended to change the nature of the Union, and Cooley simply asserted that the duty of protecting a citizen in the exercise of his fundamental rights remained with the state. Why? Because that was "where it naturally and properly belongs."[38]

An amendment that was intended by its authors to provide national protection for rights to life, liberty, and property had been transformed into an innocuous declaration of the permanence of the old federal union. Although Cooley had insisted that the amendment constitutionalized the Civil Rights Act, when it came to describing the constitutional changes wrought by the amendment, he simply ignored what the act said. Its purpose was to end interference with citizenship rights of all kinds from whatever source they arose. Lawmakers recognized that states' rights would have to be limited, and they limited them.[39]

---

historical judgment. Washington's dictum is indeed inspiring. The privileges and immunities of citizens "in the several states" are, he says, those "which are in their nature fundamental; which belong of right, to the citizens of all free governments." He includes in these the right to protection, life, liberty, property, to pursue happiness and safety, and to vote, in addition to those things noted by Cooley. But the crucial point is whether or not these are rights of state or national citizens. The weight of the evidence suggests that they are those of state citizens. See 6 *Federal Cases* 549, esp. 552. In short, Cooley was correct in his use of the *Corfield* precedent, and so was Justice Miller in his use of it in the Slaughterhouse case.

38. *Ibid.*, 659; 16 *Wallace* 82.

39. Analysis of the act reveals its intended impact on federalism. It declared that "any person [not just any state] who under color of any law, statute, ordinance, regulation or custom [the proscribed action need not be the passage of a state law]

Cooley's transformation of the amendment did not occur because of racism or a disbelief in federal sovereignty. Cooley seems never to have displayed anti-Negro sentiment, and he often displayed the contrary. He had vigorously supported the Union government during the war and had upheld the power of Congress over military Reconstruction. He was much like Justice Miller in this regard.[40]

What led Cooley to strip from the Fourteenth Amendment its intended potency was his passionate conviction that only abiding respect for constitutional traditions would provide the order necessary for the realization of his Jacksonian dreams of equal liberty. As his dreams envisioned an absence of excessive power, it is understandable that he rejected a view of the amendment so permissive of the exercise of federal power. He believed that the war had saved the old federal union, not transformed it. As demonstrated above, he was not alone in this view.

The specific instrument whereby Cooley transformed the amendment from a call to action into a victory celebration was the venerable comity clause of the Constitution. Article IV, Section 2 declares: "The citizens of each State shall be entitled to all privileges and immunities of citizens in the several states." The common meaning of this clause was that a citizen of one state would not be discriminated against in another state. For example, Georgia might not pass a law which denied citizens of other states the access to Georgia courts which her own citizens possessed. If such a discriminatory law were passed, the injured party might appeal to the federal courts for redress. But for protection for exercising a legal right which he shared equally with other citizens, a citizen was dependent on the state. In short, unequal laws were appealable; unequal protection was not.

This clause was an obvious referent for the Fourteenth Amendment. The words "privileges" and "immunities" appeared in both; the Supreme Court had rendered decisions which illuminated, albeit none too clearly, the meaning of those words within the constitu-

---

shall subject, or cause to be subjected, any inhabitant [not only citizens] of any State or Territory to the deprivation of any right secured or protected by this act" because of color or prior slavery, was deemed guilty of a misdemeanor and could be punished by a fine of $1,000 and one year in jail, or both. Federal courts had exclusive jurisdiction over violations of this act. See *Statutes at Large*, XIV, 27.

40. Fairman, *Mr. Justice Miller and the Supreme Court*, 124–140.

tional system. The comity clause was the subject of the 1823 *Corfield* case. Clearly conservatives such as Cooley could argue that the amendment's meaning was limited to what the federal system of the prewar years allowed.

This argument would have been untenable had the authors of the amendment insisted that they intended to give the phrase new meaning which would secure federal protection for important civil rights. Although this argument did appear occasionally in debates on the amendment, it was not broadcast widely, because for thirty years those abolitionists who advanced the amendment had been insisting (despite court decisions to the contrary) that the comity clause already secured that protection. Thus the amendment, in the eyes of most proponents, was declaratory—it simply made a law out of a previously existing fact. It changed nothing. But this, of course, was also Cooley's position, and those judges who studied the record for the true meaning of the amendment might conclude that both sides sought the same thing.[41]

What distinguished the two was their image of what the prewar constitutional world had been. In any argument where the weight of legal tradition mattered, Cooley's opponents were on much weaker ground than he was. Guided by the belief that slavery must die because it violated the slaves' natural rights as human beings, abolitionists grabbed for useful arguments wherever they might find them. When they accepted the need to appease the pervasive constitutionalism of their fellow citizens, they faced a difficult task. The Constitution had been written to secure the support of slave-owners; it did not yield antislavery arguments easily.

The comity clause was especially weak. While it says that citizens of a state may claim its benefits, it does not confer them on noncitizens and (more important) it does not remove from the states the right to define who shall be citizens. The clause is not a grant of federal power to do anything; it is not even a prohibition of action by a state. It merely says that whatever a state decides to offer its citizens as benefits must be offered equally to citizens of other states. Further, the clause does not define what privileges and immunities are. For clarification of these points the decision of a court was

41. Graham, "Our 'Declaratory' Fourteenth Amendment," *Everyman's Constitution*, 295–336; Jacobus ten Broek, *Equal under Law* (New York, 1965), 94–108.

required, and judges were unlikely to be moved by arguments which rested basically on the sincere wish of abolitionists that the clause mean something that would advance their cause. Victory for the abolition view depended more on moral and humanitarian sentiment than on constitutional argument.[42]

The war had generated a tremendous interest in legal and constitutional questions. Union troops had fought against what Lincoln called "the essence of anarchy" and for the rule of law. When victory for that viewpoint was assured, a society chastened by the consequences of excessive romanticism and individualism sought constitutional roots for its legislative efforts and as a foundation for reunion. Cooley, who had opposed slavery fundamentally because it endangered order, helped provide these roots by insisting on the continuity of past institutions with the war era's amendments.[43]

The Fourteenth Amendment, he insisted, was simply a restatement of the comity clause which changed the federal system not at all. His only concession to change was an admission that now the question of Negro citizenship was no longer in doubt as it had been before the war. Blacks might now claim the protection of the comity clause without question, but they would do so within an unchanged institutional framework. The provisions of the amendment, he wrote, "have not been agreed upon for the purpose of enlarging the sphere of powers of the general government, or of taking from the States of any of those just powers of government which in the original adoption of the Constitution were 'reserved to the States respectively.' The existing division of sovereignty is not disturbed by it."[44]

The imperative preliminary to the protection of equal justice was a significant alteration in the "existing division of sovereignty." To Cooley such a change was intolerable. Although deeply worried about the condition of prewar society, he had not considered the possibility that the Jacksonian dream of equal men exercising their freedom equally in a world where government played a negative

42. ten Broek, *Equal under Law*, 97–103.

43. Stampp, *And the War Came*, 221–239; Fredrickson, *The Inner Civil War*, 183–198; Basler, ed., *Collected Works of Lincoln*, IV, 268.

44. Story, *Commentaries on the Constitution*, 683–684; Cooley, *Constitutional Limitations*, 631, 497–498.

role might itself be a cause of failure. He did not ascribe the trouble to either the dream or the constitutional system. Rather, he hit upon slavery as the problem—as the corruptor of venerable institutions good in themselves and of ideals unquestionably worthy. He hit upon slavery with the same pathetic eagerness as earlier Jacksonians had hit upon the Bank of the United States as the source of all evils.

Cooley recognized that the war had produced an expanded national power, but he believed that only the necessity of destroying the great corruptor justified such power. He hoped that, with slavery and its most blatant vestiges gone, the status quo antebellum that he had dreamed of might be achieved. He therefore argued eloquently that the legal innovations of war and Reconstruction were only temporary expedients and that the true fruit of victory was a restored prewar constitutional system. Given most Americans' respect for the recently won union and their long-standing love affair with the Constitution, his argument was convincing. The nation accepted the prewar union as the prize of battle and rejected for almost one hundred years the much greater prize that had potentially been won.

Conclusion:
No Second American Revolution

The Civil War era was filled with the promise of equal rights for the Negro. The conflict harmonized two strains of American sentiment with great potential benefit to him: the humanitarian concern for his personal condition, and the widespread selfish concern of whites for the endurance of the legal and constitutional order. The efforts of abolitionists and Radical Republicans, who had long pointed to the inhumanity of slavery and who gained influence during the war, were vital in bringing about emancipation and the equality measures of Reconstruction.[1]

To this humanitarianism was joined the powerful devotion of Americans to the Constitution and the rule of law. The recognition that slavery endangered northern liberties generated a hostility against the South which made war, the only conceivable emancipator, possible. The war itself, which so clearly linked the maintenance of the Union with slavery's demise, temporarily ended the antithesis between securing liberty and maintaining order. Enlarged federal power, made imperative by the demands of national survival, was thereby unleashed as the instrument and then the protector of Negro freedom. Finally, the enduring belief that the freedman was the only reliable means to retain war-bought unity suggested the possibility of a continued commitment to equality.

While the passions of war remained, the Negro might hope. The struggle for equality and the struggle for the rule of law, the Union, and the Constitution might be the same. The two could agree on the need for expanded federal power, the sine qua non of equality, to serve their respective ends. But as war sentiment declined, it be-

---

1. McPherson, *Struggle for Equality*; Trefousse, *The Radical Republicans*.

came obvious that a continued increase in federal power served only the purpose of protecting equality. The supporters of the Union and the Constitution began to back away from wartime promises, to recall the order for which they had fought. They refused to expand national influence to the degree necessary to protect the freedmen. The federal power that had been required to save the Union was not enough to save the Negro.

The war had broadened federal influence to unprecedented dimensions. It demanded the creation and employment of a military force enormously greater than any previously known. It required federal efforts in banking, railroading, tariff legislation, and homestead measures, in addition to efforts which aided the Negro. But though these steps were new and seemed long in comparison to those previously taken, they did not bring about the degree of federal intervention necessary to guarantee equal justice.

Military forces were quickly contracted as soon as the war ended. In June, 1865, there were an estimated 202,277 troops in the South. Six months later the number was 87,550. In October, 1866, 17,679 remained. A year later, after the passage of the Reconstruction acts, the figure had increased to just over 20,000. In 1868 the number was again approximately 17,000, and by October, 1870, it had declined to 9,056.[2]

In non-military areas the increased federal activity encouraged by the war did not measurably increase the influence of the government. The war era had witnessed a substantial growth in the non-military federal expenditures. Between 1861 and 1871 the figure increased more than threefold, from approximately 18 million to more than 64 million dollars. The number of people holding federal jobs also increased moderately, from 49,200 to 53,900. But as Leonard D. White remarks, this growth "bespoke an increase in the volume of business coincident with the growth of the country rather than the addition of new functions and activities." State and local governments were far more active in expanding their functions and influence on the lives of their citizens. As late as 1884 one knowledgeable commentator on government activity concluded that "the average American citizen cares very little about politics at present,

2. Sefton, *The United States Army and Reconstruction*, 261–262.

because the [federal] government under which he lives touches his life very rarely, and only at points of little interest to him."[3]

The area of economic concern which would first attract the regulative energies of the federal government was the railroad industry, but even here the war had brought no significant expansion of federal interference. Although the Union government had had the legal power to control the nation's railroads during the war, that power was never used. Government policy was to encourage enterprise, not to control or regulate it. This policy continued after the war. For example, the enterprise which built and operated the Union Pacific railroad was free enterprise, because Washington refused to regulate and restrain a company it had helped to create. The army checked the Indians who threatened the road only when the company itself practically took over the army in the Department of the Platte and protected itself. The chicanery of "robber barons" was encouraged, if not made necessary, by the fact that the government did not use its power. Railroads were encouraged to take chances by the fact that the government neither offered nor enforced a system of rules which could guide private business. Despite railroad leaders' continual request for some national guidelines, the government simply encouraged the excesses of unregulated competition by subsidizing the roads.[4]

Not until 1887 would there be a federal agency established to regulate the economic activities of the nation. The Interstate Commerce Commission was a weak regulatory body with poorly defined functions and limited powers. It was charged with administering a law against unfair railroad practices but left with ill-defined notions of what was to be considered unfair. The commission could investigate, but it could not issue legally binding orders to the railroads. Its weakness was compounded by the fact that its head was Thomas M. Cooley.

Cooley did not believe in total laissez faire, but he took a view of his position which diminished the influence of an already weak com-

3. *Historical Statistics of the United States, 1789–1945* (Washington, 1949), 294, 300; White, *The Republican Era*, 1–5; Wayne MacVeagh, "The Next Presidency," *Century Magazine*, XXVII (1883–84), 670.

4. Wallace Farnham, "The Weakened Spring of Government: A Study in Nineteenth-century History," *American Historical Review*, LXVIII (April, 1963), 662–680; Gabriel Kolko, *Railroads and Regulation, 1877–1916* (Princeton, 1965).

mission. He was inclined to favor the interests of the roads over those of the shippers, and he thought he could best serve the commission by avoiding exercise of its power: "The less coercive power we have, the greater, I think, will be our influence." Not surprisingly, the Interstate Commerce Commission would not become an effective national regulative agency until the twentieth century.[5]

Federal courts also displayed a limited view of the dimensions of federal power. Despite the urgings of corporation lawyers for a sweeping view of federal power under the Fourteenth Amendment to protect their clients, the Supreme Court upheld the right of states to deal with corporations as they chose long after the Civil War was over. Not until the 1890s did judges feel capable of consistently overruling state police power in the name of substantive due process. Even then federal regulative power was hardly the immediate result. The Court emasculated the already puny federal efforts at regulation by defining away the federal power granted in the 1890 Sherman Antitrust Act and by consistently ruling against the ICC.[6]

In some areas of society there were proposals to expand the influence of the federal government. Populists responding to the impact of unregulated business enterprise called for public control of railroads and means of communication. From time to time some Republican congressmen demanded federal control of elections for federal offices, but these programs would not be realized until the twentieth century. Throughout the last third of the nineteenth century, the federal government exercised little control over the nation's industries and businesses.

Such an aloof posture was not notably harmful to industry, and it produced relatively mild and usually temporary inconvenience for agriculture. The needs of urban America could probably be met most effectively in the nineteenth century by state, not federal,

5. Cooley quoted in Jones, "Cooley and the Interstate Commerce Commission," 602–627; Kolko, *Railroads and Regulation*, 53–56, 69–70, 82; I. L. Sharfman, *The Interstate Commerce Commission* (New York, 1931), I, 19–34.

6. *U.S. v. E. C. Knight and Co.*, 156 *United States Reports* 1. Between 1888 and 1902 the Supreme Court heard 16 cases involving the powers of the ICC. It decided against the commission 15 times and in the other case sustained only part of the commission's order. Circuit courts of appeal had a similar record. See the very useful list of these cases in H. T. Newcomb, *The Work of the Interstate Commerce Commission* (Washington, 1905), 14–15.

action. But federal action was indispensable to Negro freedom. Barred by violence from the ballot box in practically every area of the South, blacks could organize no local or statewide organization to gain control of the instruments of government. They could pass no laws for their own protection. Districts which had returned Republican majorities when the army was present returned Democratic avalanches when troops were withdrawn; in some areas the Republican vote practically vanished. Negro leaders were murdered, intimidated, arrested, and otherwise silenced. Poll tax requirements and gerrymandering were joined with complicated election procedures, administered by whites, as devices which kept most black men powerless. By 1890 election frauds were consuming from thirty to sixty days of the working year of the House of Representatives. One member of the House Committee on Elections observed, "No fair man can sit in Committee as I have done and hear the testimony and arguments . . . without becoming thoroughly convinced of the absolute lawlessness in elections in a large portion of the South."[7]

But the protection that the Negro required was not forthcoming. He was abandoned to his own devices—or, more precisely, to the devices of those who held power and influence in the South. The reasons for this action are at first glance simple: a prevailing racism in the North made few Northerners interested in exercising themselves on behalf of the black man, and a desire to promote the benefits of unity led northern Republican leadership to court southern Whigs by sacrificing the freedmen.

But the problem is not quite that simple. Sufficient concern for the fate of the freedmen remained among Republicans that even into the 1890s conflict raged within the party over whether support should be sought from black rather than white Southerners. When the decision was made to abandon the blacks, it was made only after party

7. Quoted in Stanley P. Hirshson, *Farewell to the Bloody Shirt: Northern Republicans and the Southern Negro, 1877–93* (Bloomington, 1962), 203. See also his discussion of the elections of those years. John Hope Franklin, *From Slavery to Freedom: A History of Negro Americans* (New York, 1967), 328–334. Negroes did vote in the South all through the last quarter of the nineteenth century, but the number of voters was small in comparison with the number who were eligible to vote, and intimidation never ceased to occur. The greatest disfranchisement took place after 1895. See Franklin, *From Slavery to Freedom,* 338–343.

leaders such as Presidents Hayes and Garfield had convinced themselves that this action would benefit the blacks as well as the party.
Although the party of Lincoln said farewell to the bloody shirt, it
was a long and sometimes anguished parting.[8]

Even as the South was given control of its race relations, many
Northerners retained sincere interest in the fate of the Negro. The
Republican party platform of 1880 called for federal support of education, a measure partly directed toward securing Negro education.
Private foundations such as the Peabody and Slater funds sprang up
to subsidize black schools. President Hayes supported such efforts, as
did Morrison Waite, the Chief Justice most responsible for diminishing the extent of federal power constitutionally available to protect the freedmen. Other men of national standing combined a
sincere concern for the fate of the Negro with a willingness to let the
white South control his future. The author of the Slaughterhouse
opinion, Justice Samuel Miller, combined deep anger over outrages
against southern blacks with constitutional views that denied these
victims federal protection. A similar attitude was held by the influential Republican leader Carl Schurz, as well as by Justice Waite.
Justice Bradley apparently had similar views.[9]

It was not pure racism that condemned the Negro to his unpro-
tected state. A general disillusionment with the results of Reconstruction helped. The widely publicized corruption of southern
legislatures suggested that ethics in government were not the necessary result of enacting the ethic of liberty for untutored blacks. The
continued violence visited on freedmen by angry and frightened
whites demonstrated that all the results of freedom might not be
pleasant—especially if there was no hope of extensive protection for
the victims. In short, as the Reconstruction record was written by
southern experiences, Northerners became aware of important facts.
A policy which guaranteed to freedmen the rights that legally were
theirs would be difficult and costly to administer, disruptive of
southern domestic order, and physically dangerous to Negroes

---

8. Hirshson, *Farewell to the Bloody Shirt*.

9. C. Peter Magrath, *Morrison R. Waite* (New York, 1963), 166–171; Fairman,
Mr. Justice Miller; *Congressional Globe*, 42nd Cong., 2nd sess., pp. 699–701. Bradley
dissented in the Slaughterhouse cases, yet he wrote the opinion of the court in the
Civil Rights cases. See also *Nation*, Sept. 17, 1874.

themselves. Experience demonstrated that the price of federal intervention was very high. Promises of equal justice could be made, but not kept.

This was partly due to the limited view of federal power that manifested itself throughout the Reconstruction experience. The constitutional foundations of future protective legislation were riddled with ambiguity and evasion; the Fourteenth and Fifteenth Amendments were anything but precise declarations of federal supremacy. The major agency of assistance for the former slave, the Freedmen's Bureau, operated under a philosophy of self-reliance that suited white farmers and businessmen far better than it suited recent slaves. Even the attitude of the occupying Union Army was as often one of acting harmoniously with native whites as it was of enforcing equality. When Congress finally did enact federal laws with teeth, their effect was undercut by insufficient enforcement personnel and by the insecure support given them by the war amendments.[10]

As it became clear that the Union could not be restored with blacks as effective agents within it, Northerners accepted the argument that what could not in fact be done, might not constitutionally be done. The advanced positions taken by many egalitarians were undermined by the very constitutional framework in which they had of necessity chosen to operate. Congressional leaders might object, but the Supreme Court took the constitutional amendments they had written, interpreted them in light of a respect for federalism promoted by the war, and provided the sort of legal environment that the nation demanded.

The Slaughterhouse cases announced that the privileges and immunities that fell under federal protection had not been enlarged by the war. Newspapers which had supported vigorous Reconstruction in the late 1860s applauded the decision. The Supreme Court

---

10. See above pp. 47-59. Sefton, *United States Army and Reconstruction*, argues that, in places where the army operated, it controlled the situation in favor of federal laws. The continued incidents of violence in areas where the army was absent suggest the need for a far larger force. The Freedmen's Bureau bill gave the secretary of war great power to interfere in the life of the South. However, the insistence that the Negro make it on his own as soon as possible undercut this apparent thrust of federal power. Paul S. Pierce, *The Freedmen's Bureau* (Iowa City, 1904), 46.

declared in 1876 that Congress had viewed its power to protect the Negro too broadly under the 1870–71 Enforcement Acts; the *New York Tribune* welcomed the decision as a reminder to "future generations of Americans that no conceivable abuse of the Constitution [by the South to preserve slavery] . . . can justify disregard of the Constitution by the [North]." Other papers, even though hoping for new laws to protect the freedman, thought that the decision was proper. Then in 1883 the Court practically destroyed all hope of future federal protection. The federal government might not enact equality legislation on its own, a 8-1 court said. It could only remedy blatantly discriminatory state laws. Southern states had sufficient experience in the customs of apartheid to be unaffected by such a concession.[11] When the decision was announced at the Atlanta opera house, the white patrons erupted in applause and cheers. The black galleries sat stunned and silent.

In endorsing the federal view, the Supreme Court built upon foundations secured and expanded by the war. Secession tested the Union's ability to survive and the Constitution's ability to adapt. Both did, with the help of men like Francis Lieber, Joel Parker, Sidney George Fisher, John Norton Pomeroy, and Thomas McIntyre Cooley. These men had provided the legal-constitutional arguments that enlisted the concept of the rule of law in northern regiments. They preserved the nation's legal heritage and made it a prize of war. In one way or another, each man represented vital aspects of the legal thought that would enable the Court to abandon the Negro, and each could have found satisfaction in the ultimate results of the war.

While neither Parker nor Lieber would have been completely pleased, the actions of the court endorsed both of their views. Parker had seen in Reconstruction a fearsome expansion of federal power, and he feared that a tradition of constitutional restraint was dying. In fact, such restraint exercised its influence until at least the beginning of the twentieth century. Lieber had been worried that Americans did not possess a sufficient devotion to nationhood, but in fact nationalism was the most obvious victor in the war. Ironically, when both North and South accepted the idea of limited govern-

11. See reactions to these decisions in Charles Warren, *The Supreme Court in United States History*, (Boston, 1928), III, 263–269, 323–336.

ment within a perpetual union of enduring states, that nationalism was finally cemented. Safe behind federalism's barriers, the South was left to handle its race relations in its own way. Freed from having to face sectional blackmail on questions of race, the North could thus consign the question of the black man's future to the South. Struggles for equality would no longer endanger unity.

Fisher's unresolved dilemma, whether or not force should be used to protect the rights of undisciplined people, was settled in the negative. It was settled by the general acceptance of the constitutional ideas of Pomeroy and Cooley. They explained to the nation that its ideals of equal justice under law had been realized even as the ideal of freedom from government remained secure. They told the nation that its responsibility for equal liberty was satisfied within the limits of legal-constitutional tradition. They said, "We have done all that we could." Given the nature of the war, they were right, tragically right.

Bibliography

PRIMARY MATERIALS

MANUSCRIPTS

The only major collection of manuscripts available to me was the Francis Lieber collection at the Huntington Library in San Marino, California. Joel Parker left only a few letters of a personal nature, along with some comments describing his activities at Harvard Law School. These papers are in the Treasure Room of the law school library. No similar collection of Pomeroy papers exists, to my knowledge. The Cooley Papers are at the University of Michigan Library, Ann Arbor. Fisher left only his invaluable diary, which I have cited below.

PUBLISHED PUBLIC DOCUMENTS

Congressional Globe, 37th–41st Congresses
Federal Cases
Official Record of the War of the Rebellion
United States Statutes at Large
United States Supreme Court Reports
Alabama State Supreme Court Reports
Illinois, *Reports Made to the General Assembly of Illinois*, 34th session, 1865, Vol. 1. Springfield: Baker & Phillips, 1865.
Indiana State Supreme Court Reports
Kentucky State Supreme Court Reports
Maryland State Supreme Court Reports
Missouri State Supreme Court Reports
Wisconsin State Supreme Court Reports

PRINTED PRIMARY MATERIALS

Basler, Roy P., ed. *Collected Works of Abraham Lincoln.* 9 vols. New Brunswick, N.J.: Rutgers University Press, 1953.

Binney, Horace. *The Privilege of the Writ of Habeas Corpus.* Philadelphia: C. Sherman, 1862.

Blackstone, William. *Commentaries on the Laws of England,* ed. Thomas McIntyre Cooley. 2 vols. Chicago: Callaghan and Cockcroft, 1871.

Brown, George William. *The Relation of the Legal Profession to Society.* Baltimore: Relley & Piet, 1868.

Brownson, Orestes. *The American Republic: Its Constitution, Tendencies and Destiny.* New York: P. O'Shea, 1866.

The Constitution. New York: Society for the Diffusion of Political Knowledge, 1863–64.

Cooley, Thomas McIntyre. *Changes in the Balance of Governmental Powers, An Address to the Law Students of Michigan University, March 20, 1878.* Ann Arbor: Douglas and Co., 1878.

———. "The Guarantee of Order and Republican Government in the States." *International Review,* II (1875), 57–87.

———. *Michigan: A History of Governments.* Boston: Houghton Mifflin, 1885.

———. *A Treatise on the Constitutional Limitations Which Rest upon the Legislative Power of the States of the American Union.* Boston: Little, Brown, 1871.

Curtis, Benjamin R. *Executive Power.* Boston: Little, Brown, 1862.

Farrar, Timothy. "The Trial of the Constitution." *North American Review,* XCVII (Oct., 1863), 338–372.

Fisher, Sidney George. "The Bible and Slavery." *North American Review,* XCVIII (Jan., 1864), 48–74.

———. "Duties on Exports." *North American Review,* CI (July, 1865), 147–162.

———. "The Eight-Hour Movement." *Nation,* I (Oct. 26, 1865), 517–518.

———. *Kanzas and the Constitution.* Boston: Damrell & Moore, 1856.

———. *The Law of the Territories.* Philadelphia: C. Sherman, 1859.

———. *The Laws of Race as Connected with Slavery.* Philadelphia: Hazard, 1860.

———. "Legalized Secession." *Philadelphia North American,* Dec. 31, 1860.

———. "A National Currency." *North American Review,* XCIX (July, 1864), 204–245.

———. "The National Highways." *Nation,* I (Oct. 5, 1865), 424–425.

———. "The National Highways." *Nation,* I (Nov. 16, 1865), 616–617.

———. "The National Highways." *Nation,* II (Jan. 4, 1866), 8–9.

————. "Nominating Conventions." *North American Review*, CVI (Jan., 1868), 233–249.

————. *A Philadelphia Perspective: The Diary of Sidney George Fisher*, ed. Nicholas Wainwright. Philadelphia: Historical Society of Pennsylvania, 1967.

————. *The Trial of the Constitution*. Philadelphia: C. Sherman, 1863.

Fitzhugh, George. *Sociology for the South*. Richmond, Va.: Morris, 1854.

Godkin, E. L. "The Constitution and Its Defects." *North American Review*, XCIX (July, 1864), 117–145.

Hale, John P. *Trial by Jury: Remarks on the Attempt by Chief Justice Parker to Usurp the Prerogative of the Jury in Criminal Cases*. Exeter, N.H.: George O. Odlin, 1842.

Hurd, John Codman. "Pomeroy's Constitutional Law." *Nation*, VII (July, 1868), 53–55.

————. "Theories of Reconstruction." *American Law Review*, I (Jan., 1867), 237–264.

Julian, George. *Speeches on Political Questions*. New York: Hurd and Houghton, 1872.

Lawrence, William Beach. "International Law." *Law Reporter*, XXVI (Nov., 1863), 12–22.

Lieber, Francis. *Civil Liberty and Self Government*. Philadelphia: J. B. Lippincott, 1859.

————. *Essays on Property and Labor*. New York: Harper, 1841.

————. *Legal and Political Hermeneutics*. Boston: Little, Brown, 1839.

————. *The Life and Letters of Francis Lieber*, ed. Thomas Sergeant Perry. Boston: J. R. Osgood, 1882.

————. *Lincoln or McClellan*. New York: Loyal Publication Society, 1864.

————. *Manual of Political Ethics*, ed. Theodore D. Woolsey. Philadelphia: J. B. Lippincott, 1881.

————. *Miscellaneous Writings of Francis Lieber*, ed. Daniel C. Gilman. 2 vols. Philadelphia: J. B. Lippincott, 1880.

————. *No Party Now but All for Country*. New York: Loyal Publication Society, 1864.

————. "A Plea for the Fijians; Or, Can Nothing Be Said in Favor of Roasting One's Equals?" *Atlantic Monthly*, III (March, 1859), 342–350.

————. *The Stranger in America*. London: R. Bentley, 1835.

Leggett, William. *A Collection of the Political Writings of William*

Leggett, ed. Theodore Sedgewick. New York: Taylor and Dodd, 1840.

Lowell, James Russell. *Letters of James Russell Lowell*, ed. Charles Eliot Norton. New York: Harper, 1894.

————. "Reconstruction." *North American Review*, C (April, 1865), 540–559.

Mulford, Elisha. *The Nation*. New York: Hurd and Houghton, 1870.

Nash, Simeon. "The Legal Status of the Rebel States before and after Their Conquest." *Monthly Law Reporter*, XXVI (Aug., 1864), 532–548.

Parker, Joel. *An Address Delivered at the Centennial Celebration, in Jaffrey, August 20, 1873*. Winchendon: F. W. Ward, 1873.

————. "The Character of the Rebellion and the Conduct of the War." *North American Review*, XCV (Oct., 1862), 500–533.

————. *A Charge to the Grand Jury upon the Importance of Maintaining the Supremacy of the Laws*. Concord, N.H.: Marsh, Capen & Lyon, 1838.

————. "Constitutional Law." *North American Review*, XCIV (April, 1862), 435–463.

————. *Constitutional Law and Unconstitutional Divinity: Letters to Rev. Henry M. Dexter and to Rev. Leonard Bacon, D.D.* Cambridge: H. O. Houghton, 1863.

————. *Daniel Webster as a Jurist*. Cambridge: John Bartlett, 1853.

————. "The Domestic and Foreign Relations of the United States." *North American Review*, XCIV (Jan., 1862), 196–258.

————. *The First Charter and the Early Religious Legislation of Massachusetts*. Boston: John Wilson, 1869.

————. "Habeas Corpus and Martial Law." *North American Review*, XCIII (Oct., 1861), 471–518.

————. "International Law." *North American Review*, XCV (July, 1862), 1–56.

————. *The Law School of Harvard College*. New York: Hurd and Houghton, 1871.

————. *Revolution and Reconstruction: Two Lectures Delivered in the Law School of Harvard College in January 1865 and January 1866*. New York: Hurd and Houghton, 1866.

————. "The Right of Secession." *North American Review*, XCIII (July, 1861), 212–244.

————. *The Three Powers of Government. The Origin of the United States; and the Status of the Southern States on the Suppression of the Rebellion. The Three Dangers of the Republic. Lectures Delivered in the Law School of Harvard College and in Dartmouth College, 1867–8 and '69.* New York: Hurd and Houghton, 1869.

———. *The True Issue and the Duty of the Whigs.* Cambridge: James Munroe, 1856.

———. *The War Powers of Congress, and of the President.* Cambridge: H. O. Houghton, 1863.

Pease, William H., and Pease, Jane H., eds. *The Antislavery Argument.* Indianapolis: Bobbs Merrill, 1965.

Perkins, Howard Cecil, ed. *Northern Editorials on Secession.* 2 vols. New York: D. Appleton, 1942.

Pomeroy, John Norton. "Amnesty Measures." *Nation*, XII (Jan. 26, 1871), 52–54.

———. "Civil Law Code of California." *Albany Law Journal*, V (1871), 69–70.

———. "Criminal Procedure." *North American Review*, XCII (April, 1861), 297–318.

———. "The Force Bill." *Nation*, XII (April 20, 1871), 268–270.

———. *An Introduction to Municipal Law.* New York: D. Appleton, 1864.

———. *An Introduction to the Constitutional Law of the United States.* Boston: Houghton Mifflin, 1886.

———. "The Laws of Warfare." *American Law Review*, IX (July, 1875), 605–637.

———. "North Carolina and a New Constitution." *Nation*, XIII (July 20, 1871), 37–38.

———. "Our Duty as Regards China." *Nation*, XIII (Aug. 17, 1871), 101–103.

———. "The Pennsylvania Constitution versus the State Officers." *Nation*, XI (Dec. 4, 1873), 365–366.

———. "Police Duty." *Nation*, XII (April 27, 1871), 284–285.

———. "Political Precedents." *Nation*, XII (May 4, 1871), 300–301.

———. "The Power of Congress to Regulate Interstate Commerce." *Southern Law Review* (n.s.), IV (1878), 357–405.

———. "The Proposed Legislation for Louisiana." *Nation*, XX (Jan. 21, 1875), 37–38.

———. "The Rights of Citizens." *Nation*, XII (May 18, 1871), 335–336.

———. "The Supreme Court and Its Theory of Nationality." *Nation*, XII (June 29, 1871), 445–446.

———. "The Supreme Court and State Repudiation." *American Law Review*, XVII (Sept.-Oct., 1888), 684–734.

———. "The Use of the Supreme Court." *Nation*, VI (Feb. 20, 1868), 146–147.

Redfield, Isaac F. "John Norton Pomeroy, 'An Introduction to Municipal Law.'" *American Law Register*, XII (May, 1864), 446–448.

———. "On American Secession and State Rights." *Law Reporter*, XXVI (Dec., 1863), 70–85.

Sedgwick, Theodore. *A Treatise on the Rules Which Govern the Interpretation of Statutory Law*, ed. John Norton Pomeroy. New York: Baker, Voorhis, 1874.

Sherman, John. *Recollections of Forty Years in the House, Senate, and Cabinet: An Autobiography*. Chicago: Werner, 1895.

Story, Joseph. *Commentaries on the Constitution of the United States*, ed. Thomas McIntyre Cooley. 2 vols. Boston: Little, Brown, 1873.

Story, William W., ed. *Life and Letters of Joseph Story*. 2 vols. Boston: Little, Brown, 1851.

Thorndike, Rachel Sherman, ed. *The Sherman Letters: Correspondence between General and Senator Sherman from 1837 to 1891*. New York: Scribners, 1894.

Washburn, Emory. "Memoir of the Hon. Joel Parker, LL.D." *Proceedings of the Massachusetts Historical Society*, XIV (1875–76), 172–179.

Whiting, William. *The War Powers of the President and the Legislative Powers of Congress in Relation to Rebellion, Treason, and Slavery*. Boston: John L. Story, 1862.

SECONDARY SOURCES

Abraham, Henry J. *Freedom and the Court: Civil Rights and Civil Liberties in the United States*. New York: Oxford University Press, 1967.

Arieli, Yehoshua. *Individualism and Nationalism in American Ideology*. Cambridge: Harvard University Press, 1964.

Batchellor, Robert Stillman. "The Development of the Courts of New Hampshire." In *The New England States*, ed. William T. Davis, vol. 4. Boston: D. C. Hurd, 1897.

Bauer, Elizabeth Kelley. *Commentaries on the Constitution 1790–1860*. New York: Columbia University Press, 1952.

Belz, Herman Julius, *Reconstructing the Union: Conflicts of Theory and Policy during the Civil War*. Ithaca: Cornell University Press, 1969.

Bennett, Walter Hartwell. *American Theories of Federalism*. University: University of Alabama Press, 1964.

Bentley, George H. *A History of the Freedmen's Bureau*. Philadelphia: University of Pennsylvania Press, 1955.

Bernard, Kenneth. "Lincoln and Civil Liberties." *Abraham Lincoln Quarterly*, VI (June, 1951), 375–399.

Berthoff, Rowland. *An Unsettled People: Social Order and Disorder in American History*. New York: Harper & Row, 1971.

Berwanger, Eugene. *The Frontier against Slavery*. Urbana: University of Illinois Press, 1967.

Bestor, Arthur. "The American Civil War as a Constitutional Crisis." *American Historical Review*, LXIX (Jan., 1964), 327–352.

————. "State Sovereignty and Slavery: A Reinterpretation of Proslavery Constitutional Doctrine, 1846–60." *Journal of the Illinois State Historical Society*, LIV (Summer, 1961), 148–174.

Beth, Loren. "The Slaughterhouse Cases—Revisited." *Louisiana Law Review*, XIII (April, 1963), 490–495.

Bickel, Alexander. "The Original Understanding and the Segregation Decision." *Harvard Law Review*, LXIX (Nov., 1955), 1–65.

Bigelow, John. *The Life of Samuel J. Tilden*. 2 vols. New York: Harper, 1895.

Blau, Joseph. *Social Theories of Jacksonian Democracy*. New York: Hafner, 1947.

Blaustein, Albert P., and Ferguson, Clarence Clyde. *Desgregation and the Law*. 2nd ed. New York: Vintage, 1962.

Boorstin, Daniel J. *The Americans: The National Experience*. New York: Random House, 1965.

Brock, W. R. *An American Crisis: Congress and Reconstruction, 1865–67*. New York: St. Martin's Press, 1963.

Brodie, Fawn. *Thaddeus Stevens, Scourge of the South*. New York: Norton, 1959.

Brown, Bernard Edward. *American Conservatives: The Political Thought of Francis Lieber and John W. Burgess*. New York: Columbia University Press, 1951.

Burgess, John W. *Reconstruction and the Constitution*. New York: Scribners, 1902.

Cain, Marvin R. *Lincoln's Attorney General, Edward Bates of Missouri*. Columbia: University of Missouri Press, 1965.

Campbell, Stanley. *The Slave Catchers: Enforcement of the Fugitive Slave Law, 1850–1860*. Chapel Hill: University of North Carolina, 1968.

Carpenter, John A. "Atrocities in the Reconstruction Period." *Journal of Negro History*, XLVII (Oct., 1962), 234–247.

Centennial History of the Harvard Law School, 1817–1917. Cambridge: Harvard Law School Association, 1918.

Chalmers, David M. *Hooded Americanism: The History of the Ku Klux Klan.* New York: Doubleday, 1965.

Clancy, John J. "A Mugwump on Minorities." *Journal of Negro History,* LI (July, 1966), 174–192.

Cole, Arthur Charles. *The Era of the Civil War, 1848–70.* Springfield: Illinois Centennial Commission, 1919.

Coleman, Charles. *The Election of 1868.* New York: Columbia University Press, 1933.

Commager, Henry Steele. *Theodore Parker.* Boston: Little, Brown, 1936.

Connor, Henry G. *John Archibald Campbell, Associate Justice of the United States Supreme Court, 1853–61.* Boston: Houghton Mifflin, 1920.

Conron, Michael A. "Law, Politics and Chief Justice Taney: A Reconsideration of the Luther v. Borden Decision." *American Journal of Legal History,* XI (Oct., 1967), 377–388.

Corwin, Edward S. "Due Process of Law before the Civil War." In *American Constitutional History: Essays by Edward S. Corwin,* ed. Alpheus Mason and Gerald Garvey, pp. 46–66. New York: Harper & Row, 1964.

———. *Liberty against Government; The Rise, Flowering and Decline of a Famous Judicial Concept.* Baton Rouge: Louisiana State University Press, 1948.

———. *The President: Office and Powers, 1787–1957.* New York: New York University Press, 1957.

Cox, John, and Cox, Lawanda. "General O. O. Howard and the 'Misrepresented Bureau.'" *Journal of Southern History,* XIX (Nov., 1953), 427–456.

———. *Politics, Principle, and Prejudice, 1865–66.* New York: Free Press, 1963.

Curry, Leonard P. *Blueprint for Modern America: Nonmilitary Legislation of the First Civil War Congress.* Nashville: Vanderbilt University Press, 1968.

Curry, Richard. "The Abolitionists and Reconstruction: A Critical Appraisal." *Journal of Southern History,* XXXIV (Nov., 1968), 527–545.

Curti, Merle. "Francis Lieber and Nationalism." *Huntington Library Quarterly,* IV (1941), 263–292.

———. *The Roots of American Loyalty.* New York: Columbia University Press, 1946.

Curtis, Benjamin R., ed. *A Memoir of Benjamin Robbins Curtis.* 2 vols. Boston: Little, Brown, 1879.

Davis, Lance E., and Legler, John. "The Government in the American Economy, 1815–1902: A Quantitative Study." *Journal of Economic History*, XXVI (Dec., 1966), 514–551.

Davis, William Watson. "The Federal Enforcement Acts." In *Studies in Southern History and Politics Inscribed to William Archibald Dunning*. New York: Columbia University Press, 1914.

Dewey, Donald, ed. "Hoosier Justice: The Journal of David McDonald." *Indiana Magazine of History*, LXII (Sept., 1966), 175–232.

DiNunzio, Mario. "Lyman Trumbull, United States Senator." Ph.D. dissertation, Clark University, 1964.

Donald, David. "An Excess of Democracy: The American Civil War and the Social Process." In *Lincoln Reconsidered: Essays on the Civil War Era*, pp. 209–235. New York, Knopf, 1956.

———. *The Politics of Reconstruction*. Baton Rouge: Louisiana State University Press, 1965.

Dowd, Morgan D. "Justice Joseph Story: A Study of the Legal Philosophy of a Jeffersonian Judge." *Vanderbilt Law Review*, XVIII (March, 1965), 643–662.

Downey, Matthew T. "The Rebirth of Reform: A Study of Liberal Reform Movements." Ph.D. dissertation, Princeton University, 1963.

Dunning, William A. *Essays on the Civil War and Reconstruction*. New York: Macmillan, 1904.

———. *Reconstruction, Political and Economic, 1865–77*. New York: Harper, 1907.

Dyer, Brainard. "Francis Lieber and the American Civil War." *Huntington Library Quarterly*, II (July, 1939), 449–465.

Eaton, Clement. *The Growth of Southern Civilization, 1790–1860*. New York: Harper & Row, 1961.

Elazar, Daniel J. *The American Partnership: Intergovernmental Cooperation in the Nineteenth Century United States*. Chicago: University of Chicago Press, 1962.

———. "Comment on a Paper by Louis Hartz." In *Economic Change in the Civil War Era*, ed. David T. Gilchrist and W. Davis Lewis, pp. 94–107. Greenville: Eleutherian Mills-Hagley Foundation, 1965.

Elkins, Stanley. *Slavery: A Problem in American Institutional and Intellectual Life*. Chicago: University of Chicago Press, 1959.

Fairman, Charles. "Does the Fourteenth Amendment Incorporate the Bill of Rights? The Original Understanding." *Stanford Law Review*, II (Dec., 1949), 5–139.

———. *Mr. Justice Miller and the Supreme Court, 1862–90*. Cambridge: Harvard University Press, 1939.

————. *Reconstruction and Reunion, 1864–88*, Pt. 1. New York: Macmillan, 1971.

Farnham, Wallace D. "The Weakened Spring of Government: A Study in Nineteenth-Century History." *American Historical Review*, LXVIII (April, 1963), 662–680.

Federalism as a Democratic Process: Essays by Roscoe Pound, Charles McIlwain, Roy Franklin Nichols. New Brunswick, N.J.: Rutgers University Press, 1942.

Field, David Dudley. *Speeches, Arguments and Miscellaneous Papers*, ed. A. P. Sprague. New York: D. Appleton, 1884.

Filler, Louis. *The Crusade against Slavery, 1830–60*. New York: Harper & Row, 1960.

Fine, Sidney B. *Laissez Faire and the General Welfare State*. Ann Arbor: University of Michigan Press, 1956.

Fishel, Leslie H. "Northern Prejudice and Negro Suffrage, 1865–70." *Journal of Negro History*, XXXIX (Jan., 1954), 8–26.

Fleming, Walter, ed. *Documentary History of Reconstruction*. 2 vols. Cleveland: A. H. Clark, 1906–7.

Franklin, John Hope. *From Slavery to Freedom: A History of Negro Americans*. New York: Knopf, 1967.

————. *Reconstruction after the Civil War*. Chicago: University of Chicago Press, 1961.

Fredrickson, George M. *The Black Image in the White Mind: The Debate on Afro-American Character and Destiny, 1817–1914*. New York: Harper and Row, 1971.

————. *The Inner Civil War: Northern Intellectuals and the Crisis of the Union*. New York: Harper and Row, 1965.

Freehling, William W. *Prelude to Civil War: The Nullification Controversy in South Carolina, 1816–32*. New York: Harper and Row, 1965.

Freidel, Frank. *Francis Lieber, Nineteenth Century Liberal*. Baton Rouge: Louisiana State University Press, 1947.

————. "Francis Lieber, Charles Sumner, and Slavery." *Journal of Southern History*, IX (Feb., 1943), 75–93.

————. "General Orders 100 and Military Government." *Mississippi Valley Historical Review*, XXXII (March, 1946), 541–556.

Gabriel, Ralph Henry. "Constitutional Democracy: A Nineteenth Century Faith." In *The Constitution Reconsidered*, ed. Conyers Read, pp. 247–258. New York: Columbia University Press, 1938.

————. *The Course of American Democratic Thought*. New York: Ronald, 1956.

Gager, Edwin B. "Equity, 1701–1901." In *Two Centuries Growth of*

American Law, pp. 115–152. New York: New York University Press, 1901.

Gambill, Edward L. "Who Were the Senate Radicals?" *Civil War History*, XI (Sept., 1965), 237–244.

Gara, Larry. "Slavery and the Slave Power: A Crucial Distinction." *Civil War History*, XV (March, 1969), 5–18.

Gettell, Raymond G. *History of American Political Thought*. New York: Century, 1928.

Geyl, Peter, "The American Civil War and the Problem of Inevitability." *New England Quarterly*, XXIV (June, 1951), 147–168.

Gillette, William. *The Right to Vote: Politics and the Passage of the Fifteenth Amendment*. Baltimore: Johns Hopkins University Press, 1965.

Godkin, E. L. "The Constitution and Its Defects." *North American Review*, XCIX (July, 1864), 117–145.

Graham, Howard J. *Everyman's Constitution: Historical Essays on the Fourteenth Amendment, the 'Conspiracy Theory,' and American Constitutionalism*. Madison: State Historical Society of Wisconsin, 1968.

———. "Our 'Declaratory' Fourteenth Amendment." *Stanford Law Review*, VII (Dec., 1954), 3–39.

———. "The Waite Court and the Fourteenth Amendment." *Vanderbilt Law Review*, XVII (March, 1964), 525–547.

Gray, Wood. *The Hidden Civil War: The Story of the Copperheads*. New York: Viking, 1942.

Green, Constance McLaughlin. *Washington: Village and Capitol, 1800–1878*. Princeton: Princeton University Press, 1962.

Griffin, Clifford S. *The Ferment of Reform, 1830–60*. New York: Crowell, 1967.

Grodzins, Morton. *The Loyal and the Disloyal*. Chicago: University of Chicago Press, 1956.

Hale, George S. "Joel Parker." *American Law Review*, X (Jan., 1876), 235–269.

Hamilton, Walton H. "The Path of Due Process of Law." In *The Constitution Reconsidered*, ed. Conyers Read, pp. 167–190. New York: Columbia University Press, 1938.

Harley, Lewis R. *Francis Lieber: His Life and Political Philosophy*. New York: Columbia University Press, 1899.

Harris, Robert J. *The Quest for Equality: The Constitution, Congress, and the Supreme Court*. Baton Rouge: Louisiana State University Press, 1960.

Hartz, Louis. "Government-Business Relations." In *Economic Change in the Civil War Era*, ed. David T. Gilchrist and W. Davis Lewis. Greenville: Eleutherian Mills-Hagley Foundation, 1965.

————. *The Liberal Tradition in America: An Interpretation of American Political Thought since the Revolution.* New York: Harcourt, Brace, 1955.

Henry, Seldon. "Racial Republican Policy toward the Negro." Ph.D. dissertation, Yale University, 1963.

Hesseltine, William. *Lincoln and the War Governors.* New York: Knopf, 1948.

Hirshson, Stanley P. *Farewell to the Bloody Shirt: Northern Republicans and the Southern Negro, 1877–93.* Bloomington: Indiana University Press, 1962.

Hofstadter, Richard. *The American Political Tradition and the Men Who Made It.* New York, Knopf, 1948.

————. "The Spokesman of Jacksonian Democracy." *Political Science Quarterly*, LVIII (Dec., 1943), 581–594.

Howe, Mark De Wolfe. "Federalism and Civil Rights." *Massachusetts Historical Society Proceedings*, LXXVII (1965), 15–27.

————. "Juries as Judges of Criminal Law." *Harvard Law Review*, LII (Feb., 1939), 582–616.

————. *Justice Oliver Wendell Holmes: The Proving Years.* Cambridge: Belknap Press, 1963.

————. *Justice Oliver Wendell Holmes: The Shaping Years.* Cambridge: Belknap Press, 1957.

Howell, Roger, *The Privileges and Immunities of State Citizenship.* Baltimore: Johns Hopkins University Press, 1918.

Hughes, David F. "Salmon P. Chase: Chief Justice." *Vanderbilt Law Review*, XVIII (March, 1965), 569–614.

Hurst, James Willard. *Law and the Conditions of Freedom in the Nineteenth Century United States.* Madison: University of Wisconsin Press, 1956.

Hutchins, Harry Burns. "Thomas McIntyre Cooley, 1824–98." In *Great American Lawyers.* ed. William Draper Lewis, VII, pp. 429–492. Philadelphia: Winston, 1909.

Hyman, Harold M. *The Era of the Oath: Northern Loyalty Tests during the Civil War and Reconstruction.* Philadelphia: University of Pennsylvania Press, 1954.

————. *A More Perfect Union: The Impact of the Civil War and Reconstruction on the Constitution.* New York: Knopf, 1973.

————. "Reconstruction and Political-Constitutional Institutions: The Popular Expression." In *New Frontiers of the American Reconstruc-*

tion, ed. Harold M. Hyman, pp. 1–39. Urbana: University of Illinois Press, 1966.

――――, ed. *The Radical Republicans and Reconstruction, 1861–70.* Indianapolis: Bobbs Merrill, 1967.

Hyman, Sidney. "Rips in the Fabric of the Law." *Saturday Review*, July 11, 1970, pp. 21–23.

Jacobs, Clyde E. *Law Writers and the Courts: The Influence of Thomas M. Cooley, Christopher G. Tiedman, and John F. Dillon upon American Constitutional Law.* Berkeley: University of California Press, 1954.

James, Joseph B. *The Framing of the Fourteenth Amendment.* Urbana: University of Illinois Press, 1956.

Jellison, Charles A. *Fessenden of Maine: Civil War Senator.* Syracuse: Syracuse University Press, 1962.

Jones, Alan Robert. "The Constitutional Conservatism of Thomas McIntyre Cooley." Ph.D. dissertation, University of Michigan, 1960.

――――. "Thomas M. Cooley and 'Laissez-Faire Constitutionalism': A Reconsideration." *Journal of American History*, LIII (March, 1967), 751–771.

――――. "Thomas M. Cooley and the Interstate Commerce Commission: Continuity and Change in the Doctrine of Equal Rights." *Political Science Quarterly*, LXXXI (Dec., 1966), 602–627.

――――. "Thomas M. Cooley and the Michigan Supreme Court, 1865–85." *American Journal of Legal History*, X (April, 1966), 97–121.

Kelly, Alfred H. "Comment on Harold M. Hyman's Paper." In *New Frontiers of American Reconstruction*, ed. Harold M. Hyman, pp. 40–58. Urbana: University of Illinois Press, 1966.

――――. "The Congressional Controversy over School Segregation, 1867–75." *American Historical Review*, LXIV (April, 1959), 537–563.

――――. "The Fourteenth Amendment Reconsidered: The Segregation Question." *Michigan Law Review*, LIV (June, 1956), 1049–86.

――――. "The School Desegregation Cases." In *Quarrels That Have Shaped the Constitution*, ed. John A. Garraty, pp. 243–268. New York: Harper and Row, 1966.

Kelly, Alfred H., and Harbison, Winfred. *The American Constitution: Its Origins and Development.* New York: Norton, 1970.

Kent, Charles A. "Thomas M. Cooley." *Michigan Historical Collections*, XXIX (1899–1900), 143–155.

Kincaid, Larry George. "Legislative Origins of the Military Reconstruction Acts, 1865–67." Ph.D. dissertation, Johns Hopkins University Press, 1968.

Klein, Philip Shriver. *President James Buchanan.* University Park: Pennsylvania State University Press, 1962.

Klement, Frank. *The Copperheads in the Middle West.* Chicago: University of Chicago Press, 1960.

Kraditor, Aileen S. "A Note on Elkins and Abolitionists." *Civil War History*, XIII (Dec., 1867), 330–339.

———. *Means and Ends in American Abolitionism: Garrison and His Critics on Strategy and Tactics, 1834–50.* New York: Pantheon, 1969.

Kutler, Stanley. "Ex Parte McCardle: Judicial Impotency? The Supreme Court and Reconstruction Reconsidered." *American Historical Review*, LXXI (April, 1967), 835–851.

———. *Judicial Power and Reconstruction Politics.* Chicago: University of Chicago Press, 1968.

———. "Reconstruction and the Supreme Court: The Numbers Game Reconsidered." *Journal of Southern History*, XXXII (Feb., 1966), 42–58.

Larsen, Charles Edward. "Commentaries on the Constitution, 1865–1900." Ph.D. dissertation, Columbia University, 1952.

———. "Nationalism and States Rights in Commentaries on the Constitution after the Civil War." *American Journal of Legal History*, III (Oct., 1959), 360–369.

Leary, John C. "John Norton Pomeroy, 1828–85: A Bibliographic Sketch." *Law Library Journal*, XLVII (May, 1954), 138–144.

Lee, Charles Robert. *The Confederate Constitutions.* Chapel Hill: University of North Carolina Press, 1963.

Lein, Arnold J. *Concurring Opinion: The Privileges and Immunities Clause of the Fourteenth Amendment.* St. Louis: Washington University Press, 1957.

Lerche, Charles O. "Congressional Interpretation of the Guarantee of a Republican Form of Government during Reconstruction." *Journal of Southern History*, XV (May, 1949), 192–211.

Levy, Leonard. *The Law of the Commonwealth and Chief Justice Shaw.* Cambridge: Harvard University Press, 1957.

Lewis, Edward R. *A History of American Political Thought from the Civil War to the World War.* New York: Macmillan, 1937.

Lewis, R. W. B. *The American Adam: Innocence, Tragedy, and Tradition in the Nineteenth Century.* Chicago: University of Chicago Press, 1955.

Lewis, Walker. *Without Fear or Favor: A Biography of Chief Justice Roger Brook Taney.* Boston: Houghton Mifflin, 1965.

Litwack, Leon F. *North of Slavery: The Negro in the Free States, 1790–1860*. Chicago: University of Chicago Press, 1961.

Lynch, John R. "Some Historical Errors of James Ford Rhodes." *Journal of Negro History*, II (Oct., 1917), 345–368.

Lynch, William O. "Anti-Slavery Tendencies of the Democratic Party in the Northwest, 1848–50." *Mississippi Valley Historical Review*, XI (Dec., 1924), 319–331.

McCloskey, Robert. *The American Supreme Court*. Chicago: University of Chicago Press, 1960.

McFeely, William S. *Yankee Stepfather: General O. O. Howard and the Freedmen*. New Haven: Yale University Press, 1968.

McKitrick, Eric L. *Andrew Johnson and Reconstruction*. Chicago: University of Chicago Press, 1960.

———. "Reconstruction: Ultraconservative Revolution." In *The Comparative Approach to American History*, ed. C. Vann Woodward, pp. 140–159. New York: Basic Books, 1968.

McLaughlin, Andrew C. *A Constitutional History of the United States*. New York: Appleton-Century-Crofts, 1935.

McPherson, James M. "Abolitionists and the Civil Rights Act of 1875." *Journal of American History*, LII (Dec., 1965), 493–510.

———. *The Struggle for Equality: Abolitionists and the Negro in the Civil War and Reconstruction*. Princeton: Princeton University Press, 1964.

McWhiney, Grady, ed. *Grant, Lee, Lincoln and the Radicals*. Evanston: Northwestern University Press, 1964.

Magrath, C. Peter. *Morrison R. Waite: The Triumph of Character*. New York: Macmillan, 1963.

Mathews, Donald G. "Abolitionists on Slavery: The Critique behind the Social Movement." *Journal of Southern History*, XXXIII (May, 1967), 163–182.

Mawhinney, Eugene Alberto. "The Development of the Concept of Liberty in the Fourteenth Amendment." Ph.D. dissertation, University of Illinois, 1955.

Merk, Frederick. *Manifest Destiny and Mission in American History*. New York: Random House, 1963.

Meyers, Marvin. *The Jacksonian Persuasion*. New York: Knopf, 1957.

Miller, Loren. *The Petitioners: The Story of the Supreme Court of the United States and the Negro*. Cleveland: World, 1966.

Miller, Perry. *The Life of the Mind in America*. New York: Harcourt, Brace and World, 1965.

————. *Nature's Nation*. Cambridge: Belknap Press, 1967.

————, ed. *The Legal Mind in America, from Independence to the Civil War*. Garden City, N.Y.: Doubleday Anchor Books, 1962.

Milton, George Fort. *Lincoln and the Fifth Column*. New York: Vanguard, 1942.

Morgan, Donald. *Congress and the Constitution: A Study in Responsibility*. Cambridge: Harvard University Press, 1966.

Myers, W. J. "Privileges and Immunities of Citizens in the Several States." *Michigan Law Review*, I (1902), 286–308.

Nagel, Paul Chester. *One Nation Indivisible: The Union in American Thought*. New York: Oxford University Press, 1964.

Nevins, Allan. *The Ordeal of the Union*. 2 vols. New York: Scribners, 1947.

————. *The War for the Union*. 2 vols. New York: Scribners, 1960.

Nichols, Roy F. *American Leviathan*. New York: Harper and Row, 1966. Originally published as *Blueprints for Leviathan: American Style*. New York: Atheneum, 1963.

————, *The Disruption of American Democracy*. New York: Macmillan, 1948.

————. *Franklin Pierce*. Philadelphia: University of Pennsylvania Press, 1958.

————. "The Kansas-Nebraska Act: A Century of Historiography." *Mississippi Valley Historical Review*, XLIII (Sept., 1956), 187–212.

Nye, Russell B. *Fettered Freedom: Civil Liberties and the Slavery Controversy, 1830–60*. East Lansing: Michigan State University Press, 1963.

Paludan, Phillip S. "The American Civil War Considered as a Crisis in Law and Order." *American Historical Review*, LXXVII (Oct., 1972), 1013–1034.

————. "John Norton Pomeroy: State Rights Nationalist." *American Journal of Legal History*, XII (Oct., 1968), 275–293.

Parrington, Vernon Louis. *Main Currents in American Thought*, II: *The Romantic Revolution in America*. New York: Harcourt, Brace, 1930.

Patrick, Rembert. *The Reconstruction of the Nation*. New York: Oxford University Press, 1967.

Peterson, Merrill. *The Jefferson Image in the American Mind*. New York: Oxford University Press, 1960.

Pierson, William Whatley. *Texas versus White; A Study in Legal History*. Durham: Seeman, 1916.

Pomeroy, John Norton, Jr. "John Norton Pomeroy." In *Great Ameri-*

can Lawyers, ed. William D. Lewis, VIII, pp. 89–136. Philadelphia: John C. Winston, 1909.

Potter, David. *The South and the Sectional Conflict*. Baton Rouge: Louisiana State University Press, 1968.

Pound, Roscoe. *The Formative Era of American Law*. Boston: Little, Brown, 1938.

Pressly, Thomas J. *Americans Interpret Their Civil War*. Princeton: Princeton University Press, 1954.

Puzzo, Dante. "Racism and the Western Tradition." *Journal of the History of Ideas*, XXV (Oct.-Dec., 1964), 579–586.

Randall, James G. *Constitutional Problems under Lincoln*. Urbana: University of Illinois Press, 1951.

———. *Lincoln the Liberal Statesman*. New York: Dodd, Mead, 1947.

———. *Lincoln the President*. New York: Dodd, Mead, 1945.

———, and Donald, David. *The Civil War and Reconstruction*. Lexington, Mass.: Heath, 1969.

Rawley, James A. "The Nationalism of Abraham Lincoln." *Civil War History*, IX (Sept., 1963), 283–298.

———. *Race and Politics: "Bleeding Kansas" and the Coming of the Civil War*. Philadelphia: Lippincott, 1969.

Reid, John Philip. *Chief Justice: The Judicial World of Charles Doe*. Cambridge: Harvard University Press, 1967.

Riddleberger, Patrick W. "The Radicals' Abandonment of the Negro during Reconstruction." *Journal of Negro History*, XLV (April, 1960), 88–102.

Riker, William H. "Sidney George Fisher and the Separation of Powers during the Civil War." *Journal of the History of Ideas*, XV (June, 1954), 397–412.

Robinson, Charles. *The Kansas Conflict*. New York: Harper, 1892.

Rose, Willie Lee. *Rehearsal for Reconstruction: The Port Royal Experiment*. Indianapolis: Bobbs Merrill, 1964.

Roseboom, Eugene, *The Civil War Era, 1850–73*. Columbus: Ohio State University Press, 1944.

Rumble, Wilfred, Jr. *American Legal Realism: Skepticism, Reform, and the Judicial Process*. Ithaca: Cornell University Press, 1968.

Russ, William A. "Was There Danger of a Second Civil War during Reconstruction?" *Mississippi Valley Historical Review*, XXV (June, 1938), 39–58.

Schlesinger, Arthur, Jr. *The Age of Jackson*. Boston: Little, Brown, 1945.

———. "The Causes of the Civil War: A Note on Historical Sentimentalism." *Partisan Review*, XVI (Oct., 1949), 969–981.

Schwartz, Bernard. *The Reins of Power: A Constitutional History of the United States*. New York: Hill & Wang, 1963.

Sefton, James E. *The United States Army and Reconstruction, 1865–77*. Baton Rouge: Louisiana State University Press, 1967.

Shannon, Fred A. "State Rights and the Union Army." *Mississippi Valley Historical Review*, XII (June, 1925), 51–71.

Smith, Charles W., Jr. *Roger Brook Taney: Jacksonian Jurist*. Chapel Hill: University of North Carolina Press, 1936.

Smith, Theodore Clarkson. *The Life and Letters of James Abram Garfield*, I: 1831–77. New Haven: Yale University Press, 1925.

Somkin, Fred. *Unquiet Eagle: Memory and Desire in the Idea of American Freedom, 1815–60*. Ithaca: Cornell University Press, 1967.

Spring, Leverett Wilson. *Kansas: The Prelude to the War for the Union*. Boston: Houghton Mifflin, 1885.

Sproat, John G. *The Best Men: Liberal Reformers in the Gilded Age*. New York: Oxford University Press, 1968.

Stampp, Kenneth M. *And the War Came: The North and the Secession Crisis, 1860–61*. Baton Rouge: Louisiana State University Press, 1950.

———. *The Era of Reconstruction*. New York: Random House, 1967.

Stanton, William Ragan. *The Leopard's Spots: Scientific Attitudes toward Race in America, 1815–59*. Chicago: University of Chicago Press, 1960.

Statistical History of the United States from Colonial Times to the Present. Stamford, Conn.: Fairfield Publishers, 1965.

Steiner, Bernard. *Life of Roger Brook Taney, Chief Justice of the United States Supreme Court*. Baltimore: Williams & Wilkins, 1922.

Sutherland, Arthur E. *The Law at Harvard: A History of Ideas and Men, 1817–1967*. Cambridge: Harvard University Press, 1967.

Swinney, Everette. "Enforcing the Fifteenth Amendment, 1870–77." *Journal of Southern History*, XXVIII (May, 1962), 202–218.

Swisher, Carl Brent. *Roger Brook Taney*. New York: Macmillan, 1935.

———. *Stephen J. Field, Craftsman of the Law*. Washington: Brookings Institution, 1930.

ten Broek, Jacobus. *The Antislavery Origins of the Fourteenth Amendment*. Berkeley: University of California Press, 1951.

Thomas, Benjamin, and Hyman, Harold M. *Stanton: The Life and Times of Lincoln's Secretary of War*. New York: Knopf, 1962.

Thornbrough, Emma Lou. *Indiana in the Civil War Era, 1850–80*. Indianapolis: Indiana Historical Bureau and Indiana Historical Society, 1965.

Tooke, Charles W. "The Process of Local Government." In *Law: A Century of Progress*. New York: New York University Press, 1937.

Trefousse, Hans L. *The Radical Republicans: Lincoln's Vanguard for Radical Justice*. New York: Knopf, 1969.

Trimble, William. "The Social Philosophy of the Locophoco Democracy." *American Journal of Sociology*, XXVI (May, 1921), 705–715.

Twiss, Benjamin. *Lawyers and the Constitution*. Princeton: Princeton University Press, 1942.

Tyler, Alice Felt. *Freedom's Ferment: Phases of American Social History from the Colonial Period to the Outbreak of the Civil War*. Minneapolis: University of Minnesota Press, 1944.

Van Deusen, Glyndon. *The Jacksonian Era, 1828–48*. New York: Harper & Row, 1959.

Wainwright, Nicholas. "Sidney George Fisher—The Personality of a Diarist." *Proceedings of the American Antiquarian Society*, LXXII (April, 1962), 15–30.

Ward, John William. *Andrew Jackson, Symbol for an Age*. New York: Oxford University Press, 1955.

Warren, Charles. *History of the Harvard Law School*. New York: Lewis, 1908.

———. *The Supreme Court in United States History*. Boston: Little, Brown, 1928.

Weeden, William B. *War Government: Federal and State in Massachusetts, New York, Pennsylvania and Indiana, 1861–65*. Boston: Houghton Mifflin, 1906.

Weinberg, Albert K. *Manifest Destiny: A Study of Nationalist Expansionism in American History*. Baltimore: Johns Hopkins University Press, 1935.

Whicher, Stephen. *Freedom and Fate: An Inner Life of Ralph Waldo Emerson*. Philadelphia: University of Pennsylvania Press, 1953.

White, Horace. *The Life of Lyman Trumbull*. Boston: Houghton Mifflin, 1913.

White, Leonard D. *The Jacksonians: A Study in Administrative History, 1829–61*. New York: Macmillan, 1954.

———. *The Republican Era: A Study in Administrative History, 1869–1901*. New York: Macmillan, 1958.

Williams, Lorraine. "Northern Intellectual Reaction to Military Rule during the Civil War." *Historian*, XXVII (May, 1965), 334–349.

Wilson, Francis G. "The Revival of Organic Theory." *American Political Science Review*, XXVI (June, 1942), 454–467.

Wood, Forrest G. "On Revising Reconstruction History: Negro Suffrage, White Disfranchisement, and Common Sense." *Journal of Negro History*, LI (April, 1966), 98–113.

Woodward, C. Vann. "Equality: America's Deferred Commitment." *American Scholar*, XXVII (Autumn, 1950), 459–472.

———. "Seeds of Failure in Radical Race Policy." In *New Frontiers of American Reconstruction*, ed. Harold M. Hyman, pp. 123–147. Urbana: University of Illinois Press, 1966.

Wright, Benjamin. *American Interpretations of Natural Law*. Cambridge: Harvard University Press, 1931.

Wright, Quincy. "The American Civil War." In *The International Law of Civil War*, ed. Richard Falk. Baltimore: Johns Hopkins University Press, 1971.

Index